New Hampshire—A Visual History
Western Region

First NH Banks is proud to have a part in preserving the recorded history of the Western Region through presentation of this pictorial account of the area's development and progress.

This volume is part of a series produced to preserve the rich heritage of the Granite State. In that regard, we wish to acknowledge and express our sincere appreciation to the authors, the University of New Hampshire, and New Hampshire Public Television for their creative contributions.

Each page of the Western Region is a salute to the men and women whose untiring efforts created a region rich in cultural, educational, commercial, industrial, and charitable enterprises of which all can be justly proud.

First NH Banks is very much a part of New Hampshire's legacy, and we dedicate this book to all of our citizens—past, present, and future.

This book is lovingly dedicated
to Armand Szainer,
for his guidance, his insight and his artist's eye,
and
to the cherished memory
of Willard Richardson
(1917-1989),
who walked in the shoes of his ancestors and led those
he knew along their paths, the surest of guides.

the WESTERN REGIONS

NEW HAMPSHIRE

· A VISUAL HISTORY ·

Linda Morley

THE
DONNING COMPANY
PUBLISHERS
NORFOLK/VIRGINIA BEACH

The Donning Company/Publishers,
5659 Virginia Beach Boulevard,
Norfolk, Virginia 23502

Edited by Elizabeth B. Bobbitt
Richard A. Horwege, Senior Editor

Library of Congress Cataloging-in-Publication Data

Morley, Linda.
    Western regions, New Hampshire: a visual history / by Linda
Morley.
        p.   cm.
    Bibliography: p.
    Includes index.
    ISBM 0-89865-734-2 (lim. ed)
    1. New Hampshire—History, Local—Pictorial works. 2. New
Hampshire—Description and travel—Views. I. Title.
F35.M67   1989   974.2'0022'2—dc20   89-11750   CIP

Printed in the United States of America

CONTENTS

ACKNOWLEDGMENTS

The author is indebted to many persons for assistance, encouragement, and information. While it is impossible to thank everyone individually, I wish to express my gratitude to all those who helped along the way.

I found the public servants of New Hampshire's western regions to be gracious and generous. Many town clerks, librarians, and museum personnel went out of their ways to answer my questions, to look up obscure items, and to provide useful materials. In particular, I wish to thank Kenneth C. Carmer and Barbara Kreiger at Dartmouth College Library; Bill Copeley at the New Hampshire Historical Society; Tim Dodge, Theresa MacGregor, and Roland Goodbody in Special Collections of the University of New Hampshire's Dimond Library; John Bardwell, Ron Bergeron, Gary Samson, and the staff at the University of New Hampshire Media Center; Ellen Derby and Jim Crabtree at the Peterborough Historical Society; Jerry Kearns and Leroy Bellamy of the Prints and Photograph Division at the Library of Congress; Betty Carr at the Manchester Public Library; Patrick Pallatroni, Innkeeper of the Shaker Inn, Enfield, and Carolyn Smith, Director of the Enfield Shaker Museum.

My professional colleagues, Kenneth S. Goldstein, Sandy Ives, LeeEllen Friedland, Eleanor Wachs, Paul Berliner and David Taylor provided invaluable service over and above the continuing encouragement that I've come to count on over my career. David Watters, my esteemed colleague in the English Department at the University of New Hampshire always gives the most genial cooperation whenever called upon. Photographer David MacEachran, my dear friend, was cheerfully helpful in the most trying of circumstances.

Among knowledgeable and generous friends and associates who contributed to this effort, are Ruth Jones, Robert Richardson, Gertrude Richardson, Cora Bardwell, Margaret MacArthur, Patrick Sky, Blake Tewksbury, Bob LaPree, and Paul Dosher. I made many new friends who proved most helpful, among them Margot McLeod, Aubrey O. Hampton, Jr., and Richard E. Roy. Telephone acquaintances who deserve mention include George Hafeli, John B. Wright, Al Blake, Howard Townsend, David Draves, Cindy Patnode, and Blynn Merill.

At Donning Company, a special "thank you" must go to Beverly Hainer who kept everyone sane and to Betsy Bobbitt, a most respectful and skillful editor, every writer's dream.

This 1896 photograph evokes all the feeling and studied composition of a fine period painting. It depicts the tollgate at the Charlestown, New Hampshire end of the Cheshire Bridge over the Connecticut River. The impressive Springfield to Charlestown stage may seem a great burden for the handsome horses harnessed in front. Nevertheless, as a general rule of thumb, each workhorse would be responsible for about a ton of freight.

Bridge fees were not regulated by either townships or state. A lucrative enterprise, the return to the owner-operators of a toll bridge was between 20 and 70 percent on one's investment.

Typical nineteenth-century covered bridge tolls:
    Pedestrians, sheep, cattle, per head: 2¢
    Horses: 4¢
    Horse and rider: 6¢
    1 horse vehicle: 10¢

2 horse vehicle: 14¢
2 pair horses and vehicle: 20¢
Each extra vehicle: 4¢
1 horse wagon with load: 10¢
1 horse wagon with cord of wood or
2 horse team and wagon with load: 15¢
Courtesy of New Hampshire Historical
Society

1
THE BORDER AND EARLY SETTLEMENT

New Hampshire's western border winds against the current of the Connecticut River on its sinuous route for some 250 miles through the state's most fertile farmland up into the deep woodlands of its northern forests to the river's source in the majestic Connecticut Lakes. Lured by the region's bounty, the early European settlers pushed northward from Massachusetts and Connecticut to establish frontier communities that stabilized in the years following the French and Indian War. The towns throve around the mercantile possibilities of the area's natural resources of timber and agricultural products. From its earliest history, the territory was torn politically by regional interests and the imposition of authority from royal governorship. The land was ceded by Massachusetts but laid claim to at various stages by Massachusetts, New York, Vermont, and, of course, the royal authority headquartered at Portsmouth, New Hampshire, whose stamp shaped the foundation of the state's earlier seacoast settlements.

A placid Connecticut River flows beneath the Old Ledyard Bridge in this popular turn-of-the-century souvenir photograph of Hanover from Norwich Station. Judging by those waiting on the platform and the pickup and delivery vans and drivers visible in the station yard behind the depot, one surmises that the train is to arrive shortly. Dartmouth College crowns the heights across the river. Courtesy of Dartmouth College Library

The arbitrariness of geographical boundaries predates European settlement in the region. For the natives, boundaries were fluid anyway. The several groups of Native Americans who inhabited New Hampshire had villages along the eastern frontier as well as temporary settlements, according to their needs and the weather, in pursuit of such seasonal activities as hunting, fishing, planting, and harvesting. Indians of the Connecticut River Valley included the Ashuelots, the Pocumtucks, and the Nipmucs. The Abenakis from the mountains and lakes area and the Pennacooks of south central New Hampshire habitually traveled through or hunted in the Valley. The Mohawks of New York's Hudson River Valley, traditional enemies of New Hampshire's Indians, often raided there, sometimes claiming territory. The Indians who settled at St. Francis in Canada, thereby coming under the Christian French influence, also made periodic hostile forays along the white's frontier settlements, frequently taking captive hostages. Groups of southern New England Indians also ranged the area hunting, fishing, or moving captives inland, en route to Canada, perhaps, but certainly removed from the English towns, a strategy that likely enhanced their bargaining position when seeking ransom from the British authorities in Boston or Portsmouth.

Vivid accounts of Indian life in the early seventeenth century appear in contemporary Indian captive narratives. Mary Rowlandson's is a particularly valuable early source of information about Indian life in the region because she had a fine memory. Moreover, her powers of observation were acute and, despite the hardships she underwent, she

kept her wits about her. She and her children were forced to travel with the hostile Indians who had attacked their Massachusetts frontier village. Their destination turns out to have been the Connecticut River area of southern New Hampshire. She describes the miserable life on the trail as she trekked with the Indians, part of a large band that included many women who "travelled with all they had, bag and baggage." Before fording the Baquaug (now Miller's) River, she says that the Indians "quickly fell to cutting dry trees, to make rafts to carry them over the River; and soon my turn came to go over. By the advantage of some brush which they had laid upon the Raft to sit on; I did not wet my foot."

En route, the Indians raided English fields and barns for stock and foraged for food. According to Rowlandson's account, they traveled over the Connecticut on canoes and overland by walking or on horses. Their diet was sparse but diverse. Basic foods were bear, venison, and other game, groundnuts, peas, corn, and wild foods.

Mrs. Rowlandson's account provides insight into the needs and habits of the Indians. When she was first taken to King Phillip, she refused his offer to smoke although she later confessed to having been addicted to pipe smoking in earlier years. The pair of Indians to whom she had been sold were camped for a few days near the Connecticut River on land probably close to what is now Swanzey. During the period, King Phillip's camp was across the river to the south. There was direct and indirect contact between camps. Once he requested her to make a shirt and cap "for his Boy," and he paid her for the task.

The Old Orford Toll Bridge from the New Hampshire side. The covered bridge spanned the river from the mid- nineteenth century until the early ninteen thirties. Courtesy of Dartmouth College Library

Other Indians gave her gifts in exchange for hand-sewn shirts or knitted stockings. But the Indians whose servant she was were unkind to her. Once, hoping to curry favor with them, she invited her Indian "Master and Mistress" to share a stew made from some of her spoils. She claims that "the proud Gossip, because I served them both in one Dish, would eat nothing, except one bit that he gave her upon the point of his Knife." When desperately weary or hungry, she wandered among the wigwams looking for food or lodging and occasionally enjoying the kindness and hospitality of the women.

In such details we glimpse aspects of the basic lifestyle among this region's Native American populations. We also witness something of the acculturation process of the Indians who, by the early seventeenth century, for example, were supplementing their traditional garb with items from the white settlers. In the situation of captivity the Indians and their captives expressed a mutual loathing yet, at times, they seemed to enjoy civil social exchange. Their varying demeanor towards their captive also suggests an uneveness in social interactions and an understandable ambivalence in the attitude of the Indians to the Europeans who had so profoundly disrupted their lives.

The Connecticut River borderland was more or less common ground to the northeast Indian tribes who ranged widely, using natural resources as needed when sharing the area with other Indians of their own tribe or otherwise. To some degree, the political and economic interests of the early settlers made just as arbitrary any formal authorization of the fixed geographic border that we know today. By the mid-eighteenth century the settlers had subjugated the Indians through their success in King Phillip's War and were able to establish permanent settlements along the Connecticut River and well inland. The earliest grantees, principally of English stock, were from established settlements to the south and east. Early settlement also included demobilized fighting troops. Besides the Indians and French settlers who fought for the British during the War of the Rebellion, these included volunteer troops from all over Europe. At the close of the war, most of these former soldiers spread out into New England and to the southern and western frontiers thus explaining how the early settlers represented many nations.

Border Politics

More than one challenge to establishing New Hamsphire's western border at the Connecticut River surfaced in the region's formative period. The most important of these involved claims from the states of Massachusetts and New York, the latter culminating in independent statehood for Vermont. Although New Hampshire was unusual among its fellows in not having a charter, it proposed and passed, in January of 1776, the first constitution in the revolutionary nation, a governing code hastily composed but soon adjusted as a document that rested power in an independent electorate. The nearly immediate revision of the document reflects to

The Connecticut Lakes touch three borders; New Hampshire, Vermont, and Canada. The starkness and grandeur of the setting is well captured in this early portrait from the Monahan Studio of Hillsborough, New Hampshire. Courtesy of Dartmouth College Library

some degree the opposition of a few of the Connecticut River towns whose citizens distrusted the intentions of some of the legislators to the east.

The Connecticut River Valley's settlement was delayed until well into the eighteenth century when allegiance to royal authority had been eroded along the frontiers and elsewhere. Harsh pioneer life led to a basic distrust of authority and fostered a spirit of personal independence as frontier settlers sought economic security and self-sufficiency. They also could take advantage of the circumstance of forging homes in the wilderness in an era when, revolution in the air, many colonists were determined to take an active part in designing their own futures. Contributing to harmony among neighbors after the Battle of Lexington, there was a general migration of pro-Patriot families moving out of Boston to the countryside and Tory families moving into Boston.

The states of Massachusetts and New York each claimed exclusive rights to what is now New Hampshire and Vermont. The boundary between Massachusetts and New Hampshire was drawn in 1740, coinciding with the appointment of Benning Wentworth as the independent royal governor. Wentworth considered all the land east of New York as New Hampshire territory and he made land grants there that were disputed between New York and New Hampshire for decades. The Vermont and New Hampshire boundary as we know it was drawn in 1782,

long after the defeat of the French established Canada as an English possession.

Historian Charles Clark has described vividly the difficulties that faced the early surveyors of northern New England. The rigors of the wilderness led to great discomfort that inhibited confident progress. The unevenness of the ground and the extraordinary length (sixty-six feet or four rods) of their measuring chains required the addition of a compensatory additional length for every thirty chains of measured distance. Some surveyors substituted an inexact, shrinkable hemp line in place of the heavier chains. Incredible as it seems, many surveyors did not adjust their compasses to allow for the "local variation of the compass needle from true north."

Often, surveyors took advantage of their special knowledge of new territory in choosing their own land. For example, the early, 1741, settlement of Westmoreland by a small group of people included one of the men, Daniel How, who had surveyed the territory a few years earlier. He chose this desireable meadowland for his family and was joined in the venture by two other families from his former home of Northfield, Massachusetts. Township No. 2, or Great Meadows, was incorporated as Westmoreland in 1752. Before white settlement, the meadows had been favorite resort grounds for regional Indians.

Attempting to secure more of a say in local affairs, several of the border towns considered separating from

Seen from the north with the heights of Hanover at its eastern end, Ledyard Bridge spans the narrow bend in the Connecticut. For many years this *magnificent bridge symbolized the security of nineteenth-century rural life to its border community. The bucolic scene of this early twentieth-century* *image emphasizes the bridge's symbolic role. Courtesy of Dartmouth College Library*

New Hampshire and joining forces with some of their neighbors across the river. Vermont's attempt to rebel against the authorities of New York and New Hampshire proved timely to these plans as it did for another energetic but short-lived separatist movement. Led by some of the citizens in the Hanover area affiliated with Dartmouth College, the group hoped to create a new state, New Connecticut, comprised of towns on both sides of the border. Its capital, Dresden, was part of Dartmouth College's campus.

The various efforts of the parties concerned in all of these border disputes were brought up sharply in 1782 when, independently, the Continental Congress created the state of Vermont, setting the mutual border of New Hampshire and Vermont at the Connecticut River. Many of the town histories of the New Hampshire border carry fascinating accounts of local involvement in this and other aspects of the secessionist movement of the time —a stimulating chapter in the region's history.

Indian Stream Republic (Pittsburg)

Pittsburg was once the independent Republic of Indian Stream. Caught in a border dispute between New Hampshire and Canada, the settlers formed their own government in 1832, with constitution, assembly, court, and standing army of forty to ward off "foreign" invasion. One war with Canada was fought with stones, scythes,

guns, and catch-all weapons. The independent territory existed for five years but it took another three years of occupation by the N.H. Militia to retire it in 1840.

Border Community

The river, rather than dividing settlements, served to link settled communities on both banks. Most of the frontier towns were created by charters granted to share-holders who previously had been relatives or neighbors in various Connecticut River towns in Massachusetts or Connecticut. They traveled up the river to their new homes, making the river a center of commerce for the border towns. Frontier families shared bonds that the river served to strengthen as the locals established networks of communication, resources, mercantile exchange, and social ties. In over two hundred years of history, the people in the Connecticut River Valley maintained the distinct border identity formed in the region's early days.

People depended on each other in every facet of their lives. Although Boston area news spread to the region speedily, news from New York City took a week to reach inland and from England, it often took many weeks. Printed matter was scarce in revolutionary New England. It was not uncommon for people to share all manner of reading material: books, periodicals, tracts, letters, and copied manuscripts. Newspapers were passed around for multiple readings. As evidence of border cohesiveness, rural postal "star routes" between Bellows Falls, Vermont, and the towns in western New Hampshire continued for a hundred and fifty years.

Border life requires cooperation that defies boundaries and enduring links across the border have stood the test of time. It is often observed that there exists a greater sense of community between the citizens of Lancaster and their Lunenberg, Vermont, neighbors or between the residents of Hanover and Norwich, Cornish and Windsor, or Charlestown and Springfield than between the New Hampshire citizens of the western border towns and their fellow-staters in Concord, Manchester, or Portsmouth, all major centers of New Hampshire life. From the earliest days of settlement, the river's desirable valley land and resources built a border identity for the region and its people who not only felt stronger ties to their neighbors across the river but uncertain allegiance to the colonial government across the wilderness to the east.

A nineteenth-century popular poem poignantly illustrates this spirit of neighbors-across-the-Connecticut. "Marjorie Gray," written in, 1861, is, perhaps, a purely fictitious creation of Julia C. R. Dorr. She wrote years later, however, that "the poem was founded on a half a dozen lines that caught my eye in the newspaper, simply stating that a woman of the pioneers, being lost in the woods and unable to cross the Connecticut River, had wandered around its source and came down the other side."

In a lengthy narrative, Dorr's elaboration of the eighteenth-century incident presents a drama of the frontier in its formative years. Cast in terms of the history of our Connecticut River Valley ancestors, the story of the young mother's harrowing experience captured the imagination of those along the border and versions of Dorr's poem entered both recitation and song traditions. Even from our modern perspective, the poetic description of the rigors of frontier life seems authentic.

The following plot summary is based on a mid-twentieth-century version of Dorr's poem from the singing of Orlon Merrill of Charlestown, New Hampshire. In Mr. Merrill's ballad rendition, a young mother, Margaret Gray, loses her way returning home with her baby from a friend's cabin one April day. Her husband, Robert, begins a vain search for them, enlisting the help of his neighbors. She hears her rescuers but cannot locate them nor they her. After days of wandering and starvation, the baby dies and she buries it. She wanders through the spring and summer, surviving on acorns and berries. By journey's end in October, she wanders, half naked and distraught,

into Charlestown, where her identity is soon discovered and the townspeople hasten the joyful reunion of the Grays in a testimony to border community life. The following excerpts from Merrill's version demonstrate the emotional intensity of the story in its popular form.

Soon the scattered settlers gathered
From their clearing far and near,
And their solemn words resounded
With their voices ringing clear

Torches blazed and fires were kindled
And the horn, long pealed, rang out
Til the startled echoes answered
To the hardy woodsmen's shout;
Til in vain their sad endeavors
Night by night and day by day —
But no sign or token found they
Of the child or Margaret Gray.

. . . .

Through the dim woods she went singing
To her baby at her breast.

But when sudden terror pausing
Gazed she round in blank dismay —
Where was all the white scarred hemlock
Pointing out the lonely way?

Hark, a shout! and in the distance
She could see the torches gleam.
But, alas, she could not reach them
And they vanished like a dream.
With another shout, another
And she screamed and sobbed in vain
Rushing wildly toward the spot
She could never, never gain.

. . . .

Morning came and with the sunbeams
Hope and courage rose once more,
Thinking sure another nightfall
Her long wanderings would be o'er,
So she soothed her wailing baby
Which went faint for want of food.
She could gather nuts and acorns
That she found within the wood.

[The baby dies. Abject with grief, Margaret continues to carry her dead baby for three days.]

Til acrosst its marble beauty
Stole the plague spots of decay.
Then she knew that she must leave it
In the wilderness asleep
While the prowling wild beast only
Watch above its grave could keep.

.　.　.　.　.

One chill morning in October
When the woods were brown and bare
Through the streets of aged Charlestown
With a strange bewildered air,
Walked a gaunt and pallid woman
Whose dislevelled locks of brown
O'er her naked breasts and shoulders
In the wind was streaming down.

Then she told her piteous story,
In a vague desponded way,
And with cold white lips she murmurs,
Take me home to Robert Gray."
"But the river," says they, pondering,
"How crossed you to its eastern side,
How crossed you its rapid waters —
Deep its channel is, and wide?"

But she said she had not crossed it.
In a strange erratic course
She had wandered so far northward
Til she reached its fountain source.
Down the dark Canadian Forest
And then blindly roaming on
Through the wild New Hampshire valley,
Her bewildered feet had gone.

Ah the joy-bells sweet were ringing
On that frosty autumn air!
How the boats across the waters—
How they leaped—the tale to bear!
Oh, that wondrous, glorious sunset
Of that blest October day,
When the weary wife was folded
In the arms of Robert Gray.

That a legendary pioneer woman might lose her way only to wander more than a hundred miles up the western shore of the Connecticut River, around the Connecticut Lakes and along the river's eastern bank until reaching the frontier town many miles to the south, may seem an exaggeration in our time, but to those who live and work in the woods even today, the possibility does not seem far-fetched. According to Mrs. Flanders, who recorded this ballad version from Mr. Merrill, the singer had once "lived around the Connecticut Lakes as a trapper, guide, lumberman, and carpenter. The words describing the wandering woman come poignantly close to him . . . [he] has occasionally missed the blazed trails and has thrown a stick into a stream to determine its direction."

The poem attests to the smooth functioning of border life and celebrates the emotional ties of a close-knit community, and its popularity confirms the high value placed on the idea of border ties. There is a recent rendering of the story, an indication that Mrs. Gray's pioneer plight, as fiction or legend, continues to captivate. In 1978, Patrick Sky, a singer-songwriter of considerable reputation on the folk circuit, heard folksinger Margaret MacArthur sing "Margerie Gray." He was so attracted to it that he researched the background of the story and wrote a free verse monologue version from the pioneer wife's point-of-view. The few excerpts that follow illustrate that Sky used Mr. Merrill's version as a source. His twentieth-century rendering expresses insight into life on the river for these pioneers through a contemporary imagination that finds the story every bit as gripping as did Mrs. Dorr and the people along the border who carried the poem into tradition.

I was singing that's what did it
sometimes you can sing yourself
into two or three days
of absent mindedness.
I was just walking . . .
the baby was asleep,
I was chewing on a Wintergreen
a bunch of quail flew by
and I jumped,
it was then I knew that I was lost
The Hemlocks marked the way to Anna's
even now I cannot figure it;
how I lost my way.

.　.　.　.　.

The arrival of an 1891 surveying party contracted to demark the southwestern corner boundaries of New Hampshire at Hinsdale and Winchester, duly noted in this beautiful photograph, suggests the importance of such a venture to the local community. Courtesy of New Hampshire Historical Society

One morning
I looked across a valley
and saw the Maples
dressed in gold and red.
I knew that winter was near.
Number four, was a long way.
I decided to follow the river,
as I reached the banks
the water was so still
I had to throw in a stick
to see what direction
it was flowing,
South this time.

People were shocked
to see me that day.
I walked into Charlestown,
naked from the waist up.
They say I had been
all the way to Canada,
wandering around the Connecticut,
the river was always
on my right.

Border identity, then, as now, manifests itself in several ways as business connections and family kinship networks meander back and forth across the river and along its tributaries. Throughout our history, individuals hired out across the border, as itinerant menial or skilled workers, craftsmen, farm hands, mill hands, teamsters, or as day laborers in their communities. Today, citizens on both sides of the river cross the border for similar reasons. The river acted as catalyst for border life in the days of the settlement of the region, accommodating ferry service and a shipping route for all sorts of products originating in the towns and villages along the Connecticut to the ports of Massachusetts, Connecticut, and New York. The river continues to nurture those living nearby, not, of course, for the trade and transportation that was so vital to their pioneer ancestors, but as a source of recreation and as refuge in its superb natural beauty.

No less compelling is this documentation of the surveyors at work. A granite-bound post provides one baseline of measurement. Although precise documentation is unavailable, the wholly professional group is probably working on establishing the state's southern boundary accomplished between 1885 and 1894, and settled finally in 1901.

The growth of corn in the field along the background places the surveyor's labors in late summer. *Courtesy of New Hampshire Historical Society*

This dramatic view of a newly mown hay field on the Fellows Farm, Charlestown, illustrates the painterly eye of many of our early rural photographers. Careful scrutiny reveals harvesters at the hay wagon and a dog waiting patiently nearby. The original photograph was made with a glass negative and is part of a large collection of excellent works by turn-of-the-century New Hampshire photographer George E. Fellows who at the time of this photograph, 1900 to 1915, worked out of White River Junction, Vermont. Courtesy of Dartmouth College Library

2
AGRICULTURE AND ANIMAL HUSBANDRY

The economy of New Hampshire's western regions was agriculturally based from its settlement until late in the nineteenth century. The river valley provided fertile farmland for the farmers migrating into the northern regions of the Connecticut River Valley. Migration increased dramatically after Indian hostilities had ceased, leading to the creation in 1803 of the state's largest county, Coos, at a time when agriculture was declining elsewhere in the state. Mid-eighteenth-century settlers were spurred to the wilderness of the Connecticut River Valley by the depletion and division of fertile lands in the larger settlements of Massachusetts and Connecticut. The varied agricultural pursuits in western New Hampshire included livestock, grains, vegetables, fruits, fiber, maple sugaring, ice-harvesting and lumbering. With the mid-nineteenth-century arrival of the railroad, marketing to the cities improved for both agricultural and industrial pursuits. Declining throughout the century, farming gave way gradually to manufacturing and tourism. Census records reveal that between 1880 and 1900 New Hampshire lost 60 percent of its farms. Nevertheless, farms and farming are deeply etched into the region's sense of its identity partly, perhaps, because agricultural

In this view of an eighteenth-century farmhouse and its nineteenth-century out buildings, the anonymous photographer's panoramic technique somewhat flattens the perspective. Left to right is the farmhouse, itself, which is the small ell attached at the east end of the larger dwelling. The "first house" is observable to the right of the main house and is detached from it. By the time these photos were taken, it had been converted into a shop and icehouse. A blacksmith's shop, some distance from the south side of the big house, is out of sight behind the first house. The farm's long driveway enters the large yard shared by the house and barns between the first house and the connected barn buildings. The barn to the left is the horse and wagon barn. The barnyard begins at the fence which encloses a sheep's pen in front of the calf shed situated between the horse barn and the larger cow barn. The lilacs in the corner of the barnyard obscure the chicken house beside it. Courtesy of New Hampshire Historical Society

subjects have had an abiding popularity with the media and photographers for over a century. Additionally, the contemporary resurgence of interest in heritage has promoted research into our agricultural past and the inevitable resulting call for its preservation.

A Nineteenth Century Working Farm

It is unusual to find nineteenth-century photographs that seem to have been taken for documentary purposes. A set of photographs from the mid-1890s that show a New Hampshire farm's buildings from several vantage points were informatively annotated by a family member, a fact which sets these photos (pages 18-21) apart from the typical. It is rare, indeed, to find such a display of farm buildings taken from the rear or north and west sides.

Bringing the heritage of the region to life are the numerous anecdotes that circulate orally, through families, friends and neighbors over the years. Regional histories preserve many of these memorable accounts.

An amusing late nineteenth-century story from Andover provides a birds-eye view of one farm's approach to drying the harvested onion crop. As told by a town historian, it seems that:

> a local student, Charles F. Flanders, later destined to become a prominent physician in Manchester, was . . . paying court to Nahum (Bachelder)'s sister Bertha. One dark night, as he whirled up to the house with high-stepping horse-and-buggy to take Bertha for a ride, he failed to notice that the whole

driveway and yard had been spread with drying onions. Needless to say, the warmth of his reception was somewhat tempered by embarrassment and spiced with the aroma of freshly crushed onions. (Chaffee, page 102)

Nahum Bachelder was a highly regarded agricultural expert, serving for a time as the state Grange secretary and from 1887-1913 as secretary of the state Board of Agriculture. He served as New Hampshire's governor from 1903 to 1905. Flanders graduated from medical school in the late 1880s which dates this incident to about that time.

Hired Men

Stories about hired men are common in an agricultural region, often informing us of everyday life on the farm. One such character is Samuel Jewett of Mason, who had so poor a farm that he hired himself out for seasonal tasks, like threshing, in order to make ends meet. Neighbors remember that:

> Sammy could not distinguish one tune from another and yet he was always singing at his work— especially if matters were going well. He used to try to teach his steers which he alluded to as "them little fellers" to plow without a driver. They were small stunted animals rarely over three years old, and they tried Sammy's patience to the utmost. (Local people) used to hear him yelling at them on his farm two miles as-the-crow-flies away. All Sharon

and Peterborough, too, knew Sammy's song.... It was better heard, though, when Sammy was helping (a neighbor) with the threshing on the home farm. Sammy did not sing while he was actually swinging the flail that was too strenuous and breathtaking for song — but after each flooring had been threshed Sammy who was crippled with corns and bunyons would hobble across the barn floor to get the pitchfork to "clean up" and "put down the new flooring" and it was then that he sang, or chanted:

Doo, de doo-Doo, de doo-Doo, de doo Doo.
Doo, de doo-Doo, de doo-Doo, de doo Doo.
Doo, de doo-Doo, de doo-Doo, de doo Doo.
do Doo-do Doo-do Doo.

The rhythm (we have been told) was like that of a drum, but the voice neither rose nor fell but held to one even tone, if tone it was. (King, page 176)

This old story satisfies on two levels. It tells of a beloved town character and it tells about familiar farm animals, one of the most popular subjects of rural tales. The attempt to train animals to enlarge their potential for service brings to mind a story from Cornish about two of the buffalo that lived in Corbin's Park (about which more, later).

At the turn of the century, American journalist Ernest Harold Baynes became interested in the plight of the nation's diminishing buffalo herds. He wrote extensively on the subject and led a conservation drive to save the

This side view of the barns and barnyard provides a closeup of the barnyard from the south, and two-thirds of the horse barn at the left. Wagons were kept beneath this barn. The sheep pen's elaborate fencing illustrates the farmers concern for the security of the farm animals when left outside. The calf's shed is dwarfed by the imposing cow barn. Since, according to family sources, most of the power had been supplied by oxen, the cow barn also housed these larger work animals. At the far right is the well house. Standing in front of the sheep pen are three generations of the family whose ancestors bought the property in 1781 from the man who had built the big house, probably in the 1770s —Moses, representing the fourth generation, his daughter, Mary the fifth, her children (?), the sixth generation, and Hannah her mother, Moses' wife. Courtesy of New Hampshire Historical Society

Moses' nineteenth-century sawmill was situated some distance from the house, in a southwesterly direction. Moses stands overlooking the millpond, his wife, Hannah, sits on the bank, and Mary is in the rowboat. Perched above the sluiceway is one of the children. Perhaps it is Mary's husband who has taken these photos. While it is obvious that this is a working farm, it is worth pointing out that it was more self-sufficient than most. Not many farmers ran their own sawmills.

Family knowledge asserts that the mill was built about 1850. It had a horizontal wooden waterwheel with a vertical shaft connected to the mechanism. Among its products were shingles, clapboards, turning lathes, and firewood. Notice the track on the high bank behind where Mary is sitting in the rowboat. This would have been the path used to slide the logs or trees down to the mill hands.

The farmstead stayed in this family until 1940 when the buildings and about six acres were sold to the parents of the current owner who was eleven years old at the time. By then, the big barn and the first house were already gone. The calf shed and several of the outbuildings were in ruins. The mill is gone and the stream has become marshland, compliments of local beavers. Courtesy of New Hampshire Historical Society

animals from extinction. As part of his campaign, he praised the superiority of the buffalo's wool and touted its potential as a work animal. In pursuing this tack, he borrowed:

> two calves from the Corbin herd, whom he christened "War Whoop" and "Tomahawk,"...raised them on cow's milk and broke them to the yoke, at the cost, he admitted, of some "fine black eyes." When they were four months old, he hitched them to a stone drag, and reported that they showed "splendid strength and courage," though "to be sure, they were a trifle headstrong, and once they ran clean away with the drag." He exhibited this buffalo team at country fairs, and once won a decisive victory with them at the Central Maine Fair in a half-mile race with a remarkable steer who had been broken to a sulky. But as his buffalo calves grew up, they became impossible to control, and Baynes was forced to return them to the park herd. (Wade, page 98)

One can imagine the relish with which locals took to the idea of buffalo in the area and the fun they must have had discussing the training of the wild animals.

As extreme as such a venture seems at the end of the twentieth century, our agricultural forebears led immensely complex lives that taxed every scrap of imagination they had. Consider, for instance, the logistics that must have gone into transferring herds from summer to winter pastures or driving herds of animals (even geese) from regional farms to as far away as the Boston markets. What we can do today by truck or rail, our ancestors accomplished by wagon and on foot.

WPA Artists' Project

Unprecedented documentation of the nation's heritage and culture resulted from several of the Works Progress Administration's unemployment relief efforts in the late nineteen-thirties and early forties. New Hampshire employed writers, artists, photographers, and architectural historians under WPA's Writers', Artists' and Historic Surveys' Projects. They left a legacy of drawings, photographs, art works, research materials, and local history for later generations, many ideally suited for illustrating New Hampshire's past. New Hampshire materials are scattered throughout the state in libraries, public buildings, and archives, and at the Library of Congress in the nation's capital. Among this wealth of material is work by a few of the era's finest photographers whose artists' eyes and governmental mandate captured images of lasting interest. The artists seemed to concentrate their energies on aspects of traditional rural life, artifacts, and occupations of historical interest. L. M. A. Roy, of Henniker, for example, submitted photographs of contem-

A contemporary view shows the farmhouse and the surviving barn. The descendents of the family in the old photographs maintain ownership of the hundred-plus acres of the original farmland and woodland, but the house, surviving barn, and a few acres of the surrounding land were sold in 1940. Contemporary photographs of the homestead and outbuildings testify to the present occupant's preservationist instincts. The big house, clapboard in the old photos, has been shingled and stained a black-brown to enhance its antiquity. The first house is gone as are the connecting barns and barnyard. The lilac bushes have grown to be trees. Aside from a few new trees and the obvious growth of other trees or their replacements, the past ninety years have imposed little change on the scene. The field, though somewhat smaller than in the old photos, is kept mowed. On the foundation of the first house, a handsome fireplace and patio executed by a traditional mason in the 1940s fit unostentatiously in the dooryard. The current owners chat with the author near the lilac trees. Photo by Armand Szainer

porary maple sugaring, which he titled "Boys Gathering Sap in New Hampshire," as well as another series on oxen shoeing. His photos and others from the WPA artists' project are on page 25, and 27, to 29.

Family Story, Popular Belief

Among the WPA writers accounts are local anecdotes revealing little-known details of early rural life.

> . . . it was custom to have at least one bed in the kitchen of the home and in a house in Warner the story is told of a couple by the name of McKellips who firmly believed that if a fire was kept in the fireplace for twenty-five years that a salamander would come about the time of the 25th. anniversary period and eat up the fire.
>
> One morning the fond housewife was preparing a boiled dinner and among other things an Indian pudding was being cooked on a hook near the hot fire. She went out of the kitchen for a few minutes and upon her return was horrified to find the blazing fire out and tracks of some kind of an animal lead underneath the bed from the fireplace. Hastily calling her husband the woman watched while the brave man ? ? poked under the bed. Sure enough there was an animal that looked as though it was covered with feathers instead of the customary

This contemporary closeup shows the surviving barn, originally the horse barn. Intact, it looms handsomely in its setting. According to information that the former owners included with the photographs, the barn doors are on hinges, predating the sliding doors-on-tracks construction. Notice that the foundation and banking now enclose what had been the wagon storage. Refer to the color photograph of the house shown from the south side that appears in the color section of this volume. Photo by Armand Szainer

Stone Farm, Mount Caesar, Swanzey Center, circa 1900, was a well-built establishment refurbished and renamed Mountain House. As such, it opened on July 4, 1908, for the accommodation of tourists. Courtesy of New Hampshire Historical Society

fur o[r] perhaps in this case other covering for a salamander certainly does not have either fur or feathers. Finally with the aid of a heavy stick the man succeeded in poking out the supposed creature only to find that it was the baked [I]ndian pudding that had fallen off the hook and rolled across the kitchen floor under the bed. In falling the pudding which was in a linen sack struck a kettle of water which extinguished the fire and so the salamander did not return even if the twenty-five years was up regardless of the extinguished blaze in the fireplace. This story has been handed down as true from father to son and other inquiries reveal that it really was an old superstition regarding the return of the salamander and the eating of the fire. To keep any fire for twenty-five years winter and summer must have required a great deal of concentrated effort on the part of the entire family in any household. (WPA Writer's Project files, P. S. Scruton, worker)

This combination folktale and family reminiscence seems to have been but slightly edited by the fieldworker in setting it down. That it is the product of an early agricultural lifestyle is unquestionable. The foodways give this away.

Houses without central heating were, until mid-twentieth century, the rule rather than the exception they are today. Families used the upstairs as little as possible in the wintertime, often bringing the beds, at least of the older members of the household, downstairs for the winter. It is an interesting touch that the memory begins with that small fact which really has nothing to do with the crux of the story. The mention of this practice points to the antiquity of the lifestyle depicted in the anecdote.

Family tales that turn around superstitious behavior are popular in our culture. In this example, the old people can laugh at themselves, at each other, and invite the rest of the family to enjoy the joke, too. This suggests that the belief was a questionable one, on its way out of currency in the community and family. The anecdote acts as a sort of fond farewell to an old habit.

Among all the arboreal products of this region, so useful to man, there is nothing he appropriates more eagerly or appreciates more highly than the sugar-producing qualities of the rock-maple. Thousands of pounds of maple sugar are annually made in this town, which, being manufactured by the modern conveniences and methods, is of a very fine quality. (Worthen, page 566)

This early twentieth-century snapshot provides an unusual documentation of a county home's work crew and their overseer (far left). Prisoner-labor crews typically performed agricultural and other chores on and near the site of their incarceration. These men were at the Woodsville County Home. Courtesy of New Hampshire Historical Society

Several vital statistics of "S. S. Houghton's 'Pavillion Stock Barn,' Orford," have been meticulously copied out on the back of the original of this stereograph: "Length of front north and south: 240 feet, width: 60 feet. Length of 'T' running east: 200 feet, width: 56 feet. Height of Tower: 130 feet. Weight of Bell: 1,268 lb. Cost of Barn: $40,000.00."

These statistics turn up in numerous sources, a reflection of the public's interest in this rare showplace. Built in the late 1870s by a Boston merchant as a recreational investment, the oversized stock barn had four floors and a clock with four faces that struck the hour.

Built of a million board feet of lumber, the barn provided storage for everything including even a root cellar and an ice cellar. It accommodated 200 horses in spacious stalls or boxes and a racetrack bordered by cedar trees was situated nearby. Mr. Houghton specialized in the breeding and training of harness racehorses. The stock barn, already in semi-ruins, burned down in 1930, long after Mr. Houghton had sold the property. This century-old stereoscopic image was sold by A. T. Converse of Lyme, a dealer in novelties. Courtesy of New Hampshire Historical Society

Such posed photographs of farm workers, as this one in the Monadnock area, are not uncommon in family photo albums but they seem rarely to find their way into public photograph collections. The empty wagon seems fragile, adding a lightness to the scene that together with the softness of age makes the image seem more like a painting than a photograph. The inclusion of children reminds us of the proximity of farm work to the farmhouse. Children often worked during the harvest but in this photograph their dress suggests that they were along for other reasons. Perhaps the workers are serving as informal caretakers of the children. During the height of the harvest, it was common for homemakers or children to carry late morning lunches out to the fields. These lunches usually included generous jugfuls of the old farmer's beverage "switchel," a combination of water, honey, molasses or maple syrup, and vinegar. Switchel was reputed to be both nutritious and a satisfying thirst quencher. Courtesy of Peterborough Historical Society

This 1888 sugar house is conveniently located in the farmer's sugar orchard near Hanover. The operation is wood-fired and the outdoor work is labor intensive for both the sap gatherers and the animals, oxen and horses, that pulled the heavy sap-filled barrels through the spring snow. Pictured here are some of the workers and an ox that has drawn a heavy log for the workers to reduce to size for the constant boiling. Children's winter school vacations were timed to the sugaring season in upper New England and children provided valuable help in the woods and at the woodpile. Day laborers were often hired to augment the farmhands' ranks.

As long as the sap was running, sugaring was an around-the-clock activity. When the sap slowed during the cold nights, the slack time provided an opportunity for community socializing at the sugar house with storytelling, music, and midnight suppers. It wasn't until the middle of the twentieth century that the widespread use of plastic tubing to carry the sap from the trees directly to the sugar house eased the sugar-makers' labor. The winter vacation is entrenched in New England schools although it no longer varies in schedule to accommodate a bygone agricultural calendar. Courtesy of Dartmouth College Library

These photographs of ice-cutting in 1936 are two of a series of seven that photographer Arthur Rothstein took for the Farm Security Administration as part of the WPA documentation of rural America. Rothstein had a fine eye for visual detail and an interest in the technical processes related to rural life.

His closeup photos of people at work and at play are evidence of this. His attention to his own work log is less careful than his attendance on his craft in that he identified the setting inaccurately. Ice-cutting was common on the upper Connecticut River, however, and on its tributaries. Rothstein took most of his WPA photographs in northern Coos County and this scene may, indeed be in Coos County on the Connecticut, or on a nearby branch, either side of the state line.

Before the Second World War when refrigeration replaced it, ice-cutting was an annual activity throughout the northern United States and Canada. Large shipments of ice went from New Hampshire's Connecticut River Valley to cities and towns in Massachusetts and beyond. Ample ice was also stored locally in sawdust-lined icehouses on private property and at commercial establishments for year-round use. Today, ice-cutting is limited almost entirely to heritage program demonstrations. There are many who remember participating in an activity, that, in their youths, was customary in the cold season.

Additional examples of Rothstein's work appear elsewhere in this volume. Courtesy of Library of Congress, Photograph and Print Division

Today's residents of the region find no contradiction in this combination of the traditional and the contemporary. Indeed, many find it reassuring to observe the comfortable juxtaposition of harvesting crops on one side of the road and the mass cultural promotion of the farmer's harvest on the other as in this scene from West Lebanon, 1975. Courtesy of Dartmouth College Library

As a mark of pride in the state's agricultural heritage, the Grange encourages the owners and operators of New Hampshire's bi-centennial and century farms to publicize their antiquity. This century farm, in Enfield, was originally a Shaker farm, one of the Enfield community's working farm buildings. The Shakers lived communally, hence the absence of a conventional farmhouse. The fact of its age is painted on the roof in proportions that minimize ostentation. Today the farm grows and sells vegetables and is owned by the developers of Lower Shaker Village on Lake Mascoma. It is the farm's obvious working nature from

which its showpiece character derives, not from any romanticized presentation of a former way of life. Photo by Armand Szainer

A series of photographs follow two boys on their sap collecting route as they drive a team of yoked red shorthorns who drag a scoot carrying the sap barrel and bucket. In the first photo, two youths stop their team in the sugar orchard to gather sap from nearby sugar maples. One youth tips the contents of the sap bucket, probably collected from pails hung on tapped trees off the trail. The water pails carried by the other youth also facilitate the transport of sap from the trees to the sap barrel. The well-behaved yoked team may be steers or bullocks although the use of young heifers for such work is not unheard of on farms of the period.

As shown here, the team has pulled beyond the tree pictured on the left edge of the previous photo to wait while the youth in the leather jacket tips the pail's contents into his mate's pail as the dog surveys the scene. The emptying of one pail into the other may indicate a sluggish sap flow.

The youth wearing the shoulder yoke lugs a pair of galvanized water pails, full of sap, to the collecting barrel while his companion keeps watch over the team with a small whip, call a goad. The goad would have had a prick of some kind at the end to keep the team in place or guide it along the desired path. The placement of the sap bucket on the scoot shows clearly the handle near the bottom that the boy grasps to help distribute the weight of the sap when pouring the sap into the sap barrel.

Pails would be hung on all of the tapped sugar maple trees throughout the "sugaring" season, a two to five-week period between late February and mid-April, depending on the weather and the location. Ideal sugaring weather consists of cold nights and warm days, the sap freezing at night and flowing during the day. The emptied pails would be returned to their trees ready to receive the continually flowing sweet liquid. A scoot, or sledge, with wooden runners could travel over snow or earth but it is a rare year, indeed, when there is no snow on the ground during sugaring season.

The snow cover in the picture of the man collecting sap from the tree in the dooryard is more typical of the season in western New Hampshire. This photo and the next photo of boiling the sap were taken by an unidentified photographer in New Hampshire as part of the Massachusetts Writer's project, but their kinship with L. M. A. Roy's series of "Boys Gathering Sap in New Hampshire" leads one to speculate that they may have been Roy's, too. The old galvanized sap bucket, wider on the bottom than on the top, is a thing of the past. Galvanized water pails similar to the one in his right hand, are still in common use, however. The man's clothing is representative of the farmer's winter wear in that period.

The jacket would have been called a "jumper" by many old-timers and the high socks and leather "uppers" on sturdy boots were commonplace. More usual than his cloth cap, however, would have been a knitted cap, called a toque, a French-Canadian term brought into the state with the nineteenth-century Canadian immigrants who sought work in the region's logging operations and mills. The traditional knitted caps are still worn throughout New England. The iron pipe attached to the tree has nothing to do with sugaring. Very likely, it runs from a nearby well providing handy access to water for such outside work as watering animals or the kitchen garden.

That these photos are posed is strongly suggested by the photographs' composition; by the way the photographer is able to capture details like the yokes, buckets, and sledge; by the lack of snow cover in the woods and by the fact that, in the last of the sugaring images, the evaporator is not in operation. There is no steam rising from the pan to obscure the details of the scene from the camera's lens and the floor is littered with extraneous materials that would certainly have been a hindrance during the busy evaporation process. Sugar houses set up a continuing column of smoke from their chimneys, a sign to the neighbors that it was time to gather at the sap house for socializing and sweet smells. School winter vacation coincided with sugaring season in early New England. The farmer worked around the clock when boiling sap and everyone pitched in. He might smoke sausages from the sugar house rafters or boil eggs right in the sap. The maple flavoring made ordinary foods sweetly delectable. The probable reenactment of the action in these photos in no way diminishes their documentary value and may even explain their aesthetic power.

The shoeing of oxen is another subject that goes to the heart of the popular conception of old-time rural life. This splendid photograph shows the shoeing process so as to tell its own story. The presence of the two old-timers hanging out, intent on the smith's handiwork, reminds us that the blacksmith's shop was another center of village social life. Noteworthy is the large, carefully constructed sturdy frame which protects the smith from unwelcome kicks. The ox hangs in a sling, just clear of the floor, as he is shod. The ox's cloven hoof requires a two-part shoe, the first half of which is being nailed in this documentation. The smith's visored cap hides his features which likely include a mouth full of nails at the ready. What looks like a heat shield sits above the cap's visor. The blacksmith's toolbox serves him well. Tools rest on top of the box if needed during shoeing and are stored in the compartment below when not in use. In this picture, the hoof trimmer lies within reach. The pipe smoke adds a nice touch to the composition as does the yoked head of the ox-in-waiting, patiently observing the goings on.

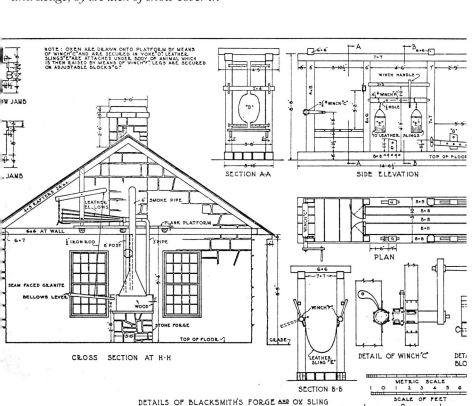

DETAILS OF BLACKSMITH'S FORGE AND OX SLING

Francis H. Brown executed this second of two drawings of the forge and ox sling in an 1840 blacksmith shop that had been moved from Chesterfield, New Hampshire, to "Storrowton," West Springfield, Massachusetts. The building was measured September 1938.

Historic American Building Survey Project No. 464-14-3-6, Survey No. N.H. 41. Courtesy of the Library of Congress, Photograph and Print Division

The lettering on the log in the foreground of this H.H.H. Langill photo reads "Lower Olcott Falls," a spot in the Connecticut River at Lebanon that often caused bottlenecks in the downriver log drives. The quieter water and the riverbanks afforded temporary resting places for excess logs until the crew could isolate them and send them individually, or in pairs, along their way. Hartford, Connecticut, was one destination of the drive. There, the logs would be sawn into boards for local sale or to be sent on to New York. Raft loads of lumber were also sent downriver from New Hampshire sawmills to various points in Massachusetts, Connecticut, and beyond. Langill had a turn-of-the-century photographic studio in Hanover. Courtesy of Dartmouth College Library

3
LOGGING AND MILLS

The magnificent forests of western New Hampshire early drew logging interests to the region. Indeed the timber industry remains identified with the upper Connecticut River Valley to the present day. Work animals made possible judicious cutting of timber in well managed forests. Long aware of the value of its forest resources, the state began to purchase and preserve its forest in 1881, an effort energetically reinforced by the work of the Society for the Protection of New Hampshire Forests, a private organization founded in 1901.

The rigors of lumbering drew powerful men to dangerous work and a strong camaraderie developed among workmates. The last of the great log drives down the Connecticut in 1915 drew loggers from throughout the north country and Canada.

Robert Pike recounts a story involving some of the men who worked on the stupendous "last drive down the Connecticut." The anecdote reveals a lot about the character and lifestyle of the men who worked in the woods.

Black Bill Fuller, 'Phonse Roby, Jigger Johnson, and Vern Davison, who told the story to Pike, rented a fringe-top surrey from a livery stable in North Stratford and started for the Connecticut Lakes to go fishing.

This snapshot of a team dragging a sizeable log on a yarding sled was taken around 1938 at Roger Andrew's Ravine Camp on Mount Mooselauke. Other snapshots taken at the same time show a small lumbering operation, including a sawmill, on the site. Both stationary and portable sawmills were common throughout the region.

In deep snow, the team would have worn heavy shoes with caulks for easier passage over a slippery surface. The driver sits sidewise on a cushioned spot at the front of the log wearing what looks like a racoon-skin hat. Another logger walks the trail ahead of the load. Usually, the butt end of the log was placed on the bunk of the yarding sled (the connecting portion between the two runners), while the tips of the logs dragged behind. *Courtesy of Dartmouth College Library*

...Vern sported a large handlebar moustache, Jigger was shaved clean, but both 'Phonse and Bill wore great black beards [hence, Fuller's nickname]...They stopped to buy two gallons of Canadian high wines, as pure alcohol is called along the border.

...The four friends stopped (at Cold Spring) to cut the liquor, and had a drink or two. It was warm, and they had all left their coats in the surrey. In his vest pocket Jigger had his whole winter's wages, more than five hundred dollars in bills. Because it was warm, he took off his vest and hung it on a limb.

"We sat there a while," said Vern, "and had a couple more drinks, and finally we started north again. We rolled along for more than fifteen miles, clear up to First Lake, before we noted Jigger didn't have his vest. 'Phonse and I wanted to go back and get it, but Jigger says, 'Oh, to hell with it! We're going fishing!' So we go over to the East Branch and stay ten days until our bait is all gone, and then we come back to the lake and get our team and start back to North Stratford."

" 'When we come to the Spring,' Jigger says, 'just stop a minute while I go down and get my vest.' And so help me, there it was, still on the limb where he'd left it, and all the money still in the pocket." (Pike, pages 243-244)

Songs, music, and stories provided the entertainment in the logging camps with a repertory drawn from English and French tradition. Radio, recordings, and non-English speaking European immigrants who entered the workforce at the turn of the century led to the eventual decline of these old ways.

Primeval Forests

Forestry in the western regions virtually wiped out the primeval forests that awaited the settlers. Heritage conscious citizens did manage to preserve a few of the ancient stands.

The WPA Guide to New Hampshire mentions that the town of Sutton jointly with the Society for the Preservation of New Hampshire Forests, owns a grove of twenty-one primeval pines, one mile north of North Sutton Village.

There is an 1890 description of this stand of trees, untouched in a forest that had by that time reached its second and third generation growth of trees.

Fortunately a few large pines were left uncut, a mile or two below the North Village, and they yet remain to show to this generation to what height and size a pine tree can attain, though they are long past their prime, and some of them *lean* considerably. (*Worthen,* page 565)

Not surprisingly, the trees have not survived to the present, but "The Sutton Pines," about four acres of land off Route 89 in North Sutton is cared for by the Society for its historic meaning. (The state took some of the land to build the highway.) This remnant of an old growth pine

Among the most captivating occupational subjects are those of the log drive, an essential aspect of traditional logging operations. The movement of logs down the river was as thrilling as it was dangerous and numerous tales and songs celebrate its place in the history of the woods. All the logs taken out of the woods through the long winters were run down to market with the spring ice-outs. At the height of the industry in the late nineteenth century this could comprise from ten to sixty million feet of lumber. Log drives were feasible almost the entire length of the Connecticut River, a fact important to the establishment of a thriving lumber trade in the eighteenth century. In fact, it has been noted that the Connecticut River was the largest log drive in New Hampshire and, at over three hundred miles, the length of the Connecticut from near the Canadian border to Long Island Sound, was the longest log drive in the world. The rigorous labor required exceptional strength and skill that in the drive's most spectacular moments presented a drama to onlookers that even action films of the 1980s do not rival.

The anonymous photographer of this spectacular view of drivers guiding logs over the falls highlights the daring of the men perched along the edge of the gorge and dam, greatly enhancing the action contained in the scene. They wore spiked boots to help their footing, to be sure, but the work was treacherous just the same. At such places in the river, the log drive became labor intensive, the placement of each log requiring utmost precision. This view of the drive testifies the observation that Robert Pike makes in his engrossing history of logging in New England. He says, that "the Connecticut drive was not only the longest in New England, it was one of the toughest. Everything to bother a riverman was there: falls, rapids, dams to be sluiced past, mill-owners to fight with, dry ledges to break a horse's legs on, freshets, droughts, ox-bows, bridges built on piers, . . . God! How the rivermen hated those bridges!" *Courtesy of Dartmouth College Library*

This 1912 summer scene of Ledyard Bridge, looking west, informs the viewer of just how laborious the log drives were. Every man is busy keeping the logs moving. Bridge footings are vulnerable to damage in a log jam or by uncontrollable timber pileups and a large number of men attend the effort to keep the logs moving around the bridge piers. Robert Pike comments that "the old covered Ledyard bridge at Hanover, beloved by so many Dartmouth students, sturdily withstood all the attacks of the rivermen, though many great jams piled up behind it." The last drive on the Connecticut River occurred three years after this photo was taken. It began with forty million feet of logs and before it was over, sixty-five million feet of lumber was bobbing down the river. Courtesy of Dartmouth College Library

stand represents one of the Society's earliest gifts. Robert H. Davis and his sister, Gertrude Davis Clay, gave the land to the Society in 1914. The trees were separately owned, however, and the Society's first fundraising drive was for their purchase. A few dead stems and a large bronze plaque today mark the place of the historic trees.

Neighboring Bradford has its claim to forest history in a stand of pines known popularly as the "King's Pines" because they were incised with the royal insignia that claimed them for the colonial king's navy. The Broad Arrow, hatchet marks in the shape of a crow's foot, is an ancient symbol indicating naval property. A 1729 statute required the mark to be placed on all New Hampshire white pines over forty inches in diameter on public land. Public protests against the statute erupted across the state, the most violent occurring in Weare in 1772.

The Bradford Pines are owned and managed by the state as a historic site. For their protection, the state has attached lightning rods to them, resulting in a curious combination of heritage and technology. Easily accessible from the road, the historic pines stand near the intersection of Routes 114 and 103.

One of the many wide-ranging activities sponsored or supported by the Society for the Preservation of New Hampshire Forests was an outstanding 1974 art exhibition on the Grand Monadnock at the Louise E. Thorne Art Gallery, Kent State College. Works by Keene's most famous painters, Barry Faulkner (1881-1966), Abbott Henderson Thayer (1849-1914) and local signpainter, later painter, William Preston Phelps (1848-1923) were among the selections.

The Mills

The sound of running water was the magnet that

attracted the pioneers to those sites in western New Hampshire suited to rude sawmills and gristmills. Villages clustered about the brooks, streams, and rivers that promised secure future settlements. By the time photography came on the scene, sawmills were great, efficient operations and gristmills were, by and large, passe, their buildings converted to other uses. Small mills were on the decline and large manufactories were making towns out of villages and cities out of towns.

An anecdote reflecting the dry wit of some of our forebears illustrates how important it was to choose a mill site with ample water power. Sometime around the turn of the nineteenth century, a Peterborough joiner named

> Mosey Morison went to Londonderry, Vt., and built a mill for a man by the name of Patterson, and after his return he called to see Wm. Smith, Esq., and wife (his sister.) "Well," said S[mith], "have you built a good mill for Patterson," "yes very good," was the reply. "Well, has he got a good millseat?" "Yes, very good." "Well, has he got plenty of water?" "yes, plenty, but he will have to cart it four miles." (Peterborough Historical Society, 1938, page 161)

According to the Cheshire County Registry of Deeds, in 1775, Elisha Briggs "built the canal and dam on the Ashuelot River that provided power for a grist mill north of the road to Ash Swamp and a sawmill south of the road. The mills were operated by the Blake family. Nathan Blake bought the mills on May 1, 1778 for £134/5. These mills were the site of the Faulkner and Colony mill that brought industrial growth to Keene in the nineteenth century." (Sanger, page 72)

To distinguish it from the mill nearby the Sanger home on the highway north of Keene, Abner Sanger, in a journal entry for April 29, 1776, refers to the Elisha Briggs mill as the "Mill at Keene town." On June 24th of that

Perhaps the last log drive in the region was in May, 1959. Here, the pulp logs are bulldozed into the fast moving current of the Swift Diamond River near Stewartstown on the Dartmouth College Grant, a legacy of the original land grants made to Dartmouth by the royal governor. The timber seems of a more manageable size although it employed many more than the three-man crew appearing in this photo. The tree at the far left in the photo, barely beyond the bud stage, is testament to the lateness of spring in the northern reaches of the state. *Courtesy of Dartmouth College Library*

The lumberman's work was only partially over when the logs arrived at their destination, most often a sawmill. The skills associated with the various tasks of getting the sawn boards to market were also specialized. This fully loaded flatbed, its burden carefully balanced and chained, sits outside a lumberyard in Lisbon, an impressive tribute to the skill of the workers who erected it board by board. Both the sight of the load and the thought of what went into it give pause. Snow chains on the tires, once an absolute necessity in winter snow, are completely obsolete at century's end. The handcrafted cab completes the aesthetic appeal of this subject that so deserves to have been caught by an anonymous photographer's eye and camera. *Courtesy of New Hampshire Historical Society*

The northern Connecticut River valley's bustling paper, pulp, and lumber industry drew WPA photographer Arthur Rothstein who documented the mills for the Farm Security Administration. A sampling of his photos appears earlier. This photo of "pulpwood cut by a cooperative farmer's organization" gives further evidence of his insightful work. Cooperative agencies were of particular interest as the Depression wound down, a reflection of a national policy that encouraged self-help. This way of life was second nature to the rural population of western New Hampshire where neighbor regularly helps neighbor in such cooperative seasonal chores as haying or laying in the winter's wood supply. Note the stencil-lettered sign: "This wood is the property of the State of New Hampshire." *Courtesy of Library of Congress, Photograph and Print Division*

35

"The Champion Load of Wood" featured in this priceless stereograph view sold by the J. A. French Studio of Keene was drawn to the Cheshire Railroad Company at the city of Keene, February 6, 1875, by Roger C. Osgood of Sullivan. Photographed at Keene's City Square, the load's dimensions are: 10 ft. 8 in. wide; 11 ft. 3 in. high; 12 ft. long making 1440 cubic feet or eleven cords. These dimensions were certified by C. G. Gale, "A Measurer of Wood for the City of Keene."

Mr. Osgood stands proudly by his formidable team of oxen. He is wearing the traditional farmer's smock, an antiquated garment even then. According to the stereographer's advertisement that

completed the information on the reverse of the image, this was one of a hundred stereograph subjects from Keene in

French's stock of over two thousand souvenir views. Courtesy of New Hampshire Historical Society

year, he records that he "[went] to work afternoon for young Nathan Blake at Elisha Brigg's mill for a bushel of rye. Abel Blake to mill [meaning that he was also there]."

The Faulkner and Colony Company is a good example of a mill with a long, continuing history in the region. It was founded by a descendent of John Colony, a Roger's Ranger, in partnership with another local entrepreneur in 1815. During the nineteenth century its staple product was a flannel cloth, twenty-seven inches wide, in primary colors. Red was the favorite color of shirts for the "Forty-niners" and blue for New Orleans stevedores. After 1900 and until it closed, the firm specialized in white flannels and women's dress goods. Today, the revitalization of Keene may be symbolized by the refurbishing of these same mills as a shopping center and gathering place.

Textiles and shoes were the most important commercial factory products, historically, in western New Hampshire. Cotton and linen, processed by a workforce of Scottish and Irish immigrants, were especially important. The first shoe factory in New Hampshire was built at Weare in 1823.

Sawmills

Many north country sawmills operated only in the winter, closing down for the summer while owners and workers attended to farm chores. During the winter, when the farm chores were light, women and children could take care of noon feeding for the animals while the men worked in the woods and at the sawmill. Production varied according to the size of the operations. Logs would be hauled over snow and ice. In an open winter, the logs piled up until there was enough snow to haul them to the mill.

When needed, women pitched in for all manner of hard "men's" work, including driving teams. Famous in the Lyme-Haverhill area for her skill with horse teams, was Ruth Park, ninety-two years of age when the following commentary was published in 1976.

> Miss Park's teamsters and her father's before her, drew over that road en route to the railroad station at East Thetford.
>
> When getting logs out of the woods, an early thaw might mean working continuous shifts and feeding the horses while "on the road." On such an occasion, it was not beneath Miss Park to take the reins herself. Residents recall her doing so in 1926, drawing pulp with a four-horse team through Lyme Center at two or three o'clock in the morning. (Cole, page 174)

The variety of sawmill sites and of architectural style defies categorization, as these photographs illustrate. By the end of the nineteenth century, portable steam-powered sawmills made it possible to haul logs *and* boards out of the woods. A sawmill might occupy one of the several outbuildings to be found on a prosperous farm. Some were family businesses run out of the home, and at times actually sharing the farmhouse dooryard. Every town had its commercial sawmill and some had several. Good historical records of sawmill operations, including portable sawmills working locally, are available for many towns. Andover is an example:

> Few years have passed since 1900 when there were no portable sawmills operating in the town. Steam was the main motive power until about 1920, generated by burning the slabwood under the boilers. These mills were set up on or near the timber lots to be sawed, and the lumber "stuck up"

The Old Bell Mill on River Street, Peterborough, burned down in January 1922, a great loss in terms of local architectural and industrial heritage. Jonathan Morison, an original settler of Peterborough, built the first gristmill and sawmill on the site, Lot No. 112. In addition to the sawmill in vigorous operation at the time this photograph was taken, Old Bell Mill has hosted several other manufactories including cider, piano keys, shoe shanks, and baskets. In this attractive photograph, the proportions and design of the building are nicely balanced by the massive logs artfully scattered along the roadside. Courtesy of Peterborough Historical Society

Knight Saw Mill in Dublin appears to be a small but efficient operation of conventional architecture and layout. Courtesy of Peterborough Historical Society

A. Eddy of Claremont took this photograph of a busy nearby sawmill. The empty yardsled is an uncommon sight in the old photographs of the area. The crew look to be healthy men in their twenties and thirties, although a companion photograph, probably taken the same day, shows a boy no older than fifteen among the workers. In photographing the workers, Eddy thoughtfully includes the large workhorses. Courtesy of New Hampshire Historical Society

to season for a year or so before being shipped out by rail. . . .

It would be pointless to list all the portable sawmills which have operated in Andover in the past sixty-five years, for the number has been great. In some years, notably between 1918 and 1924, as many as ten have been going at one time, scattered all over the town. A few of the sawmill operators since that time have been Herbert Sevigny of Lebanon, Max Israel of Henniker, Fred Flanders and William Wood of Hopkinton, Walter Gardner of Laconia, Chadwick & Kidder of Franklin, Webster and Calley of Andover, and lastly Frank Pobuda of Lebanon. There are none in town in 1965. (Chaffee, page 90)

The Historic American Buildings Survey, another Works Progress Administration public works project, generated selected inventories for towns, cities, counties and church archives throughout the state but mostly in the Seacoast region. In New Hampshire, as elsewhere, selected buildings of historical interest were carefully documented, including a number of mill sites, mostly abandoned. The workers produced photographs, drawings,

historical accounts, and miscellaneous notes and surveys. Interest has centered on the elegant examples of historic homes that WPA surveyors documented and many publications have featured them in the fifty years since. Vernacular buildings were studied, as well, and their sites searched for evidence of machine and building parts. Mills clustered around the banks of fast-moving water locations on the rivers, streams, and brooks throughout the region. The mills often formed the nucleus of the earliest villages in a settlement and some proprietor's maps indicate that these sites were designated for the establishment of grist- and sawmills, the two most necessary to the building of a new town. The smithy would always be found in the heart of the village and became the traditional center of male social life.

The Cheshire Mill

The Cheshire Mill, known locally as Lower Mills, is situated in Harrisville, one of the most beautiful mill villages in New England. The town was among the first in the state to seek historic district status, having been well documented by the Historic American Buildings Survey.

This artistic document of a busy lumberyard in the Claremont area may also be an Eddy photograph. The teams, oxen and horses, add greatly to the awareness of the strenuous life of north country lumbermen. Courtesy of New Hampshire Historical Society

Stereograph: Bachelder's Saw Mills, Wilmot. Courtesy of New Hampshire Historical Society

Stereograph: Falls at Bachelder's Mills, Wilmot. Courtesy of New Hampshire Historicald Society

These two stereographs, of a series of "Views Near Kearsarge" photographed and offered for sale by John Bachelder of Andover, are of a permanent mill site nicely situated by an active waterfall. The photo of the actual operations of Bachelder's Mills at Wilmot includes one workman sitting on a log, center foreground. The mill falls are barely visible at the left and top left of the building. A careful perusal of the other photograph, featuring the mill falls, reveals several people perched at various dry vantage points near and about the falls. The boardwalk and the wooden sluiceway, angling in at opposite corners of the falls offer a strong element of design that lifts this photograph above the ordinary or the merely clever. The Bachelders, of neighboring Andover, are a distinguished family, Nahum J. Bachelder having been governor of New Hampshire from 1902 to 1904. Courtesy of New Hampshire Historical Society

The original building in the drawing, the section with the bell tower, was built for Cyrus Harris between 1846 and 1847 by Asa Greenwood, a noted stonemason and an investor in the new mill.

At night that summer ox teams straining with the large granite blocks could be heard coming up the eight-mile winding dirt road from the quarry in Marlborough to Harrisville. To avoid the heat, a driver and team would leave Harrisville in late afternoon, pick up the blocks that had been made ready and, if nothing broke down, arrive back at the construction site sometime before work began the next morning. Thus, he wasted no time and built it well. Cyrus Harris, superintending the construction, must have answered many question[s] about the mill's appearance, for it was unlike that of the factories of Massachusetts and northern New England. The four-story building had fine large windows on all sides, roof windows running its length, a slate roof, and, instead of the usual wooden ones, solid granite eaves. At the front of the building was a square granite tower which housed the stairs and supported the cupola. Architecturally, the mill resembled those found in Rhode Island and their English prototypes. In fact, it has been called "the purest form of old English industrial architecture north of Rhode Island." (Armstrong, pages 28-29)

Harris's untimely death of consumption in 1848, led to the sale of the building, pond, and water rights to Faulkner and Colony of Keene. By the time it began operating, two of Josiah Colony's sons had acquired the company and Henry Colony became the mill's first president in 1851. The company remains in the family.

The drawing of the Cheshire Mill, Harrisville, is by Otto H. Barker who rendered it in 1888 for the October issue of *Century Magazine*. The view is of the northerly direction. It is on the second floor of this building that the women pictured in the companion photograph are working. The historical and architectural documentation of this important Harrisville mill is the most complete of any mill in western New Hampshire.

Other images presented here are meant to illustrate the variety of mill operations in western New Hampshire. A few express something of the lifestyle that went along with them.

There are few working mills in western New Hampshire in the last decades of the twentieth century. Mid-century town planners in the region, like their counterparts across America, devalued the architectural or historical importance of their mill buildings, demolishing many of them between the 1920s and 1960s. Successful adaptation of mill complexes in mill towns elsewhere and the increasing costs of building large new edifices made an impact by the 1970s, however, and today, many mills have been renovated, rarely as mills. Keene's Colony

The building in which this documentary photo was taken is located on the southeast corner of Main and Grove streets, Harrisville, Cheshire County (New Hampshire Historic American Buildings Survey No. NH-173). Jack E. Boucher succeeds in achieving the appearance of a candid photo in this view of women working under rather primitive conditions at Cheshire Mill, in May 1969. He captions this New England Mill Survey photograph, "No. 1 Mill, Second Floor Interior." Courtesy of Library of Congress, Photograph and Print Division

Cheshire Mill, 1847, Harrisville. Courtesy of Library of Congress, Photograph and Print Division

This building which was on the site of the Needham Basket Company, Peterborough, was known as Eagle Factory and was open from 1851 to 1875 when it burned down. It was rebuilt as Felt's Machine Shop. The history of this mill site is a familiar one for the area. "Daniel Abbott came [to Peterborough] from Lyndeborough as a boy to learn the carpenter's trade. When very young he worked on the construction of the Old Meeting House. . . . In 1795, . . . twenty-six years old, he established a cabinet-and-chair-making business in a shop he built on the south side of the Nubanusit River immediately east of Elm Street. Power for his shop was taken from the Elm Street dam. The manufacturing of cotton yarns, however, seemed to give more promise, so in 1813, he, with others, converted the building into a spinning mill known as the Eagle Factory, with machinery built in town by Moses Dodge. A year later he sold out to Thomas Baker and Joseph Tubbs. (Morison, pages 363-364)

They manufactured cotton yarns, batting, and candlewicking. After fire damaged the building in 1833, they sold out to a new cotton and woolen factory which, in turn, sold to a pump manufactory. The building suffered fire again in 1875. The unhurt portion was used as a machine shop until Needham Basket company acquired the property in 1893 and rebuilt it. To lure Needham's business from Worcester, the town excused the basket company from town taxes for five years.

In 1909, the building became an underwear factory. From 1917 Hagen's art neckties were made there. A. Erland Goyette acquired the building for a museum in 1935 (Morison, pages 363-344) Goyette auctioned off the contents of his museum not long ago. Today, the building is a warehouse and distribution center for Rugged Bear, a local manufacturer. Courtesy of Peterborough Historical Society

Some of the workers at this Peterborough shoe shop line up as for a formal photograph while others lean out of the windows and stand on the porch and porch roof. The building was built in 1884 by the Peterboro Improvement Company and leased as a manufactory. Later, it was sold to a piano and piano key manufacturer who, in turn, sold it to Needham Basket Company. It was taken down in the early twenties, a period when a number of other Peterborough buildings were demolished. (Note the bicycle with the large front wheel in the right foreground.) The pianos had been manufactured by a German firm, Hagen & Ruefer, which employed several Germans in the plant, some of whom settled in the area. One local historian recalls that the German families, "in those days caused at least mild discussion by the number of cases of beer that appeared on Saturday night." The remark reveals a degree of prejudice characteristic of mill town populations as European and Canadian immigration increased. (Morison, page 8) Courtesy of Peterborough Historical Society

The H. B. Needham Basket Manufactory, an imposing presence in Peterborough at the intersection of Elm and River streets, occupies the site of the Eagle Factory. Besides textiles, Peterborough was a major center for basket manufacturing for over a century. The mill town of Peterborough reveals its early rural character in this photo. Private residences situated among mill buildings throughout the town gave Peterborough an architectural aspect that appealed very much to the photographic artist. This photograph was taken by M. G. W. Machinist. Courtesy of Peterborough Historical Society

Nellie Boutwell gave this photograph of mill workers from the White Mills (earlier the White Machine Shop), West Peterborough, to the local historical society. It well represents such portraits, revealing a tidy workforce of varying ages. Women supplemented family incomes with very low factory wages. The foremen were always men whose wages were somewhat better. Peterborough was a major mill center in southern New Hampshire attracting a large number of new residents. It was not until the late nineteenth century that westward migration began to drain the workforce of local factories. Courtesy of Peterborough Historical Society

An important step in the manufacture of textiles for sale was the inspection of the finished cloth. Large inspection tables situated handy to the folding machines made this an efficient job. As much as possible the room is designed to allow adequate lighting for the inspection, done by trained inspectors, men or women, who looked through a half-dozen lengths from every bolt. Final inspection took place after the folding. New Hampshire textile mills took pride in the quality of their fabrics and workers were trained to look for flaws at every stage of manufacture. It was the responsibility of these inspectors, however, to certify the quality of the mills output. The original of this photo reads

"the folding machines and inspecting tables of the Old Mill at Jackson Mills, near Newport." Courtesy of New Hampshire Historical Society

Early tanneries were established on property away from the village and town population centers, often on a remote area of a local farm. By the middle of the nineteenth century, however, town locations were common for the larger commercial tanneries, close to the pool of workers. An unpleasant and physically rigorous operation, tanneries employed male workers, almost exclusively, to execute the process. This was one of three different portraits of Burnap's Tannery that J. A. French offered among his views of Keene and vicinity. Taken in October, 1873, it was sold in Marlow by E. N. Howe, "Dealer in Drugs, Medicines, Fancy Goods." Courtesy of New Hampshire Historical Society

This striking portrait of the workers at the Hillsborough Mills in Milford document the inescapable fact of child employment in the New Hampshire textile mills. These enormous spooling and shuttle rooms are in the 180 foot by 50 foot Hillsborough Mills. Hillsborough Mills was one of Milford's largest textile mills, specializing in carpet yarns, blankets, and "cassimeres." The two hundred or so workers "were picked up from Milford and the surrounding towns by horse-drawn wagons and carried to their work at the mill." (Wright, page 234) Mill buildings had operated on the site known as Pine Valley as early as 1814. Several buildings had been successively destroyed by fire before this brick structure was built in 1873. It was situated within less than a mile of the principal village of Wilton. The mill was supplied with "an engine of sufficient power to make good any lack of water power during the dry season."

Fires at mills were all too common, caused by various hazards inherent to the trade from spontaneous combustion of grain dust to ignition from sparks resulting from friction of machine parts. The hand-pump that Mr. Johnson and his Boy Scouts from Troy, shown on page 139, proudly demonstrate, at a 1959 regional muster would very likely have fought several mill fires in its day. Courtesy of New Hampshire Historical Society

Mill Marketplace represents one of the many successful adaptations. Chamber of Commerce literature invites the public to "experience New England under one roof in this beautifully restored 150-year-old woolen mill which now houses more than forty stores featuring unique New England products and goods of exceptional quality and value." Local patrons find little exaggeration in this public relations statement. Other buildings await decisions as to their eventual use and still others have become apartment or condominium complexes.

The history of mill towns shifting from north to south, a steady trickle throughout the second half of the nineteenth century and a great flow during the twentieth, is well documented. Local opinion reflects the larger view that electricity, by enabling factories to move away from sites of water power, sparked the demise of New Hampshire's mills.

TIME TABLE

OF THE

PETERBOROUGH MILLS,

TO TAKE EFFECT MARCH 20, 1858.

From March 20th to September 19th, inclusive.

COMMENCE WORK, at 6.30 A. M.   LEAVE OFF WORK, at 7.00 P. M., except on Saturday Evenings.

BREAKFAST, at 6.00 A. M.   DINNER, at 12.15 P. M.   COMMENCE WORK, after Dinner, 1.00 P. M.

From September 20th to March 19th, inclusive.

COMMENCE WORK at 7.00 A. M.   LEAVE OFF WORK at 7.15 P. M., except on Saturday Evenings.

BREAKFAST at 6.30 A. M.   DINNER 12.30 P. M.   COMMENCE WORK after Dinner at 1.10 P. M.

BELLS.

From March 20th to September 19th, inclusive.

Morning Bells.	Dinner Bells.	Evening Bells.
First Bell, - - - - - - 4.45 A. M.	Ring out, - - - - - 12.15 P. M.	Ring out at 7.00 P. M., or as
Second, - - 5.45. Third - - 6.22	Ring in, - - - - - - 12.52 P. M	near that time as the Machinery can be run by daylight, except on Saturday Evenings.

From September 20th to March 19th, inclusive.

Morning Bells.	Dinner Bells.	Evening Bells.
First Bell, - - - - - - 5.00 A. M.	Ring out, - - - - - 12.30 P. M.	Ring out, - - - - - - 7.15 P. M.,
Second, - - 6.15. Third, - - 6.52.	Ring in, - - - - - - - - 1.02 P. M.	Except on Saturday Evenings.

SATURDAY EVENING BELLS.

During April, May, June, July, August and September, Ring out at 5.00 P. M.

The remaining Saturday Evenings ring out as follows :

October.	December.	February.
2 First Saturdays ring out 4.45.	2 First Saturdays ring out 3.50.	2 First Saturdays ring out 4.45.
2 Second " " " 4.30.	2 Second " " " 4.00.	2 Second " " " 5.00.

November.	January.	March.
2 First Saturdays ring out 4.15.	2 First Saturdays ring out 4.15.	2 First Saturdays ring out 5.00.
2 Second " " " 4.00	2 Second " " " 4.25.	2 Second " " " 5.00.

₊ SPEED GATES commence hoisting three minutes before commencing work. *₊*

Broadside courtesy of Peterborough Historical Society

Formerly Munson's Cotton Mill, Colony Mill was purchased by Lewis J. Colony, of Keene, a few years after his marriage in 1858. He apparently operated it as a cotton mill until 1871. He was one of the first manufacturers of rocking chairs and large office chairs. Soon after 1877, the Munsonville mill began producing splint-seat chairs. They were finished and sold at a paint shop and storehouse that Colony owned on Wilson Street in Keene. This French & Sawyer photograph was sold out of their Bridgeman Block Gallery in Keene, only ten miles west of the mill pictured here. Courtesy of New Hampshire Historical Society

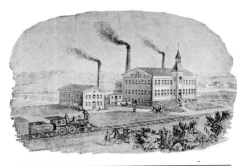

Mill sites were popular subjects for the engraver as they were for the photographer and painter. This depicts Peterborough's Noone Mill, the last of the old Peterborough textile mills to close in a town that was once an important textile center. It specialized in woolen cloth and felt for the paper industry. Situated south of town on the Jaffrey Road, the buildings have been converted to shops and eateries. The Noone Mill's handsome belfry was torn off in the hurricane of September 21, 1938, and never replaced. Albert W. Noone, proprietor, was one of twelve long-time residents, all men, to be named a "Peterborough Elder of 1930." Courtesy of Peterborough Historical Society

Millponds often made ideal settings for adaptation of a former mill to a summer resort after the working mill had been closed. The buildings on mill sites, though plain, were often large and sturdy with little interior division. This is the "Old Mill and Algonquin Lodge" in New London. The original of this photo is dated July 1897. However it is probable that it was taken a year earlier when W. A. Wright of Ayer, Massachusetts, was on a photographing trip through western New Hampshire, including the Monadnock, Keene, Claremont, and Sunapee regions. Courtesy of New Hampshire Historical Society

Phoenix Factory, as it was called, commissioned this and other photographs of the plant for use in company publications. The view, northwest across the millyard, shows up the beautiful twin bell towers. A large wooden mill built in 1793 had previously stood on the site. Its fate is vividly described in the Annals of 1828: "On the 18th of December, the New part of the Phoenix Factory was burned. This was the largest building [ever] destroyed by fire in town. It took fire in the upper story probably from the stove which was used for warming the room. . . notwithstanding the vast quantities of water thrown by the engines, every effort to save the building proved unavailing. . . . The walls were left standing and some parts of the floors and machinery in the north part of the building. (Peterborough Historical Society, 1938, page 173)

The large Phoenix Mill complex pictured here, that once occupied much of Peterborough's business district, replaced the ruined building in 1829 and was built of brick as a hedge against fire. A two-story house was added to the factory in 1840. The handsome factory complex was torn down in 1922. Courtesy of Peterborough Historical Society

Groveton is the lumber capital of the northern Connecticut River Valley. Every spring and summer, the vast cordage of lumber that had been stored in booms strung along miles of the length of the Upper Ammonoosuc and its tributaries would be released to the mills in Groveton. The town took due pride in the success of their major industry. This handsome scene is reproduced from a folded color postcard sold at one time to tourists throughout the northern tier of the state. Courtesy of New Hampshire Historical Society

Odell Mills, Groveton, N.H.

What WPA photographer Arthur Rothstein calls a Pulp Paper Mill is easily identified in the photo as the Groveton Paper Company. In 1936, Rothstein took a lengthy series of photographs at this thriving industrial site which is certainly impressive enough to justify his attention. Logging attracted the lenses of many of the artists who photographed rural America for the Works Progress Administration. A talented and versatile artist, Rothstein took well designed images of visually interesting sights throughout the mill such as these of "Stacked Logs in the Mill Yard" and "Working the Log Pile." Courtesy of Library of Congress, Photograph and Print Division

47

Trying to pin down the sites of Marion Post Wolcott's photographs of Coos County is hindered by the careless annotation of her field photographs. In this, she finds good company in Rothstein and many other WPA photographers. To these artists, impeccable images counted, not historical details. The archived microfilm is labeled simply, "Coos County, N.H." Such trains traveled regularly to the Groveton mills and lumber mills throughout the area. Courtesy of Library of Congress, Photograph and Print Division

For many years one of Newport's principal factories, The Newport Shoe Manufacturing Corporation has only recently gone out of business. The buildings sprawled around this tower are utilized now by various small businesses that rent space in the complex of well-preserved buildings sitting low between the road and the river just south of Newport's downtown. Photo by Armand Szainer

The site of this newly renovated mill on the Sugar River in downtown Claremont, with its millstream and rushing waters, retains the beauty in 1988 that nineteenth-century builders found there. Claremont has been fortunate enough to retain most of its original brick mill buildings, some already handsomely reclaimed, others awaiting their turn at rehabilitation. Renovated mill buildings in the area are multi-purpose, combining businesses, offices, and residential units. Photo by Armand Szainer

The Dorr Woolen Company continues to operate in Guild, outside of Newport. The textile mill, long a family run business, is now operated by the Pendleton Company. The mill continues to weave fabrics, mostly used to make women's suits and dresses, for the parent company and a number of New York garment houses which purchase through Pendleton's New York offices. The Dorr family retains the Dorr factory store situated across the road from the mill pictured here. The factory store carries a complete line of fabrics and sewing notions, crafts supplies, and similar wares as well as being an outlet for Pendleton clothes. Photo by Armand Szainer

Local gossip has it that this and several other former mills along the river in Claremont are destined for renovation as residences, a happy choice given their location. The building once housed a machine factory that included a foundary on its north end. Claremont is one of the most unspoiled mill cities in the state with a downtown area that shows off its period architecture. The human scale of the city streets invites the pedestrian to wander comfortably among stores that are well preserved, having undergone little reconstruction. Photo by Armand Szainer

This drawing of the bail dogs from the Nicholas Rowell Saw Mill, Sutton Mill Village, is from the Historic American Buildings Survey records. The bail dogs held the log in place on the carriage to keep it from rolling as it was sawn into boards. The bail dog is similar in design and function to the dogs on the end of a logger's sled that held the timber together and kept the load off of the horses' heels. At the sawmill, the dogs sit at the front of the log carriage head block. The dogs can get very close to the saw blade when it is in operation but they so place the wood that the blade, as one old-timer puts it, "won't quite ever hit these metal parts."

In the up-and-down sawmills, one sawyer would stand in the pit below the carriage and another would stand on the mill floor above. Up-and-down sawing was muscle-building work and the men would trade off their work positions. When working in the pit, the sawyer wore a wide-brimmed hat to keep the sawdust out of his face.

In 1829, Captain Nicholas Rowell erected his sawmill, apparently on the

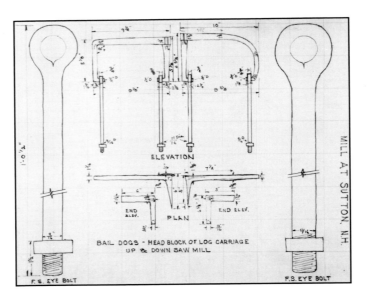

site of Quimby's gristmill at Mill Village, Sutton, the first mill site in that town. Quimby had built his mill in the 1760s. A local anecdote is revealing:

The early saw mills were of rude construction. The foot- and head-blocks were stationary. They had overshot water wheels, and the water

was poured on to them from a trough. Ezekiel Davis [1773-1852] carried the crank of one of them, weighing one hundred and fifty pounds, over [Mount] Kearsarge, from where is now Franklin, to Sutton. (Worthen, pages 228, 290)

A number of photographs and drawings exist from the Historic American Buildings Survey of the Butterfield Mill in Washington, including this drawing of part of a waterwheel and balance. When surveyed, for the Historic Records Survey (1936-1941), the up-and-down sawmill was in ruins and these parts were scattered over the site, some in the Ashuelot River itself. The history of the Butterfield Mill is fully discussed in the most recent local history. It was located in the Cherry Valley area of Washington, now part of Pillsbury State Park. It was built in 1842 and was active until 1915 (although a map dates it as active until 1922). The millpond was located adjacent to cultivated farmland, a fact that placed limitations on the mill's water rights. An early deed states that the buyer acquires an acre of

land: ". . . with a sawmill standing thereon, together with the privilege to raise the water in said pond to certain holes drilled in three stones in said pond. . . for the purpose of showing how high the water might be raised." (Jager and Jager, Portrait of a Hill Town, page 430)

Such legal attention to the needs of neighbors illustrates both a respect for the historical use of land and a practical reinforcement of the lifestyle of cooperation that was imperative to our ancestors. The older generation apparently saw fit to secure in law the neighborly habits they took for granted in the first years of settlement. A few years after the WPA surveys, mill parts all over the nation was salvaged for use in the war effort.

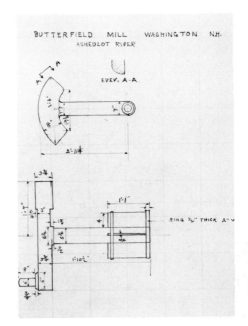

The accompanying photograph provides satisfying technical details of antiquated mill machinery parts. Resting between the two halves of the "Rosewheel" (waterwheel) containing the water buckets, the anchor-shaped part appears to be made of iron and probably served to regulate the movement of the wheel as the water poured into the buckets causing the mill gears to operate. Butterfield Mill offered an array of services and products. Photo by E. B. Philbrick

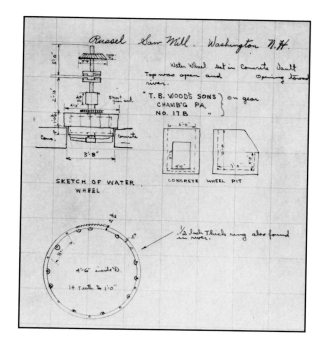

Russel Saw Mill. Washington N.H.

SKETCH OF WATER WHEEL

CONCRETE WHEEL PIT

By 1880, Russell's sawmill, located below Ashuelot Pond on the Ashuelot River in Washington, was owned and operated by Edgar Farnsworth. John Wilcox worked it briefly after he took it over in 1897 but it did not survive as an active mill into the twentieth century. The mechanical drawing of waterwheel parts from Russell's mill details what a functioning waterwheel is like in situ.

The photograph of the iron rag wheel and shaft with its wooden arbor and wooden pins complements the several drawings the surveyor made of it and other mill parts. The iron rag wheel sets the log carriage ahead by water power but it is returned by hand power. The photographs of the Russel[l] Saw Mill parts were taken by E. B. Philbrick in July 1936 for the Historic American Buildings Survey, a project of the WPA.

When these drawings and photographs were taken, few early mill buildings were standing. A fine exception, although somewhat deteriorated even then, is the abandoned Charles Kelly Mill of South Sutton, photographed for the Historic American Buildings Survey by E. W. Clark. Charles Kelly, unmentioned in Sutton's town history, was probably not the owner most identified with this mill site in town records.

Harry Tanzi delights the local crowd at Hanover's 1961 bi-centennial parade, as he wheels the original turn-of-the-century pushcart that started a successful family business. Bananas, peaches, grapes, and onions aptly encapsulate the history of the street vendor-turned-storekeeper, a conventional route to success for many immigrants to America, then and now. The Tanzis operated their family greengrocers store on Hanover's Main Street until 1969. Courtesy of Dartmouth College Library

4
ENTREPRENEURS AND INVENTORS

The diversity of businesses in the region follows the normal development of small town economy in New Hampshire throughout its history. The basic services that came first, grist-and sawmills, for example, were followed in time by the industries dependent on local natural resources. The coming of the railroad invited the proliferation of business opportunities in the communities it served. Fortunes ebbed and flowed with the tides of local, state, national, and international fashion. In the Connecticut River Valley and environs, villages and towns fostered a personal relationship between the population and its business community. Citizens wore several hats. It was not uncommon for a leading figure of local commerce to serve concurrently as local or state politicians, officers in the local militia, or lay authorities in their local church.

The demographics of the region's economy is fully documented in town and state records, census figures, and statistical studies. To its neighbors and patrons, a business is both the people and the physical plant—outside, a plate-glass-windowed storefront, and within, a multitude of parts. The ambiance of a store emanates from the combination of the well-laden counters, the appointments and decorations, the unique scent of the merchandise, and the faces of the workers—these are all familiar to the regular customer. The physical setting and the social exchange that takes place there remain in the minds and emotions of local residents. In small

The three Tanzi brothers, Charles, Harry and Leon, look up at the photographer from their normal activities of uncrating, bagging, and making change as the heavily burdened customer waits. A potential customer inspects the produce display in the window. The year is 1947.

Tanzi's specialty food store is extremely well-organized; the trash can is handy to the produce (a wilted leaf or a cardboard divider can be discarded before produce goes on display); bags are at hand on their own shelf beneath the counter and the cash register is in the center of things where it belongs. Tanzi's was more than a food store; it provided lessons in geography and nutrition. Exotic and imported foods (dromedary dates) developed the palate and expanded the vocabulary. Advertising broadsides are discretely placed. Colorful fruits and vegetables lie in open boxes and neatly aligned foodstuffs sit on the shelves, placed to attract the customer's eye.

The clock sits in view of the street for the convenience of passersby. "Sen-Sen"

advertised in the window recalls the time prior to mouth sprays. The product was especially popular with teenagers and college students who wished to mask the odor of tobacco or alcohol after a night on the town.

The Tanzis, garbed in their tidy caps and protective white shirts (despite the one torn sleeve), appear to be professional food handlers, their cleanliness inspiring confidence in their wares. Courtesy of Dartmouth College Library

communities, local businesses are like homes away from home. Whereas one's aesthetic sense develops and changes with training and schooling, one's emotional attachments result from familiarity, repetition, and personal communication.

The era of the traveling salesman followed hard on the heels of the peddler, many of whom settled in established communities and founded dry goods stores. Seemingly everything could be purchased from the traveling salesman who would sometimes write to various businesses in a region to announce an impending sales trip. To add the veneer of professionalism, many companies had form letters or circulars with prescribed spaces for writing the name of the company's representative and pertinent dates.

In this section are images that reflect the meaning that business people and places have for those who interact with them throughout a lifetime. Included are a few examples of businesses, like large building movers, that may not have had a specific shop, storefront, or office location, but which gradually evolved into contracting firms, large-machine operations, moving companies, and similar businesses. A few businesses have made the transition from the nineteenth to the twentieth century with only cosmetic changes. Auctioneering is one. Fuel companies are another.

Also included are photographs that graphically depict the changing landscape of the area's business districts, whether village, town, or city. Many other photographs depicting businesses are to be found elsewhere in the book as useful illustrations for other aspects of the social history of the regions.

John A. Wright

According to A. Harold Kendall, John A. Wright was an inventor and businessman, co-proprietor of the Eagle Hotel.

[One day, he] was driving his horse and buggy in Troy, when he came upon a cow stuck in a roadside bog. He stopped to pull the animal out, with the help of a farmer he called upon for help. As bits of mud dried on the cow, its body turned an extraordinary white. Deeply interested, Wright began experimenting with the mud. Noticing a cleansing effect on the silver spoon with which he was mixing it, he realized the mud was a fine grade of diatomaceous earth, a substance famed since ancient times for its cleansing powers. With this discovery, he produced a silver cleaner which he first used in his own hotel. Word about the new polish spread to the surrounding towns, and he soon found himself in business making Wright's Silver Cream. The first factory was in a remodeled house on Cypress Street. The business was incorporated as J. A. Wright and Company in 1893. After the death of John A. Wright in 1896, Arthur L.

This trio surveys their wares at Putnam's Drug Store on Hanover's Main Street in this Adrian Bouchard photo. The precisely organized products seem interchangeable with those of many mid-twentieth-century drugstores all over America. Most commonly requested items are situated conveniently, scented powders and colognes are under the counter. Bromo Seltzer, a big-seller in a town where all but one of its many eateries has some kind of alcohol license, sits near at hand on the counter. The gleaming countertop mirrors its burdens, a reflection of the shop's ship-shape atmosphere. Photo by Adrian Bouchard; courtesy of Dartmouth College Library

and Frank A. Wright, sons of the founder, carried on the business. Once the company had found the materials suitable for its polish, the formula never changed. . . . John P. Wright, the founder's grandson, entered the firm in 1927, and after the death of his father in 1928 and his uncle in 1929, became chief executive officer. In 1940 the company built a factory on Dunbar Street, which it now occupies. John M. and Thomas P. Wright, sons of John P., came into the business in 1955. The three men are the executive officers of the company today. (Keene History Committee, pages 490-491)

The above information remains current except to add that yet another generation has entered the firm since Kendall wrote in 1968. John B. Wright, son of John M., came on board in 1980 and is now the firm's director of marketing.

The photograph of the company's founder is a rare and wonderful document of an entrepreneurial venture, probably similar to many such endeavors our ancestors leapt to when the virgin soil of a new land offered its riches without restriction. Details in the photo (page 61) demand examination. The methodological extraction of the earth, shaped into small rounds, set out in the open air perhaps for drying or simply waiting to be gathered up and carted away speaks well of Wright's organizational skills. Is the small building, so precisely constructed and so obviously new, a drying place, a storage shed, or a

Old Hanover Businesses as they were photographed in 1867.

Separate stores for dry goods, groceries, tin and hollow ware (with samples hanging in the window), and the barber's painted post in front of the smaller building, taken together, provide what the department store would later sell under one roof. This diversification of tradesmen's wares is the natural outgrowth of the craftsman-based manufacturing economy of early America. As the industrial age advanced, individual stores consolidated. This photograph depicts something of a middle stage of merchandising in the town. Outside, pony and horses wait patiently in the traces of their vehicles. The young trees speak for the newness of the scene.

The near wood-frame building houses H. O. Bly's "Photographic Gallery" on an upper floor. Bly took this photograph prior to 1875 when the inn next door came down, here in its full glory, a row of granite hitching posts lining the front boardwalk. The photo's inclusion in an album belonging to a Dartmouth student, Class of 1869, dates the image to at least a half-dozen years earlier yet. At about this time, Dudley and Babcock's Meat Market occupied the basement. Other shops were Clough

Storrs & Co. and a printing office. The tin coffee pot on the post lends interest to the scene. Albert Wainwright, tinsmith, was the first owner of Hanover Hardware Company and operator of the Hanover Wilmot stagecoach line. This section of Main Street became known as the Tontine Block.

Hanover's semi-isolation apparently inhibited the development of large

department stores. As a result, the business section has made a handsome transition from one generation of small merchants to another. There is even today the sense of both continuity and of change in Hanover's mercantile district. The town's architectural scale remains relatively small but a manifestly healthy commerce persists today.
Courtesy of Dartmouth College Library

place to get out of the sun and have lunch? The chimney does not appear to be emitting smoke. The straw hats and coatless workers proclaim it to be summer. A crew of at least three men indicates an ambitious effort. The well-wrought basket arrests the eye. The tools are simple; a handmade ladder, sturdy wheelbarrow, simple planks, probably spades for digging. Wright's neatly groomed beard, high crowned hat, watch chain, and carnation boutonniere define a man well aware of his standing in the business community.

Ambrose L. Shattuck

Ambrose Shattuck (1849-1939) founded the coal, wood, and ice purveyors business in 1873 and ran it for over forty years from Grove Street. He lived long enough to rank among the Peterborough Elders of 1930, a dozen distinguished citizens, all male, designated as twentieth-century counterparts to the gallery of Peterborough's Apostolic Twelve. "The Apostles" were local men photographed at random by a Mr. Ollis as a promotional gambit sometime in the mid-nineteenth century. Vintage prints of the original Twelve Apostles are in the collection of the Peterborough Historical Society. The men became something of a town treasure, each one eulogized, in

turn, by the Transcript in sometimes touching obituaries.

The photographs of these twelve early citizens demonstrate how effectively the camera shapes our sense of history. By the mere accident of their having been available to be photographed, these men acquired a status in the community far higher than many of them would have achieved on their own. Quite the opposite is true of the Peterborough elders of 1930. Each of them was a highly regarded and popular local personage. Small reproductions of all twenty-four photos appear in the heritage pamphlet produced by the town in honor of the nation's bicentennial in 1976.

Shattuck sold his business to the Woodward brothers on Concord Street. They ran it for several years and sold to Martin Hafeli and Silva Santerre in the late twenties. Hafeli bought out his partner a few years later and continued the business, remaining at the Concord Street location. "I peddled ice behind a horse, too," Martin's son, George, said when asked about the photo on page 61. "That was in about 1928. I remember old Mr. Shattuck. He was elderly then, quite a man."

Martin Hafeli had been town road agent and later was elected as town selectman. He expanded the business to include fuel oil and bottled gas. George kept the business going after his father died in 1946, eventually

selling out to the Mann family. The Manns kept the name, Hafeli Fuels, continuing to operate out of Concord Street, where Monadnock Workshop is now. A few years ago, A. W. Peters, Inc., bought Hafeli's which remains in the fuel business on Summer Street, going strong after over a century of uninterrupted service to the community.

Older residents of Peterborough remember when ice was cut up at Batchelder's Pond. Shattuck's truck very likely carried ice from the pond in this very wagon. George Hafeli remembers when "we had big ice houses over at Batchelder's Pond. They were big, too, actually under one roof, but there were four separate houses in there. I hesitate to give measurements. Each one must have been 30' by 60'. They were big houses. They were high, too. Let's see, they must have been 35' high. We had to get ice for the whole summer. Everybody had ice refrigerators then."

Building Moving

Our ancestors thought nothing of moving even substantial buildings from one site to another. Town histories are full of reference to the moving of meeting houses, schools, and numerous other kinds of buildings. Some of the first settlers along the river would build on

Everything of importance in the small commercial riding stable stands in front of Bachand's Riding Stable in this undated portrait. The fully harnessed horses and all hands pose for the camera. Included, as well, are their near neighbors at the Hanover Diner. The impressive carved horse, a handsome example of the early American trade sign, stands guard over the scene. The diner's Indian head placard, an invitation to college-associated customers, eyes the Hot Dog sign with its abstract flourish, a promise of plain, cheap food that goes easy on the student pocket. Allen Street, once the site of the old stagecoach stables, in this photo is little more than the "Allen's Lane" of the last century, where Ira Allen kept his stables and stagecoach. By the seventies, the diner housed a Chinese restaurant before being overtaken by the Dartmouth Coop and Bookstore.

The livery stable provided flexible transportation services to the entire community from the private individual to the large business. Summer boarders and other transients relied heavily on the local livery stables. One Charlestown resident remembers when "there were also many drummers to be taken to Springfield [Vermont]. Fred Miller was often the man to drive for these salesmen and he told with a chuckle how, with the approach of a thunder shower, he would drive his horse at full speed to reach the shelter of the covered Cheshire Bridge before the storm broke." (Frizzell et al., page 281) Courtesy of Dartmouth College Library

The arrangement of vehicles, horses, and human figures in this photo effects a warm portrait of the busy W. W. Davis Stables in the middle of Warner Village. It is typical of the small town livery establishment that catered to local and visiting traffic, renting out or providing space and upkeep as needed. Notice the woman looking out of the window just under the W. W. Davis Stables sign. The rambling structure, according to a handwritten note on the original photograph is, "the house next door to the Variety Store." William W. Davis was one of twenty Warner residents who, in May of 1875, petitioned to form the Harris [Masonic] Lodge and was installed as one of its officers at the ceremonies constituting the Lodge at Warner Town Hall, September 30 of the same year.

Livery stables were eventually transformed into automobile garages or replaced by them. By the 1920s, few were in business in the region. Charlestown, for example, collected its

last taxes from the livery business, a stable with twelve horses, in 1911. It had been in continual operation for at least eighty years. It is said of one owner of the stables in question, that "during all

his business life he never took a vacation and never left the livery barn at night until the last horse was in." (Frizzell et al., page 280) Courtesy of New Hampshire Historical Society

choice meadowlands that flooded in the spring freshets or rising river waters necessitating relocation of houses unwisely built along the low-lying river plains. Occasionally, a flood would accomplish in a few minutes what it would take oxen, log rollers, and a large crew of men to orchestrate over several days. Be that as it may, it is obvious that our ancestors possessed the know-how and the oxen power needed to approach the task deliberately and with confidence. Moving structures was a cooperative affair, moreover, and our ancestors lived by the rule of cooperation. Logs, trimmed to rollers, would be placed under structures to be moved. Workers would keep moving them ahead, picking them up from the rear as the building moved off the back log, then running the freed log up ahead to place in the front for the building to move forward over. The process continually repeated itself until the building reached its new foundation. If logs were being trimmed for such a purpose at the sawmill, "the dogs," as illustrated earlier in the drawing from the Nicholas Rowell Saw Mill in Sutton, would hold the logs in place while the sawyers trimmed them down.

Auctioneering

The person who arranged for the publication of this photographic souvenir apparently knew the people of New Ipswich very well. The printed text on the back gives full identification. It reads as follows:

Group at Auction

Of Edward M. Issac's Store about 1860.

The photograph car of Newton Brooks stood near

The shops of Charles Fletcher and Josiah Webber.

On the spectator's left is Hosea Eaton. The one hidden by him is probably Emerson Howe. Next is the auctioneer William W. Johnson, with his arm raised. Next him, in a tall hat, is Charles A. Whitney who bought the store. Looking out from the car window is Stephen Thayer, and below him, leaning against the car, is Edward A. Barrett. Gilman Brickett, in a tall hat, and with head down stands next, and next him is Captain William Churchill. Just seen over Churchill's shoulder is Henry A. Whitney, in a tall hat. Next stands David Thomas in a white coat; his wife was sister of Mrs. Howe and Mrs. Webber. Next to Thomas is William A. Preston, and next comes Deacon William Hassall, who is whittling. Next the Deacon is John Preston with a cane, and at the spectator's right hand is William Bailey. The little boy with his back to the spectator is Jimmie Fairbanks, whose mother was daughter of William Searle. (Courtesy of New Hampshire Historical Society)

George S. Bond bought the Granite State Novelty Works, makers of fiddle cases, in October 1880. The Charlestown factory building was lost in a spectacular fire on July 13, 1893. Bond then purchased property between the railroad and South West Street and "built a two story [wooden] building, 125 x 40 feet, which was dedicated with at least 600 people present at a grand concert and ball on October 26, 1893." Sadly, this building, too, succumbed to a devastating fire at midday, August 15, 1900. Only a small ell part survived.

Valiantly, Mr. Bond began rebuilding less than two weeks later, immediately after forming a partnership with James Hunt. The new building went up on the same foundation and included a two-story addition. Forty workers made cases for violins, violincellos, zithers, autoharps, cornets, and other instruments. "The cases were made of basswood, many covered with leather and imitations of leather... The cases were sold all over the world, a soldier from Charlestown buying a case in the Philippines which proved to be a Bond case."

It is this second new building that George E. Fellows captures in this clean photograph. Notice the face peeking out of the lower window. The window awnings create a cheerful decorative appearance to the plain line of the structure. By the end of the decade, the business divided and diversified. Another fire razed this building two days before Christmas 1912 and a third building was built, wisely, of concrete block. The business did not survive this series of disasters unscathed and five years later went into receivership. The effects of this spunky local firm were sold at auction June 1923. Courtesy of Dartmouth College Library

Group at Auction, New Ipswich, circa 1860. Photo by Newton Brooks; courtesy of New Hampshire Historical Society

Joe Magny pauses long enough for an anonymous photographer to commit to posterity the process of graveling the road in Lisbon. The traditional time in northern New England for honing the roads is after mud season. Magny's powerful workhorses stand patiently enough for a clear image. The sturdy construction of the truck bed is evident, with wheels even heavier than those on Shattuck's wagon. The old early automobiles in the background are dealer-new, symbolic of the soon-to-be-phased-out scene they turn their backs on. Courtesy of New Hampshire Historical Society

"That's all gone now," one town native said when he looked at this photograph. "Yankee is now where the depot was. At one time the A&P and Dyer's Drug Store were there. They're both on the Plaza on the south side of [Route] 101 now. And other stores. . ." His voice trailed off as he scrutinized the photo more closely.

At the time the former Piano Factory was moved, it was Anderson's storehouse. The American Express office was located there for many years. It seems a formidable task, indeed, to draw it across the Boston & Maine Railroad tracks. Courtesy of Peterborough Historical Society

John Artemus Wright stands near a workman at the diatomaceous earth bog he discovered in Troy in 1873 and which led him to experiment for the formula for Wright's Silver Cream that became the basis for a family business that still thrives. Courtesy of New Hampshire Historical Society

A. L. Shattuck's Ice Company horse-drawn wagon was a familiar sight in Peterborough before trucks and then refrigeration relegated the memorable iceman to distant memory. The wagon's large back wheels allowed good workhorses to pull a very heavy load. Courtesy of Peterborough Historical Society

Things have not changed all that much. When a local business is put up for auction, everyone in town wants to be in on the action. Going to the auction is a favorite pastime for residents of the area and a tourist attraction, as well. There are still regular weekly auctions held in the region. They are well attended, some of them drawing buyers from as far away as Boston and New York.

Francestown Soapstone Quarry

The Francestown Soapstone Quarry became the most important center of the soapstone industry after the Civil War. The fine documentation of its central works was a popular stereographic souvenir. The photo of the heavily worked cut at the Francestown quarry is clearly visible in the W. A. Wright photo, taken in July of 1896 when Wright, of Ayer, Massachusetts, was on an extensive photographing trip through the area. The quarry (page 65) was on its way out of production by this time.

The story of the Francestown quarry is an interesting one. Sometime in the 1790s, farmer Daniel Fuller discovered a deposit of soapstone while plowing on one of his 514 acres. He found it peculiar that the

". . .plough and harrow did not make any gritting noise in passing over [one] ledge, while it did on others, and on examining the rock, found it to be a soft variety of soapstone."

What Fuller had discovered was the world's purest source of steatite, commonly called "freestone"—because it could so freely be sawed, carved and shaped—or "soapstone" owing to the texture or "feel" of the substance. Technically, it is a soft variety of talcose rock, composed entirely of the interlaced crystals of laminae of talc. (Schott, page 59)

In 1802, he and his son began to quarry the stone in a small way. The stone was of such quality that it "never failed to fetch the highest prices for soapstone on the Boston market."

The Fullers quarried at the site until 1847 when the elder Daniel died. His son continued the business until he, too, died a decade later. John West, a nephew, and Abner Woodward, a family hired hand, inherited the property. In 1865, they formed and incorporated the Francestown Soapstone Company. The business prospered. In the first years, "four six-horse teams [ran] continually all summer long convey[ing] twenty tons of freestone to the Boston market daily." Francestown soapstone was in great demand by manufacturers far and near, so superior a grade it was and admirably suited to a great many uses.

A competing quarry, the Union Soapstone Company, operated in the town beginning in 1884. By 1891, the depth of the original quarry had reached 134′, well below the water's natural drainage level. The enterprise became too expensive to run and went into bankruptcy receivership in 1905.

The New Francestown Soapstone Company, under different owners, operated seasonally between 1906 and 1912 when dynamite started a devastating fire that destroyed the quarry buildings and works and two valuable nearby farmhouses. The business never opened again.

Although the title of "Colonel" could be honorary or a rank in the local militia, Daniel Fuller was probably a Revolutionary Soldier. He had been among the first generation of families to have moved from South Dedham, Massachusetts, to Francestown between 1763 and 1790. He, along with several other local businessmen, was a patron and proprietor of Francestown Academy, incorporated by the legislature June 24, 1819. (Schott, pages 17, 58-67, 87)

Anecdotes About Trading

The various businesses pictured here are places where, in the local parlance, people "do their trading." The term, still used in the region, has lost almost entirely its older, literal meaning, of paying for purchases all or in part with products of the farm. Local history is replete with examples of the term in its original usage, however.

The economy of the settlers depended on trading and our ancestors made a fine art of it. Stories such as the one about Moor Robb, recounted in the 1897 history of Stoddard, illustrates the point. The subtlety of the story's message may seem, at first, to take the idea of a contract too lightly, but the seller's persistence in his clever ruse thrusts forward the shared value that our forebears expected all parties in a bargain to behave by a rule of fair play.

An early resident of Stoddard, Moor Robb had relocated just over the Stoddard line, in Antrim. Finding his former town convenient for trading, he had gone back to Stoddard:

[to sell a quantity of grass seed to] the trader there

for less than the worth of it, not knowing the price, and was to carry it up the next time he went. He soon found he had made a bad bargain, and did not carry it as he had agreed and the following dialogue took place.

Trader says: "Uncle Moor did you bring that grass seed?"

Moor: "No."

Trader: "Well, I depend upon it."

Moor: "Did you say you didn't want it?"

Trader: "No, I said I *did* want it."

Moor: "Ah! well, you needn't have it if you don't want it."

Trader: "But I *do* want it, I depend upon it."

Moor: "I thought it was a fair bargain enough but you needn't have it."

Trader: "But dam it I do want it, I depend upon it, I promised it."

Moor: "I can sell it to Hancock [the town of] and you needn't have it." As he was about to leave the store, he says, "Then you say you won't take that grass seed."

The engaging tale may, indeed, be apocryphal. In style, it is like so many rural jokes of the period and the pretense to being hard-of-hearing is a recurring motif in many tales. The disgruntled yankee's name, Moor Robb, seems a clever pun, indeed, on the moral of the tale. Of course, the attitude it expresses is entirely authentic. No one likes to be cheated and, if "Moor Robb" learned by the unpleasant experience, his clever put-down on the cheater much more than evened the score. This little cautionary story, moreover, has taught the lesson to generations of local traders.

Indian Trading

August 30, 1838, diary entry of Denison Gould, Hillsborough:

Some cloudy this morning. There were 5 cart loads of Indians landed near Deacon Sawyer's containing 23 persons. They make baskets very curiously wrought and make them very fast. There have been more than 1000 people to call on them already. They began this morning before 8 o'clock to canter along. The whole lot cleared the place to some other spot. They behaved very regular and appeared quite well.

Situated on a busy two-way road in Newbury, on the shore of Lake Sunapee, Blake's Antiques beckons to the traveler. The merchandise is varied and well-presented, the service, friendly and unpressured. An abiding attraction to tourists is the opportunity to interact with local business people on a one-to-one basis. Roadside shops such as Blake's serve this need exceptionally well. The proprietor, Al Blake, stands in his shop doorway. Photo by Armand Szainer

The used clothing and soft goods at a yard sale by the side of the road appeal to the rummage sale and flea market hounds who invade the rural areas in the warm weather. Such itinerant businesses date back to the days of the settlers, and continue to thrive in the region. Photo by Armand Szainer, 1988

Another trade that came over the waters with the first settlers, shoemaking continues as a living craft in our time. Such old-time shops as Cooper's are virtually extinct although they linger in recent memory and a few have withstood the degree of change that most other traditional trades have experienced. In this White Studio photo, Cobbler Cooper works in his Hanover shop. Courtesy of Dartmouth College Library

Ores were mined on more than one Ore Hill in the northern mountains of New Hampshire. This mine at Warren was among the largest mineral mines in the state. Although it was owned and worked by a succession of owners, not ceasing production until 1914, it operated most profitably in the middle of the nineteenth century. The chief ores mined were copper, zinc, silver, and lead. In addition to employing locals, mining in the area drew immigrant labor from Canada, England, and to a lesser degree, from continental Europe. The iron industry was profitable in the region until the railroad made it feasible for the large iron ore mines of Pennsylvania to dominate iron ore mining. Courtesy of New Hampshire Historical Society

Some of the most beautiful buildings and monuments in the United States were faced with New Hampshire granite and some of the finest stone in the Granite State was mined in southwestern New Hampshire. The Webb Granite Quarries pictured here in 1899 were opened at the beginning of the nineteenth century by Asa Greenwood. It was worked by several other owners through the century and went into full production after George

D. Webb purchased it in 1891. The next year, the company laid a private railroad track from the mine to the B&M railroad line. The quarry specialized in paving stones although some dressed stones were produced for buildings, one being Marlborough's own Frost Free Library. Courtesy of New Hampshire Historical Society

The rail line and curious spectators add considerably to the visual interest in this stereograph identified in handwriting as the "Sunapee Ledge," Probably, the word "ledge" is used, mistakenly or euphemistically, in place of "lead." For, according to a local historican, a thriving graphite mine was located in nearby Warner at the turn of the present century. Graphite, used in pencils, is called "lead" in popular parlance. Andover's town history reports from an undated Franklin Journal-Transcript item that the American Graphite Company of Baltimore expected to employ twenty-five men to ship graphite from Potter Place over the winter of 1901 to 1902. "The graphite came from what is commonly known as the 'lead mine' just over the line in Warner on the slope of Kearsarge Mountain." (Chaffee, page 210) Courtesy of New Hampshire Historical Society

Francestown Soapstone Quarry Works. Stereograph Courtesy of New Hampshire Historical Society

Francestown Soapstone Quarry, July 1896. Photo by W. A. Wright, Ayer, Massachusetts. Courtesy of New Hampshire Historical Society

The Mother and Child *sculpture was made from soapstone found at Francestown Quarry. The artist carved this work (16 ½" high) in about 1960 from a large piece of soapstone he picked up on the approach to the deserted Francestown quarry. An immigrant from Europe, he was fond of driving through the countryside. He says he had never worked soapstone but he "welcomed the challenge. I found this quarry and was surprised by its existence there in this lovely small town," he recalls. "And I had just learned that soapstone was used for sculpture. I had seen some beautiful Eskimo carvings at the homes of friends and learned that Eskimos worked mainly in soapstone. Before I came here I never knew about it. Then, I came across this quarry and noticed many pieces lying around in a ditch. I took a couple of pieces home to my studio. I found that soapstone was easy to carve and I went to work to make this figure. I left the stone almost as it was. The raw stone suggested to me the figure of the mother and child. I didn't have to chisel off very much. Of course, the quarry stone was not used for sculpture. They made sinks out of it back then." Photo by the author*

The former importance of the Francestown quarry made it a likely documentation site for the WPA survey. Soapstone was a very important material for sinks, stoves, griddles, and fireplace inserts in the nineteenth century. E. W. Clark worked for the Historic American Buildings Survey in July 1936 when he made a series of photographs at what he calls the "Soapstone Mill, Francestown, N.H."

Clark describes the image on HAB photograph, No. N. H. 34, 17, as a "detail showing tool marks on soapstone made at the quarry." Courtesy of UNH Dimond Library

Woodsville's large and varied patronage for commerce is evident from this photograph of a gentlemen's haberdashery. The well-outfitted businessman, entrepreneur, or man-about-town could easily fill his needs choosing from among the diversified assortment of quality merchandise handsomely presented in this establishment. The shirt collars and antique hand-held telephone date this to no later than the 1920s. Lace curtains behind the window displays doubtlessly discouraged customers seeking work clothes. The cosmopolitan nature of the shop's merchandise confirms that Woodsville was, indeed, a thriving crossroads of commerce after 1853, when the railroad gave its strategic location a huge economic boost. Courtesy of Dartmouth College Library

The country store, like the Crossroads Store at Haverhill, caught by WPA photographer Marion Post Wolcott, is the trading post for basic and general necessities whose prices reflect the overhead costs of a no-frills operation. It is in such a store where locals purchase their work clothes, outdoor gear, and, in fact, any of the great variety of goods needed to keep a rural community fully supplied.

Such down-to-earth dry goods as denims, rubber boots, plaid wool slouch hats, sacks of grain, boxes of laundry soap, and cans of shortening, all visible in the window, sit in stark contrast to the wire bird's cage just visible through the glass in the door just above the clean-swept front step. It is such crossroads, defining this simpler lifestyle of the region, that attracted many WPA artists. Wolcott's reputation as a first rate photographer has stood the test of time. *Courtesy Library of Congress, Photograph and Print Division*

The bustling city of Claremont calls for a "groceteria" that addresses the forward-looking values of the emerging Yankee urbanite. The rising middle-class attitude is well expressed in the message hand-lettered on the plate-glass window: "Everything in clean sanitary packages fairly priced." The inviting window displays, the bread storage box, the wrapping paper roller, well-stocked shelves of standardized tinned goods, and "Fine Teas from Ceylon" (advertised in the left-window handbill) promise value and satisfaction.

In mid-twentieth century, chain stores began to proliferate in the less populated centers of the country. One variation allowed for the stores to use local names but to offer primarily the chain's brand of items, thus providing opportunity for such discounts as the emerging supermarkets were able to effect with their vast bulk purchasing potential. The repetitious labeling of goods visible in this store suggests that it may have been such a venture. *Courtesy of New Hampshire Historical Society*

5
ART AND ARCHITECTURE

I n examples of architecture, fine art, folk art, and
artists' colonies, the western regions of New
Hampshire harbor some of the state's most prized artistic
works. The Historic American Buildings Survey confirms
the deep appreciation that all levels of society have for
first-rate representations of diverse styles of American
architecture. Interest in the dwellings of famous
personages, sites of meaning to the social and political
history of the country as well as interesting, perhaps
unique, miscellaneous structures is supported by major
academic, governmental, and commercial institutions.
Numerous handsome publications in praise of American
architecture exist. Excellent universities foster the study
and conservation of architectural landmarks and many
tax-supported programs have encouraged attention to the
documentation and preservation of architectural
landmarks. Of the WPA artists' and writers' programs, only
the Historic American Buildings Survey continued—
through the Offices of Historic Preservation.

The western regions of New Hampshire have had
great appeal to artists and writers throughout their history.
Dublin, long a summer resort for the well-to-do, has been
the permanent home of such artists as Abbott Thayer,
George deForest Brush, and Joseph Linden Smith, among
many others. A great number of distinguished illustrators
make or have made New Hampshire their home. Trina
Schart Hyman, Tomie dePaola, Wallace Tripp, Erik Von
Schmidt, John Steptoe to name but a few, reside in
communities scattered throughout the western regions of
the state.

Folk art provides an ideal vehicle for talking about many of the values associated with the history of western New Hampshire. Rural in its beginnings and rural-identified even today, the region clings affectionately to a traditional self image. People are particularly proud of those among their neighbors who are skilled in the arts and crafts of their ancestors because they symbolize the vitality of earlier attitudes and priorities in a fast-moving society.

Families of artists, such as the Richardsons of Peterborough, entertain through their creative output. Their works also remind us that the skilled, practical, and inventive among us are the ones who carry on "the old ways" with success in the modern world. Descended from Moses Eaton, Jr., the renowned itinerant stenciller, Robert and Willard Richardson and their sister Louisa Richardson Fairfield, keep alive the family tradition of artists in every generation. Their pursuits reflect their farming heritage and their collective knowledge of how to make indifferent nature bountiful. Among the color plates of photographs are works by folk artists Louisa, Robert, and Willard from one of the region's most talented families of artists. Their illustrious ancestors, Moses Eaton and Moses Eaton, Jr., painted their original stencil designs in fine old homes throughout northern New England. The small sculptures of Moses and Rebeckah that their great-grandson Robert Richardson carved are pictured in this volume among the color plates.

Willard recalls their father telling him of his great-grandfather, Malachi, urging him to puff a cigar and sip whiskey when he was a toddler. Young as his father was, Willard says, he always remembered the incident, later claiming that he had "just about died." Moses, Jr., and Malachi are among the "five old people" page 72.

A forerunner to the development of artists colonies in Cornish and Peterborough existed in Walpole. At the end of the eighteenth century, a literary club of some local fame, comprised of men of letters from Walpole and surrounding communities, met at Maj. Asa Bullard's Walpole Tavern.

Bullard, who earlier had run a coffeehouse on the corner of what is now Main and Dunbar streets in Keene, was that community's first postmaster. He had earned the rank of captain through his Revolutionary War service, rising to the rank of major in the local militia. The first post office was at his coffeehouse, a building that later was called the "plastered-house" because it was plastered on the outside. (Keene History Committee, pages 40, 233-234)

Among the places in New Hampshire most notable for the arts is Saint-Gaudens National Historic Site in Cornish where the home, gardens, and studios of Augustus Saint-Gaudens (1848-1907), one of the most important of American sculptors, are open to the public. After Saint-Gaudens began summering in Cornish in the mid-1880s, the area became an important center for the arts, attracting numerous artists and writers. Homer Saint-Gaudens, the son of the sculptor, describes the circumstances under which his father and other "city folks" settled there, the vanguard of what became a thriving artists' colony. His commentary, in William H. Child's *History of the Town of Cornish*, reads like a *Who's Who* of publishing and the arts at the turn-of-the-century. No wonder, then, that Cornish carried the nickname, Little New York.

The summer community in Cornish counted many distinguished artists, entrepreneurs, and political figures among its ranks. The beauty of the scenery and the stimulation provided by a group of talented neighbors inspired such artists and writers as George deForest Brush (who eventually settled in the Monadnock region), Maxfield Parrish (in Plainfield) and the St. Louis writer, Winston Churchill, poet Witter Bynner, and numerous lesser well-known personalities. Others came for short visits.

Despite Homer Saint-Gauden's forthright acknowledgment of the outsider status of the residents of the colony, the town's historian proudly includes Saint-Gaudens, Winston Churchill and several others, either year-round or summer residents, among the town genealogies. About Saint-Gaudens, he writes:

AUGUSTUS SAINT—GAUDENS, the celebrated sculptor, was b. March 1, 1848, in Dublin, Ire. His father was b. in Southern France and his mother in Dublin. They came to Cornish about 1885 and purchased the old brick mansion long known as "Huggins Folly." This he greatly improved, intending it at first only as a summer residence. His artistic and cultured taste soon transformed the place into "a thing of beauty." This, together with his fame as an artist, attracted many friends of kindred tastes to his home and vicinity, and in this way it became "the center of the world to him," so that in 1898 he decided to make it his permanent home. He had, in 1877, m. Augusta F. Homer of New York. They had but one child: Homer, b. Sept. 28, 1880, who is

Huggins Folly, renamed Aspect by Saint-Gaudens, had once served as an inn on the stagecoach road between Meriden, New Hampshire, and Windsor, Vermont, across the river from Cornish. Its handsome columned porch, the focal point of this photo, was an early addition the sculptor made to the building. This photo was taken from the portico of the Little Studio. Photo by Armand Szainer

The house contains the artist's original furnishings. The emphasis in the informal sitting room is on comfort and conversation. It is simply furnished, including few of the reproductions of work that appear in number throughout the rest of the public rooms of the house. The photograph is the work of Mattie Edwards Hewitt, a New York photographer. St. Gauden's wife and son founded the Memorial as a way to exhibit his work and encourage aspiring sculptors by providing studio space and living quarters. Few artists applied for the residencies and they were discontinued until revived after mid-century. In 1964, the residence and grounds were accepted by the National Park Service and named a National Historic Site in 1965. Courtesy of New Hampshire Historical Society

The Heald house in Temple remained in the family of Maj. Ephraim Heald (Jr.) until about 1853. It sits on Lot 4, Range 8, originally granted in draft No. 17 to Peter Powers but acquired soon thereafter by Ephraim Heald, Sr., of Townsend, Massachusetts. The 1860 date on the sketch made by Bradley Heald, apparently a descendent of the Major, makes it a family historical document. The family was fortunate enough to have someone whose skill with the pencil was up to the task of respectable documentation. Courtesy of New Hampshire Historical Society

This old family photograph pictures the four great-grandparents of the Richardsons. Family members affectionately identify the snapshot as "The Five Old People." Taken in the early 1880s in Dublin, New Hampshire, it depicts, left to right: Malachi Richardson (1798-1887); his wife, Tamasin Greenwood Richardson (1810-1901); Lucy Brewer Pratt Richardson (1805-1893), widow of Luke Richardson, Malachi's brother; Rebeckah Pratt Eaton (1798-1892), wife of Moses and sister of Lucy Pratt; and, Moses Eaton, Jr. (1796-1886). Robert says that his grandmother, Mary Rebeckah, "took care of these old people, along with taking care of three growing boys and running a household, feeding everyone including several hired men, etc." He adds, "My father was born in 1878. He could remember them all well." Courtesy of Robert Richardson and family

giving abundant promise of high rank in the literary world. Augustus Saint-Gaudens d. Aug. 3, 1907, aged 59 years, 5 months, 2 days. (William H. Child, page 323)

A longer, informal "sketch," one of several on local personages that precedes the geneological section of the *History,* gives fuller details of his life. Augustus Saint-Gaudens had apprenticed at thirteen-years of age to a New York cameo cutter, the probable foundation of his later specialization in low relief sculpture. Among his most famous works are the Shaw Memorial on the Boston Common and the Statue of Lincoln near the Chicago Public Library. He enjoyed an international reputation which garnered him numerous public and private commissions. His brother, Louis, an accomplished sculptor in his own right, worked somewhat in his brother's shadow, having spent many years assisting Augustus in his New York studio. He moved to Cornish in 1901 to work for his brother, built his own home two years later, and settled there. He, too, had many public commissions including the sculptural appointments of the Union Station in Washington, D.C., completed about 1912.

Orozco at Dartmouth

Dartmouth College anticipated the WPA historical murals project by a few years, having invited the world-renowned Mexican muralist, Jose Clemente Orozco, to paint a series of murals as artist-in-residence at the College. Orozco had painted murals at Pomona College and at the New School for Social Research but his frescoes at Dartmouth are considered to be among his finest work. In his explanatory pamphlet on the murals distributed to visitors at Baker Library, Churchill P. Lathrop interprets his "climatic panel," reproduced on page 68. He says,

We see a tremendous Christ-like figure bathed in a fiery light, his angry upraised fist challenging us to spiritual action. Behind him is a junk-pile of discarded symbols, symbols of outworn faith in the false powers of military weapons, of imperial grandeur, of dogmatic religions. To this junk-pile he has just added his own cross, chopped down by his own hand, in disgust at man's far-too-often-abuse of this symbol to sanction aggression and to terrorize the weak and the oppressed. He subordinates the cross in order more fully to emphasize his sacrificial wounds, his flayed skin of penitence and the bright warm light of his spiritual leadership. He is arousing us from lethargy, asking us to be alert, to be concerned, to make commitment. He is offering leadership in a new migration, a migration this time of mind and spirit to seek and . . . to find a better America. . . . It is a powerful finale to the visual symphony.

Orozco writes affectionately of his experience at Dartmouth in his 1962 autobiography. He says,

On the ground floor of [Baker] Library, I painted a series of murals for the Department of Fine Arts, whose Director was Mr. Artemus Packard . . . . The Administration and the 2500 students of the College were enthusiastic in their support of the Fine Arts project, and so I set to work. I had complete freedom to express my ideas; no suggestion or criticism of any sort was ever made.

In the beginning there had been some opposition to the idea of a foreigner's painting the walls of an institution which is one of the sanctuaries of that Idealism upon which the great country of the North

"Pilgrim Scene" from 1910 Pageant of Peterborough, MacDowell Colony. Library of Congress, Photograph and Print Division

"Indian Wedding" from the 1910 Pageant of Peterborough, MacDowell Colony. Courtesy of Library of Congress, Photograph and Print Division

Finale with full cast, 1910 Pageant of Peterborough, MacDowell Colony.

Courtesy of Library of Congress, Photograph and Print Division

The MacDowell Colony is the pride of New Hampshire's art scene attracting to the region some of the nation's finest artists, budding or established, in all media, for short-term residencies in an atmosphere conducive to creativity. The Colony was established in 1907 in memory of Edward MacDowell, distinguished American composer, on the site of his Peterborough home. The Colony was endowed, organized, and administered for many years by his widow, Marian.

Among the informal activities of the Colony, in its early period, were a half dozen pageants, the first held in 1910. The Peterborough Pageants, as they are called, were joint efforts of the Colony and the townspeople put on for the benefit of the MacDowell Memorial Association. Among the more important benefits of these events, however, seems to have been the warmth of the relationship that developed between the Colony and the people of Peterborough in the Colony's formative years.

The first Peterborough Pageant was staged by Harvard's Professor George P. Baker with lyrics by Hermann Hagedorn. The choral and orchestral music was adapted from Edward MacDowell's own compositions by Chalmers Clifton. The Pageant narrated the story of the Peterborough region from settlement through the Civil War. Numerous photographs of the first pageant production exist, a few at the local Historical Society and a number of others, with their glass negatives, in the Library of Congress's MacDowell Colony Papers where we learn that "the pageant pressed into service every available Peterborough man, woman and child and attracted hundreds of visitors from outside the state."

The second pageant was held almost ten years later, in 1919, also set in the open-air ampitheater amid groves of trees and groups of shrubs. On a clear day Mount Monadnock could be seen by the audience. Most of the actors were from Peterborough and included both locals and summer residents as participants. A few artists-in-residence from the Colony joined in, as well. Members of the Boston Symphony Orchestra provided the music. The program included an opening and closing Dance to the Muses and an old English country dance, in two sets. The costumes were on loan from the Metropolitan Opera Company.

The Samuel Morey house, pictured here in the soft light of early morning, is the result of at least three separate building stages. The first, a small dwelling which was enlarged from the back and finally expanded to the front by an addition that makes up the present one-and-one-half-story section visible from the street. "[Its] hewn pine ridgepole is one continuous beam extending forty-five feet from end to end." (Hodgson, page 14). As the sign on the fence reads, the ell was built in 1773 by Rev. Obadiah Noble, the first dwelling to be built on The Ridge, and the front, by Samuel Morey, in 1804. Particularly fine features are its hipped roof neatly framed by brick chimneys, its fanlighted doorway with Palladian arched window above and its small window lights. Photo by the author

was founded. But the protests came from Boston, not Hanover. Many of them bore signatures with the difficult consonants of Central Europe, and those who signed protested in the name of one-hundred-percent Americanism, without comprehending that precisely the position Dartmouth was taking expressed one of the most highly prized of American virtues: freedom—of speech and thought, of conscience and the press—the freedoms of which the American people have always been justifiably proud.

The murals consist of fourteen pictures of approximately ten by thirteen feet in dimension, and ten smaller ones.

In the first of them the theme is that of "Quetzalcoatl." but the final paintings bear no very clear relation to this. (Orozco, pages 158-159)

Some Houses of the Area

An old or historic house in New England very often carries the proper name of its owner, or, more frequently, in fact, of its former owner or a former owner whose name is popularly recognized. It can carry hyphenated names, combining the surnames of two or more such persons. Maj. Ephraim Heald's house, Temple (p. 71), identified in the town history as the Heald-Bragdon-Register house, is a typical example. Ephraim Heald (1734-1815) and his wife Sarah, both of Townsend, Massachusetts, were among the first settlers in Temple, having purchased their homesite lot from Heald's father in 1756. In 1783, the Healds built a saltbox house to the east of his first cabin which was annexed to the new building. Its central chimney provided for five fireplaces.

According to the town history, Major Heald was commissioned under the English king in the colonial militia. Active in town affairs and a leading taxpayer, on

September 7, 1768, Heald called the first town meeting in Temple by authority of the royal governor. He was a leader of the revolutionary movement in Temple, marching with his townsmen to Cambridge after the alarm of April 19, 1775. A renowned hunter, Heald built his fortune "by chaffer [bargaining] in the hides" of wild animal skins.

Along the upper reaches of the Connecticut River, in Orford, are a row of seven mansions that together comprise what may well be the finest architectural treasure in the state. They perch up high, along the edge of a prehistoric riverbed known locally as The Ridge, overlooking the single street of the town. A beautiful tree-lined mall runs parallel to them at street level. Sweeping lawns appointed with well-tended trees and shrubbery, connect them to the mall. The most fully documented of these houses is the General Wheeler house, the southernmost of the dwellings. Wheeler Family tradition has the great architect Charles Bulfinch as having visited the property when it was being constructed.

Samuel Morey was a son of Israel Morey, blacksmith by trade, an original settler of Orford and the patriarch of an enterprising family. Samuel was a three-year-old when the Moreys arrived in Orford in January 1766, having traveled by ox sled up the Connecticut River from Charlestown. Among other ventures, the Moreys held large lumber interests which they worked. Until the first bridge was built over the river at Orford, the family also held the ferry rights.

Samuel Morey was an engineer, inventor, and lumberman whose original innovations in steamboat design led to the commercial development of the steamboat. In 1793, Morey had designed and built a small steamboat which he launched on the Connecticut River fully seventeen years before Robert Fulton's boat made its maiden voyage on the Hudson River. Morey acquired many patents and his steam engines were also used in

WM. KING,

TAKER OF PROFILE LIKENESSES,

RESPECTFULLY informs the Ladies and Gentlemen of Hanover and its vicinity, that he has taken a Room at Mr. *James Wheelock's*, where he intends to stay one week to take

Profile Likeneſſes,

with his Patent Delineating Pencil.

He takes the Profiles in ſix minutes, on a beautiful *wove paper*, with the greateſt poſſible correctneſs, which is well known, he having taken above twenty thouſand in *Salem, Newburyport, Portſmouth, Portland*, and their adjoining towns ; and from them he has ſelected a few as ſpecimens, which may be viewed at his Room.

His price for two Profiles of one perſon is *Twenty-five Cents*—and frames them in a handſome manner, with black glaſs, in elegant oval, round or ſquare Frames, gilt or black—Price from *Fifty Cents* to *Two Dollars* each.

Mr. KING reſpectfully ſolicits the early attendance of thoſe Ladies and Gentlemen, who intend to have their Profiles taken, as he muſt leave town at the above named time.——Conſtant attendance from 8 in the morning till 10 in the evening.

March 24, 1806.

N. B. Thoſe who are not ſatisfied with their Profiles previous to their leaving his Room, may have their money returned.

Certainly one of the most popular examples of early American anonymous artifacts are the carved wooden trade signs. Of these, surely none evokes more nostalgia to the twentieth-century historical art buff than the Cigar Store Indian. It is understandable, then, that such vestiges of the nation's popular mercantile past would attract the lens of Harold Kimble, WPA Artist, working in Keene at the end of the 1930s. Kimble identifies the subject simply as the "Carpenter Store Indian."

An earlier photo of the same carving places it in Roxbury Street, in the Chelsea House Block extension next to the Dreamland Movie House which opened in April 1909 for about five years. Perhaps it is symbolic of the value placed on such figures that the original print is splendidly oversized. Although the figure is conventional, it is a striking example of the genre. Courtesy of UNH Dimond Library

Before the mid-nineteenth century, itinerant portrait artists were familiar figures in early America, the only portraitist available to most citizens outside the major cities. The wealthy could afford to commission portraits of itinerant artists or, perhaps, travel to New York or Boston. In western New Hampshire, painters summering in the region would also, one assumes, have been available for locally commissioned portraits.

A very popular and far more affordable form of portraiture was the silhouette. The wording of William King's advertisement, reproduced here, amuses the contemporary reader, with its description of quality work and promises of specimens to facilitate the decision making. It is to be expected that careful Yankee customers, besides wanting value for their money, would be cautious about committing their cash to anything that took a mere six minutes to make. On the other hand, local people were efficient workers themselves and respected true craftsmanship. They must certainly have appreciated the industriousness implied by a fourteen-hour work day. The money-back guarantee indicates that the artist was paid before the profile was executed, however. The hard sell of the traveling salesman is undoubtedly as old as commerce. The line that he "must leave town at the above named time" brings to mind the large repertory of salesman jokes that have circulated since time immemorial.

William King had posted a version of this advertisement, in February, a month earlier, informing the people of Keene that he was to be in their city for a few days. This schedule would have allowed the itinerant artist time for several other stops along the Connecticut River between these documented visits to Hanover and Keene. Courtesy of Dartmouth College Library

Built in 1840 to replace the earlier open wooden bridge that was the second to span the Connecticut River in New Hampshire, the Tucker Toll Bridge was built by Walpole's Sanford Granger. Of the Town-lattice type, the design was adapted by Issac Damon and Lyman Kingsley. Nathaniel Tucker, who became the bridge's proprietor when his wife inherited the bridge from her father, financed and ran the bridge. Tucker's bridge was on the main traffic artery from Boston to Vermont. The stone double-arched Cheshire Railroad Bridge visible behind its covered bridge companion, rests where the first New Hampshire railroad bridge crossed the Connecticut River to Bellows Falls. Built for anticipated heavy traffic, the bridge carried two pair of tracks. The original had "twin entrances graced with stone-work portals set into the interior of the wooden bridge" and was built under Lucius Boomer's direction in 1849.

(Morse, page 30) The Howe design railroad bridge was 280 feet long and its two spans survived until 1899. Its double-arched stone bridge replacement, seen in this photo, is uncovered. The photo showing the Tucker Toll Bridge (so-called even after it became free in 1904) and the second Cheshire Railroad Bridge dates from the first decade of this century. They straddle the rapids where the Connecticut River bends between the two towns. The house visible underneath the stone arch

on the right sits above the river on the Walpole bank. In 1930, the modern Vilos Bridge replaced this famous old landmark.

It is the juxtaposition of these two bridges, stone next to wooden covered bridge, that makes this such a remarkable image. Notice the ladder up to the railroad bridge from the rocks that crop out below, blending with the bridge piling. Courtesy of New Hampshire Historical Society

manufacturing. It is alleged that Fulton usurped Morey's double-paddle wheel idea, obtaining a patent on it. Morey had neglected to include the double-wheel idea specifically in his patent applications. Apparently, Fulton moved in, as well, on important financial backing previously pledged to Morey. Nevertheless, history does credit Morey's inventive genius, acknowledging numerous other inventions. Of equal or greater importance is his invention of the internal combustion engine. In fact, Morey's first patent, granted in 1793 for a steam-powered spit was, itself, a welcome invention that eased an onerous, uncomfortable task.

Bridges

Early photographers found an attractive subject in bridges, in particular the wooden covered bridges that crossed rivers, streams, and brooks all over the region. The first state-chartered toll road and bridge across the Connecticut were built by Col. Enoch Hale in 1783. The first, and between 1785 and 1796 the only, bridge across the Connecticut River between New Hampshire and Vermont was at Walpole, below Bellows Falls, a toll bridge, that had a 360 foot span and rose fifty feet above the river. The bridge joined Walpole and Bellows Falls, an early center of commercial activity because its mill sites clustered around the splendid water power there. The second bridge was built at Hanover in 1796. Like all early bridges and ferries, they were privately owned.

Why many bridges were covered to begin with is disputable but the widely accepted explanation is that the roof extended the life of the structure by protecting its floor from weathering. On average, a covered bridge would be newly roofed about every twenty-five years. Thus, the upkeep of these bridges was minimal unless

violent weather intervened. In the winter, the bridge had to be "snowed" so that vehicles with runners could pass through the otherwise dry bridge. This was considered children's work for which boys were paid a few pennies. Bridge openings had to accomodate a load of hay, the key measure for size. Railroad "through bridges," as they were sometimes called, had train engines as their guide for measurement.

For many, the covered bridge is symbolic of New England, for some of the most beautiful and well-known covered bridges span New Hampshire's Connecticut River and its tributaries. There can be quite a bit of history behind these outstanding structures. It has been pointed out, for example, that the Haverhill-Bath Bridge over the Ammonossic at Woodsville was built in 1829, twenty-five years before the railroad's incursion into Woodsville, a township of Haverhill, made it the most important of the three settlements. Tradition persists. The bridge remains the "Haverhill-Bath Bridge" to this day, despite Woodville's prominence.

Cheshire Bridge

Towns record all formal transactions concerning bridges in their annual reports. Ferry rights can include eventual bridge-building rights or, as in Charlestown, the ferry rights granted in 1827 "were not to prevent the building of a bridge within the limits described."

Charlestown's Cheshire Bridge was chartered in 1804 with toll rates that included: foot passengers: 1¢; horse and rider, 6¢; horse and chaise or sulkey, 12½¢; four-wheeled carriage for passengers, 25¢. Consistent with practices everywhere, the charter called for gates to be left open when there was no toll gatherer in attendance. This provision led to the general practice on

This historic photograph of Walpole, New Hampshire, and Bellows Falls, Vermont, gives an aerial view of the two bridges described earlier. Forming a great V, the Tucker Toll Bridge and the first Cheshire Railroad Bridge stand side by side across the Connecticut over the falls in the river bend. The scene is unique in covered bridge history. Nowhere else in the world have four covered bridges joined the same two towns. The third bridge is the Sullivan County Railroad Bridge, situated at the upper right of the photo where the river curves and narrows over the rapids, and the fourth, to the left of the Sullivan County Bridge, crosses the canal leading to the depot in Bellows Falls. The water power that made these towns the center of industry in the region's early history is partially visible in this aerial image taken about 1880. Other items of interest in Walpole include the tremendous wood piles in the foreground between the road and the railway tracks with their rows of idle boxcars, and, across the tracks, the railroad car barn, looking like a miniature of the Cheshire Railroad Bridge nearby. The huge, circular turntable in the yard allowed engines or cars to be positioned either coming or going. The great Comerford Power Plant on the Connecticut River at Fifteen Mile Falls, not far from this spot, was documented by the WPA. A photo of it appears in the WPA Guide. Courtesy of Richard E. Roy

The boxy look of this covered bridge with the train on top makes it a startlingly idiosyncratic period piece. Its huge proportions and its handsome design cause the vintage locomotive on top to look like a model train set. The double-decker wooden bridge was built in 1853 when the Boston, Concord & Montreal Railroad Company succeeded in locating its junction point at Woodsville. This former township of Haverhill thereafter became a major transportation center where five railroad lines came together and were supplemented by excellent highways. Trains ran atop the bridge, as seen here, and highway traffic proceeded through it to or from the tollhouse west of the river.

The building of the bridge settled a fierce competitive rivalry between the Passumpsic Rail Company, which, until the early 1850s, held sway over the Boston and New York routes. It was all very political. The Passumpsic Company, with Vermont Governor Erastus Fairbanks as president, tried to prevent the BC&M access, carrying it to the courts and losing. The joint highway/railway use served as the compromise that settled the matter. The trains had easy straight-away access and egress at both ends of the bridge. Teamsters were served less well, however. At either end of the lower bridge, stone walls forced vehicles to make rather tight turns. The entrances came to be called "rat-in-the-wainscot" by some unhappy drovers. (Allen, page 96) A steel double-decker replaced the wooden bridge in 1904. Courtesy of New Hampshire Historical Society

At 460', the Cornish-Windsor Bridge is the longest covered bridge in New Hampshire. It is also among the oldest, having celebrated its centennial in 1966. It is the first and last of the private toll bridges in the state, having collected tolls from 1785 until 1906 when New Hampshire purchased it. The faded paint of the block letters on the wooden sign that rides like a banner above the entrance reads: WALK YOUR HORSES OR PAY 10 DOLLARS FINE. According to the commemorative plaque placed by the Covered Bridge Association of New Hampshire, it is Covered Bridge No. 70. Photo by Armand Szainer

many bridges of unattended gates at night.

Tolls were a source of anger and frustration to frequent users of bridge and ferry services, leading to many complaints to the local and state authorities. In 1835, the New Hampshire legislature approved "An Act to Regulate the Toll of Cheshire Bridge" with tolls set that "were to remain unaltered at least 12 years." Among further restrictions in the Act was one limiting "net proceeds to 12% per annum on the cost of the building, repairing and (operation)" of the bridge.

When the old wooden Cheshire Bridge was replaced by a new bridge, constructed by the East Berlin, Connecticut Bridge Company, they employed "all the horses and dump carts available in two townships during the summer of 1896. Stone for raising the piers was blasted from the ledges south of #225 [i.e. town lot] . . . . The waste from the demolition of the old bridge was dumped into the river where some of it was salvaged for building purposes." (Frizzell et al., pages 126-127)

In 1933, the state responded to repeated efforts to "free the Connecticut River bridges" by appointing a commission to study the situations of the Cheshire and Cornish bridges with the result that Cornish was freed but Cheshire was not. Cheshire was to be the last toll bridge over the Connecticut River.

Cornish-Windsor Bridge

The southernmost of the covered bridges across the Connecticut River, the present bridge, fourth to occupy the site, was built in 1866 by James Tasker, a popular builder in the area who, it is reputed, could neither read nor write. Tasker advertised by taking a model bridge around to the agricultural fairs. The bridge is of the lattice-truss design known as the Town-truss type, patented in 1835 by Connecticut born Ithiel Town. He leased the rights to the plans, charging by the foot and

doubling the amount if payment was made after the bridge's completion.

The pedestrian walking east at the far end of the bridge has ignored the posted restrictions that were in effect when the above photo was taken in the summer of 1988. Plans underway to refurbish this bridge, one of the historical landmarks of the region, are not without controversy. The decision pending is whether or not to employ traditional wooden-frame building techniques.

In the days when Windsor was a dry town and Cornish not, the toll agent encouraged business by charging but two cents for patrons going to New Hampshire. He made his profit by charging three cents for the return trip. Sheep farming was at its height in the area between 1824 and 1840, before the railroad reduced the importance of the Cornish Bridge as "a truly great artery for commerce." Tollhouse journal records (with original spellings) testify to these facts:

Sheep and cattle in gret numbers passed over the bridge from the North and West on their way to market. On the Sabbaath day, October 23, 1825, there crossed the bridge, 450 cattle; on November 7, 920 shep and 236 cattle; on December 4, 470 cattle. The record for that year was about 9,500 sheep and 2,600 cattle. The droves went to market chiefly in the autumn and early winter. The records for the years 1837 to 1841 show the total numbers of sheep and cattle as follows:

YEAR.	SHEEP.	CATTLE.
1837	13,233	2,420
1838	14,084	2,208
1839	12,229	1,705
1840	11,451	2,657
1841	11,513	2,988

Shaker Bridge, Mascoma Lake, Enfield. Courtesy of New Hampshire Historical Society

The Old Ledyard Bridge connecting the towns of Hanover, New Hampshire, and Norwich, Vermont, across the Connecticut River. The bridge was constructed in 1859 through the cooperative efforts of both towns and Dartmouth College. The bridge has the distinction of being the first free bridge over the Connecticut River and for many years it was the only one at which tolls were not charged. Courtesy of Dartmouth College Library*

The arch and arcade of the old Ledyard Bridge frame this vintage auto on its way to Hanover across the Connecticut. A curious passenger takes a peek at the camera out of the back window. The inevitable notice restricting the speed of vehicles greets all travelers who cross the span. Courtesy of Dartmouth College Library

The largest drove in one day which the writer [H. S. Wardner] has found recorded was on September 30, 1833, when 1,000 sheep crossed. . .historically, the most interesting item of the year [1825] was noted on Tuesday, June 28, when "Marquis Fayette passed with his Suit." [The journal Wardner quotes from was written by Colonel Brown between 1825 and 1836.] (William, H. Child, pages 214-215)

Shaker Bridge

This unique bridge, whose log crosspieces seem to be floating, is another span built as a result of compromise and the extension of the Boston & Maine railroad. In 1847 the railroad, seeking to extend its line westward through Enfield, expected to follow the old stagecoach road. In Enfield, the stage ran right through Shaker property, a situation that had benefited the community for many years. The Shakers had always been alert to innovations in industry and technology that would enhance efficency and further their business. The Shakers welcomed the idea of access to markets and increased mobility that a nearby railroad depot would offer. They did not, however, wish the train to cut their village in two. To build the depot on the other side of Lake Mascoma would resolve the issue, the Shakers thought, to benefit all. The problem to be solved was to reduce the lengthy drive around the lake to the depot.

Elder Caleb Dyer, village administrator, working on behalf of the Shakers and their near neighbors, devised a plan that was eventually accepted. His group proposed a bridge across the lake at its narrowest point, approximately one-half mile, and the gift to the railroad of a piece of land on the lake's northern shore. The Shakers offered to build the bridge, no mean feat, as the lake was thirty feet deep with a soft mud bottom of similar depth. Reaching an agreement on all sides, the Shakers cut, peeled, and set sixty-foot log pilings every ten meters across the lake in two straight lines. On the winter ice, they built wooden cribs around each piling and loaded them with stones for weight. When the ice went out of the lake in the spring, they sank to the bottom, securing the pilings. The bridge was completed in 1849 and accepted by the town at a late summer town meeting. The town paid the Shakers five thousand dollars for the bridge and the Shakers agreed to keep it in repair for ten years in lieu of highway taxes. The bridge proved troublesome to maintain but it did survive for almost ninety years, until the 1938 hurricane blew it out.

When WPA workers repaired the bridge, they found many sound original timbers which they used in the reconstruction. Apparently, some are still in place holding the present Shaker Bridge connecting the opposite lake shores.

For cooperating with the railroad, the Boston & Maine gave Caleb Dyer a lifetime pass on the line, a common practice later outlawed.

The undulating lines of the structure make it seem fragile and impermanent but the road traffic is well organized as seen by the STOP sign at the edge of the stonewall in the foreground where vehicles must wait before proceeding on to the bridge. What looks like a storage place for logs, perhaps a log boom, is visible to

the left of the far end of the bridge. The current Shaker Bridge has two lanes and rests on three piers.

Old Ledyard Bridge

The Old Ledyard Bridge connects the towns of Hanover, New Hampshire and Norwich, Vermont, across the Connecticut River. The bridge was constructed in 1859 through the cooperative efforts of both towns and Dartmouth College. The bridge has the distinction of being the first free bridge over the Connecticut River and for many years it was the only one at which tolls were not charged.

Completed in June of 1859, the bridge soon became the pride of the upper river valley. Replacing the privately-owned toll bridge with a free bridge was not accomplished without difficulties. The original owners and many local residents bitterly opposed the plans. Professors Sanborn and Crosby had been vocal and, sometimes, combative advocates for the free bridge. The diplomacy of Dartmouth President Nathan Lord is credited with having smoothed the ruffled feathers of the opposing locals, most of them Mill Villagers (Etna), who didn't think they would benefit enough from use of the bridge. By the decisive town meeting of November 19, 1858, he had wrought "the spirit of compromise" that led to the townspeople voting in favor of a new bridge.

On July 1, 1859, to celebrate its formal opening and the happy ending of the long and bitter controversy,

a large and respectable audience from Norwich and

Hanover gathered in the College Church. After speeches by Professor Sanborn, Dr. Crosby and others, William H. Duncan, who had been one of the officers of the Bridge Corporation, remarked "of the Old Bridge, let us say, 'Peace to its ashes,' and may all the ill will, hard feelings and bad blood that may have been engendered by its ashes in the deep waters of the river be buried." At the close of Mr. Duncan's remarks, Dr. Crosby said, "it is important that our Bridge should have a name" and suggested that it be christened the "Ledyard Free Bridge" in honor of John Ledyard, one time Dartmouth student and famous "American Traveler." Dr. Crosby's motion was put and unanimously approved. (John K. Lord, pages 21-22)

Old Ledyard Bridge survived two outstanding floods, "the freshet of 1869 [and] the even greater flood of 1927. . .no doubt due to its well constructed abutments and central pier, as well as to its height above the water." (Lord, page 26)

That John Ledyard is one of thirty-three signatories to a bond in favor of Eleazar Wheelock Esquire, Dartmouth's Founder, recorded in the early court records of Hanover (February 6, 1773), places him among the first residents of the town. The bond levied a fine or a flogging for "defamation in manner and form as alleged against another man." (Lord, page 149)

Ledyard, from a distinguished Connecticut family, had been, in fact, a friend of Eleazar Wheelock in Connecticut. He followed Wheelock to Hanover in 1772 to enter the newly opened Dartmouth College and to

The "New Ledyard Bridge was constructed by Davison Construction Company at a cost of $153,000, an amount shared by Hanover and Norwich, the states of New Hampshire and Vermont, and the federal government. Of steel and concrete, it has a sidewalk on the northern side. Two concrete abutments and two concrete piers replace the old stone abutments and center pier.

This Ralph W. Brown photograph showing modern techniques of bridge construction is of the present Ledyard Bridge, which in 1936 replaced the much-loved Ledyard covered bridge that had survived the pounding of numerous floods, log drives and the vicissitudes of raging storms. The work is concentrated down at the Norwich end of the structure where a crane cable is the focus of the workers' attention. The cement mixer sits at the Hanover end, where the first section of concrete appears to have set. Three men busy themselves between the cement section and the first concrete pier.

The big pile of slab lumber in the farmyard, at the top of the photo in the background, is poor man's wood, used for heating and a variety of other purposes on a thrifty farm. Courtesy of Dartmouth College Library

work among the Indians. Apparently, the bridge's namesake stayed only a few weeks before beginning his life of adventure and romance by running away from the College and journeying down the Connecticut River to the sea in a canoe of his own fashioning. Among his exploits was sailing with the famous Captain Cook. He traveled to Russia and the Far East at the instigation of Thomas Jefferson who urged him to find an eastern route to America's west coast. He had become something of a legend in the college town by the time he died suddenly, at thirty-eight, in Egypt.

The many anecdotes about John Ledyard confirm him to be a local hero of legendary status. One memorializes "Ledyard and his fellow-students who in 1722 climbed Velvet Rock and slept all night in the snow in the dead of winter," an act that one historian implies to be somewhat prophetic of the winter sports craze at the College epitomized in the twentieth century by the

Dartmouth Outing Club. (Childs, page 181)

The beautiful span stood for seventy-five years before it failed to live up to traffic needs. A modern Ledyard Bridge replaced it in the mid-nineteen thirties.

Rebuilding the Stone Bridge

The citizens of Peterborough chose to rebuild the stone bridge over the Contoocook River at Main Street after it had washed out in the hurricane and flood of 1938. The decision is a testament to prescient community planning. The town suffered greatly as a result of the flood and the concurrent great fire that destroyed a beautiful stone landmark, an early gristmill, and the surrounding block of businesses.

A local resident remembers with pleasure an anecdote he heard many times about a group of indomitable elderly ladies who lived in the apartments

upstairs in the Brennan Block. He says,

a row of them sat on the porch watching the flood. having a high old time. It took both the fire chief *and* the police chief to convince them to go. I don't think they ever believed there was danger. They just loved the excitement of it.

Gone from the scene, as well, are "O'Malley's Filling Station" and the tavern, behind which was an automobile repair shop that people reached by going down the driveway alongside the tavern. The Old Central School, visible on the hill, is now the parking lot for the Catholic Church (photo, page 85).

The people of Peterborough may have had moments of regret during the period of rebuilding, itself. One old-timer, seeing the photo, immediately recalled how "the old steam-driven engine pounded away on the iron piles

The railroad bridge angling into the view from the right and the great double arch commanding the eye from the left are two of the elements of design that make this such a powerfully aesthetic image. The pedestrians walking in small groups, pairs, and singly and the horse-drawn vehicle emerging from the far side of West Walpole's "Arched Bridge," all seem to be going to New Hampshire. The two youths standing idly by the river in Bellows Falls near what looks like a horse's hitching post and dismounting block, seem also to be drawn to the New Hampshire view. The serene scene is surprisingly peopled, the pedestrians in neat attire. Are they, perhaps, going early to church on a quiet Sunday morning? The anonymous photo is undated. The arches were removed from the bridge when it was repaired in the early 1980s. Courtesy of New Hampshire Historical Society

Remnants of old advertisement bill-boards still cling to the sides of the entrance way: ". . .'s Wild West." The protected interiors of the old covered bridges were ideal bulletin boards for such advertising posters, broadsides, and notices to pedestrians. A man approaches the pedestrian's walk on the near side of the bridge. The simple construction emphasizes sturdiness in the trusses, three across on each side of the bridge. George E. Fellows took this photograph of Enfield's South Street Bridge between 1900 and 1915. Courtesy of Dartmouth College Library

day and night, for weeks, driving them in." His wife, at the time a bride and new to the town, added softly, "you could hear the noise all over town." They both laughed.

Bridges sometimes contributed to social commerce in unexpected ways. In 1976, town historians incorporated the memories of old-time Lyme resident, Roy Balch, into a published history. Of a great local teamster he recollected:

> One man working for Frank Pushee drove a six-horse team and thus a larger load. He was Henry McMann (1873-1931), remembered by many for the ease with which he could handle four, six, or eight horses. He showed others how to hold all the "ribbons" (reins) but few could do it as well. Mr. McMann drove the town's road machine, a mammoth horse-drawn piece of equipment which was the forerunner of today's grader. It is said that he could turn his team around "on a dime." Money passed hands the day he turned six horses and the road machine around inside a covered bridge, emerging in the direction from which he had just come. It helps to know the road machine was set on two small wheels so that it could turn like a swivel, but that does not diminish the awesomeness of the feat, nor did it "help turn the heels of the horses around!" (Cole, pages 172-173)

Balch's admirable understatements increase one's appreciation of the combination of fun and hard work that often characterizes the people of the region. It seems that they are quick to take advantage of any opportunity to lighten the load with laughter.

Mink Brook Bridge 1914
Hanover N H

The Mink Brook Bridge spans a waterway known for the series of waterfalls that once powered several mills including a gristmill and a sawmill, in what is now Etna. In the early days of settlement, Etna carried the common name, Mill Village, or occasionally, Mill Neighborhood.

This anonymous photo of stone-arched bridge construction is inherently interesting to the contemporary viewer. The careful poses of the workers, some carrying tools, others archly casual, look like the result of a fastidious artist's meticulous direction. The cooperation of the men reveals a deep pride in their work, an attitude shared by skilled laborers everywhere. Their work is, indeed, fascinating. That many old stone-arched bridges survive in fine condition is a source of pride to the people of the region and heightens the interest of the viewer in the techniques of the trade. The worker's calm assurance as they stand on the thin scaffolding betrays its soundness. The combination of finely engineered instruments and handmade equipment attests to the many layers of know-how that go into the building of these handsome structures. In the finished bridge, long slabs neatly top a crazy quilt pattern of stones that fill the parapet between its perfect arch and capstone. The Mink Brook Bridge was completed in 1915. Courtesy of Dartmouth College Library

No less appealing to the chronicler than the bridge in full span, is the bridge being built or in repair, innards and structural components exposed to the curious. Like construction sites everywhere, there is the focal activity to observe, such as the two groups of workers, one at each of the scaffolding sets, the caterpillar bulldozer at the ready on the hillside across the river, and the neatly coiled cable thrown down near the parked automobiles on the Vermont side of the river. And there is the inevitable line-up of the workers' personal vehicles in which they come and go. Among this sampling, the license plate on the vehicle with old fashioned running boards and bug-eye headlamps reads, VT: 2S 40 67. The bridge under construction is in West Chesterfield on Route 9, built around 1939. It spans the Connecticut River at the southern end of Brattleboro, Vermont. Courtesy of New Hampshire Historical Society

The bustle of bridge building in this effective photograph, is done against the background of a Main Street that has faded from memory. Gone is Peterborough's Brennan Block, where Brennan had a stone monument shop on the ground floor, next to the First National grocery, managed at the time by Vernon Harris. Center Town has grown up in the spot. Courtesy of Peterborough Historical Society

Quadrille Bands played for dances and took their name from the dances in squares popular at the time with four pairs of dancers to a standard square. At the dance itself, contras and other popular dances were also performed and the band was expected to be able to accompany them all. C. E. Bullard of Peterborough took the striking portrait of this band on January 20, 1888. Personnel included F. V. Barrett, first violin; E. Upton, second violin; L. J. Dean, flute; F. H. Osborn, clarinet; F. G. Livingston, cornet; H. E. Miller, trombone; and F. E. Longley, basso.

The formality of the instrumentation designations, printed on back of the photo, might simply reflect a somewhat sophisticated level of musical education. Perhaps these young men played for the more formal community dances instead of the barn dances in the area. However, many musicians crossed the line, happy enough to have any

opportunity to play with other musicians. Community concerts were also popular at the time and the instrumentation of this group would certainly have made possible such performances as well. Courtesy of Peterborough Historical Society

6

ENTERTAINMENT AND TOURISM

The settlers of the Connecticut River Valley and their descendents were self-sufficient people. Work engaged their hours fully. Many social events merely attached a social aspect to community work. Most familiar of these were the bees: corn husking bees, maple sugar bees, apple paring bees, and the like. The laborious effort at these intensely busy events was lightened somewhat by the dance party and feast that followed. Opportunity for social interaction was tied in to religious organizations, the schools, and official town activities. Otherwise, neighbors visited among themselves. By the last quarter of the nineteenth century, however, family parties and visiting the region's tourist sights became more common.

Dancing

There have been those in Charlestown who claimed that "if the people in this town educated their heads half as much as their heels we would soon be a brilliant community." There have been plenty who were ready to take a whirl. According to Mrs. Johnson dancing on the new boards was a pleasure in the early days, and has continued so through the popularity of Kitchen Junkets, Hops, Balls of all descriptions and plain Social Dances. There were dance halls in the old Darrah Tavern, Parker Tavern, Cheshire Bridge House, Connecticut River House. Assemblies were held at the Eagle, and Hops for the summer boarders on the piazza at the

87

The fairgrounds come to life in this photo taken in 1910, about thirty years after the previous image was taken. The work of E. G. Dewey of Hanover, this view of the fair gives a sense of how great a variety of activities was possible even in a small country fair like Etna's. The sports and attractions take no more precedence, it seems, than the agricultural features, ostensibly the raison d'etre for these events. But it is the social life, the "visiting" that is taking place throughout the grounds that defines what may very well be the greatest motivation of all. Courtesy of Dartmouth College Library

Evans House. The Casino at Fairy Dell, the Hoyt Casino, the old Hall Grist Mill were scenes of dancing parties. After the building of the Town Hall the Balls and many of the less pretentious dances were held there. During the Gay Nineties, Annual Balls were held by many of the organizations in town — Grange, Odd Fellows, Red Men. The Bond Shop had an Annual Ball at which a prize of a violin case was given to the woman voted the most beautiful or the best dancer, and a guitar and case to the homeliest man present. (Frizell et al., page 298)

Kitchen Junkets was one phrase used to describe dances at private homes where the furniture in kitchen and living room might be moved out onto the porch or into the yard to clear the room for sets of dancers. The musicians, perhaps a lone fiddler, would stand in the doorway between the rooms or on the stairway. Children would be put to sleep in the upstairs bedrooms on beds laden with the coats and hats of visitors. Some of these parties began Friday night and didn't end until Sunday morning. Historically, many descriptions of dances, callers, musicians, and dancers, like the one that follows, have found their way into regional publications.

When George S. Bond dedicated his new fiddle case factory in Charlestown, October 26, 1893, "at least 600 people (were) present at a grand concert and ball." An anonymous eyewitness account has been preserved. Except for size, the event is typical of community entertainment at important gatherings, and holiday festivities throughout the region.

The spacious interior was a beautiful scene, the walls draped with the attractive scarlet and blue material used for lining the cases manufactued by the firm and the raised dais on which the music was stationed and the waiting room were draped and curtained with the same. Over all were the rainbow hues of the colored electric lights adding new tints to the brilliant picture. The music by Comstock's Orchestra was excellent and the solo by Allen Wood was accorded an enthusiastic double encore. Promptly at 9 o'clock Mr. and Mrs. Bond commenced the grand march, 121 couples following.

On the reverse of the original stereograph of the Etna Fairgrounds, taken September 12, 1877, the photographer is identified as "Artist, Currier, Bradford, N.H.," possibly Herman J. Currier of New London who also operated The Elms. Many township charters required an annual market if the town was to maintain rights to the district. Fairs, a mid-nineteenth-century development, are a natural outgrowth of the early market days. Etna's fairgrounds are little more than open space but nicely graded for the purpose. Courtesy of New Hampshire Historical Society

The 100 X 40 foot floor space was densely crowded and ability was taxed in divisioning for the first quadrille. While the dance went merrily on the guests were sightseeing in the spacious building and that portion of the machinery department where Charles H. Hodgkins of the C & C Electric Motor Company of Boston was stationed in charge of the electric dynamos. At 11 o'clock the ladies of St. Luke's Church served an elegant supper in the machinery department. (Frizell et al., page 230)

Such community dances as described above are in the living memories of many old-timers. A few old-time dance callers, musicians, and dancers are still active in the region. In addition, there is a strong contradance revival in place today. One of the persons behind the success of the revival of New England dancing was Keene's own Ralph Page.

In the nineteenth century, America was fond of music and theater. Sight reading and singing and declamation were standard in the public school curriculum. Singing, storytelling, and reciting at school and in the home were commonplace. Concerts, lectures, and theatrical evenings were heavily attended. Culture was on the rise. Just about every institution in the community reinforced these interests.

Peterborough has had at least one community band since the early part of the nineteenth century. A Fife and Drum Corps "furnished music on Training Days and Military Musters." The Peterborough Brass Band was "a long standing town organization" that had its first concert at the Town Hall on March 20, 1852.

It furnished excellent music and was particularly effective at the Fourth of July celebrations during the period before the Civil War. (Morison, pages 581-582)

Newport's musical history goes back to the eighteenth century with military muster fife and drum corps and bands. A town band was active and popular for many years after its founding by Col. William Cheney in 1815. The Newport Cornet Band

The winter sports industry has done away with the small town winter carnival in our time. In this scene, the sense of community is strong, perhaps because the playground is right in the middle of the town. Lancaster even today gives the impression of being almost completely a residential town. The business district is tightly contained at a crossroads and many residents can walk from their homes to shop there. The toboggan slide is a temporary structure, built for the occasion. There is genuine charm in the posture of the three young skiers to the left, who appear to be exchanging pointers and drawing courage from each other. WPA photographer, Arthur Rothstein took several photos of this carnival for the Farm Security Administration in February, 1936. Courtesy Library of Congress, Photograph and Print Division

made its first appearance in public in July, 1860. Two years after, in October, 1862, the full band, eighteen pieces, enlisted for the war in the nine months service. (Wheeler, page 216)

One of the most impressive examples of community musicianship in the nineteenth century was the musical convention. These were four-day events devoted to the rehearsal and performance of music by amateur and professional artists who gathered together for the purpose of making music. At first, these conventions were organized by town or county musical associations. They took place at various times of the year, weather not seeming to be a significant factor in the planning. Annual musical conventions, conducted and organized by local professional musicians, went on for over twenty-five years, beginning in the 1860s.

Eventually, a state musical convention, proposed by three Concord music teachers, John H. Morey, Benjamin B. Davis and John Jackman, took place in Concord on January 26, 1864. Devised as a "festival . . . open to the

attendance of singers from all parts of the state, (it) was to be held annually. . . .

Banks of seats were built up from the stage to accommodate the chorus singers, who came from all parts of the state. Noted conductors and soloists were brought from Boston. . . . The convention lasted four days and grand concerts of classical music were given on Thursday and Friday evenings. Wednesday afternoon was devoted to the entertainment of the children. . . . These conventions did much to stimulate the musical taste . . . of the state.

The people of Concord welcomed with ready hospitality the numerous visitors in attendance. . . . [There were] daytime rehearsals and evening concerts in which a chorus of more than five hundred voices participated. (Lyford, page 1078)

The Sullivan County Musical Association had its first Newport meeting in June, 1848, "an occasion of much interest, and . . . fully attended." It met again in Newport

A far more ambitious winter carnival happens every year at Dartmouth College, Hanover. Although it is primarily a college sponsored function, local communities find many ways to participate. In this delightful snapshot from 1950 the members of the Claremont Skating Club wait in the dressing tent for their turn to perform at the Outdoor Evening Show, the extravaganza event of the weekend's festivities. Courtesy of Dartmouth College Library

in 1851. "again full of interest, and most satisfactory." Throughout the state, county and local musical conventions were popular events for thirty years or more beginning in the 1840s.

The event pictured on p. 97, the first Sullivan County Musical Association Convention, September 26, 1873, was the first of several annual conventions. The Association had been formed a year earlier, almost to the day, and became "one of the most popular and successful institutions of the kind ever held in the county." The committee was comprised of town dignitaries, music professionals and clergymen. At this meeting,

> Solon Wilder was conductor and Joseph P. Cobb, of Boston, pianist and humorist. At the close of this convention, which was holden in the new town hall, they were so well pleased with their accommodations in all respects, that they voted unanimously that the annual meetings of the association be permanently located in this town. (Wheeler, page 216)

The choral singers, musicians and principals pose on the stage, the site of the convention rehearsals and concerts.

Town Fairs

In any community, the annual town fair was a major opportunity for business news, socializing, and fun. Etna's Village Improvement Society ran their annual fairs,

> their most colorful activity. . .held on one of the commons. There were big tents for meals and exhibits. Some years more than a hundred cattle were shown. There was always a big parade

complete with floats, horses, horribles, bicycles and sometimes a twenty-piece band from Norwich. A horse-drawn, merry-go-round sort of ride was very popular. Eight forty-foot poles with seats on the ends which would hold five adults or eight children were fastened to a tall mast. You could ride for five minutes for five cents which was hardly long enough to read all the advertisements which fluttered overhead. (Lillian Kenison Bailey in *Hanover Bicentennial Book.* pages 78-79)

The town of Stoddard's first fair, limited to local participants, was held August 22, 1851. Its sponsors, the Stoddard Agricultural Association, stipulated that all stock entered for a premium must either have been raised in town or if bought from abroad, must be owned in town at least three months before the exhibition. . .ladies in particular were requested to bring such articles of domestic manufacture or of fancy and ingenuity as their convenience will admit. (Stoddard Historical Society, page 159)

Winter Carnivals

Winter weather sometimes limits revelers' mobility, but our early ancestors braved the elements if the occasion warranted it.

The Dartmouth Winter Carnival attracts spectators from all over the Northeast and is very well publicized. Hundreds of stunning photographs exist documenting the annual event. The portrait chosen for inclusion here, however, is a verbal one, penned by Jose Clemente Orozsco

When Orozsco was artist in residence at Dartmouth, he found the annual Carnivals to be such memorable

experiences that he wrote about them most feelingly in his autobiography. "Dartmouth is delicious in winter," he begins.

It stands on the Connecticut River, surrounded by forest-covered mountains....

In February, a famous Carnival is held which attracts young ladies from the most aristocratic women's colleges and, Dartmouth being a school for men only, they are fully entertained in dances and skating parties.

One of the most important events in the winter fiesta is a competition in ice sculpture. The students are most skillful in erecting figures, and even monuments of great size. Each fraternity erects its own in front of the fraternity house and illuminates it by night. The effect is stupendous. While there I was a member of the jury to award prizes for these figures. (Orozco, page 159)

Coaching Parades

A few White Mountain towns held successful "coaching parades," as they were called, and Lancaster held two very successful events in the summers of 1895 and 1896.

After considerable correspondence with the managers of other coaching parades, railroads, and proprietors of the mountain hotels and boarding-houses, committees were appointed at a public meeting called at the Lancaster House for that purpose, and all necessary arrangements were made for a gala day on August 15, 1895.... The railroads, especially the Maine Central, cooperated to its success. This [rail]road generously loaned the committee enough bunting to decorate all the public buildings of the village. The citizens took a deep interest in the movement, and by contribu-

tions of money and the elaborate decoration of their houses guaranteed its success. The enterprise was well advertised; and when the day came it was one of those glorious days of summer that puts every living thing at its best. Heavy rains a few days before had laid the dust and refreshed all nature. The day broke with a clear sky, and by eight o'clock the streets began to fill up with people. Streams of teams kept coming over the hills, and large excursion trains arrived from all the railroads, so that by ten o'clock there was such a throng of people as is rarely seen in a country village. Gov. Charles A. Busiel, and many distinguished citizens from abroad, were present to witness the event. Scores of finely-decorated coaches and carriages were in line as well as a variety of exhibitions of the various industries and enterprises of the town. Two bands, the Berlin Comet Band and the Saranac Band, of Littleton, discoursed music on the occasion. Taken all in all, it was an indescribable profusion of beauty and pleasure, a scene never to be forgotten....
(Somers, pages 161-162)

Traveling Circuses

William Dewey of Hanover writes in his diary, for 1845:
...an unusual rush of all kinds of people [attended Dartmouth Commencement] from the circumstance that there was uncommon attractions for them. A somewhat extensive Menagerie of wild animals (in most miserable plight however)—The Boston Band of Musicians and the famous foreign Violin player named Ole Bull—and 4 Albinos or white negros—everything to pick away money and lead the minds of people from the great concerns of eternity and their duties of charity to their needy fellow citizens and the perishing heathen. Even clergymen were so enraptured with the mere report

of the fame of Ole Bull that they could not resist the inclination to hand out their half dollar to hear him scrape his catgut and another quarter to hear the brass band perform. (Childs, page 271)

Childhood Escapades

An anecdote that illustrates how the early telephones challenged the imaginations and the daring of local children, told by an anonymous resident, found its way into Hanover's bicentennial history:

> Our first telephone was an enormous instrument on the wall, with a dial, something like a cribbage board. There was a little peg hanging on a chain. You put the peg in the number and drew the lever down to the peg and released it. One of my pals was the son of the Episcopal minister. My father came home one afternoon and found a whole string of children across our kitchen, holding hands. At one end of the line was this boy, with his hand in a strategic spot in the telephone apparatus, and the last child in the line had his hand in a bucket of water in the sink. When Henry would do something to the phone, an electric shock would run through the hands and arms of the children, to their howls of delight. (Speny, page 51)

Ball Games

Peterborough *Annals* include excerpts of a letter sent to John H. Morison, town historian, by Daniel Abbott,

native of Peterborough, in which Abbott reminisced about the days which Jonathan Smith, *Annals* editor, describes as "just after the close of the Revolution, when the laxity of habits and the general social conditions, customs and manners of the people in the country towns in the years immediately following the Revolutionary struggle...."

Abbott describes a ball game played by some members of the local militia the morning after their first postwar meeting. Picking up Abbot's description immediately at the close of elections of officers, he says:

> The training commenced and the rum was made free use of so that by evening they were not only rich but merry and apparently very happy, and to make their happiness complete they commenced a knock-down between Peterboro and (now) Sharon men. Mathew Wallace put some of them under keepers for swearing, and in fact swore as much himself as they had done. You mentioned the bbl. of rum with the head knocked out. By the bye the bbl. of rum was all gone by evening and they sent for a half bbl. which John Smith and James had procured to do their roling with. In the evening the rum became a little too fiery, and a large tub was placed in the middle of the floor and filled with Grog and with many bowls and dippers every one helped himself to as much as he pleased, and perhaps to as much as was necessary....Many stayed all night and the next morning found them in good spirit. Second day, a great game of ball (which was much practiced at that day) was proposed on Scott's hill and the two Captains chose their men, from forty to

fifty on each side. The game went on with great exertion on both sides till each side had but one to make, and Capt. Smith had the ground. At the last knock Ensign Houston caught the ball by which means Capt. McCloud won the victory. "Well Capt. McC." (said Capt. S.) "you have beat me but you could not do it again." Night being at hand and the rum all spent an adjournment took place as a matter of course. (Peterborough Historical Society, page 160)

Tourism

Once communities achieved basic physical and financial security, hospitality, and sociability blossomed in the region, as elsewhere. Festivities, picnics, and outings gradually found their place in the social life of the region. Stagecoach trips to friends and relatives for a summer in the mountains or on the farm were common enough by the end of the eighteenth century but it was railroad development that gave tourism an economic boost in New Hampshire. Such choice vacation spots as the towns around Lake Sunapee and Mount Monadnock drew visitors from New York and Boston for the summer holidays. Even towns with few spectacular attractions hosted summer residents whose only demand was the temporary bucolic experience of rural life. The Connecticut River Valley towns north of Hanover, former-ly reachable only by wagon and stagecoach came into their own with the railroads. With the ascendency of automobile travel since the Second World War, the region prospers with a year-round vacation and weekend tourism industry.

The well-to-do clientele of high-toned summer resorts like Lake Sunapee was well served by the railroad's expansion into the small communities of western New Hampshire. But the iron horse age also gave birth to

dozens of small rail lines, later to become trolley lines, some along the routes of the earlier horse-drawn car lines. These small lines, emanating from almost every large town and certainly from every city in the region, made excursions to the country easy and affordable to the working class. For the modest sum of five cents, a rider could join the crowds on board bent on spending an afternoon picnicking near one or another of the many attractions, natural or man-made, that the rural areas of the state served up in abundance. (pages 87-88)

In 1903, the trolley lines that completed the network of public transportation in the hinterlands of New Hampshire begun by the railroad were electrified. Rural trolleys catered to the needs of the communities along their routes. They ran frequently, every half hour in larger communities. The cars had freight compartments for mail and cargo. Sunday excursions from the larger towns into the country were part of the regular local rail schedules.

Trolleys ran until mid-century in some of the communities in western New Hampshire, passenger trains ran into the 1950s, and freight trains still roll the rails. No matter how primitive their accommodations seem to us at the end of the twentieth century, to our ancestors, the car lines were a vast improvement over the discomfort of wagons or stagecoaches. Indeed, we can envy the flexibility and availability of turn-of-the-century public transportation, local and long distance, served by what seems to us to have been unlimited choice of connections in all four directions of the compass.

Resort hotels, guest houses, private homes, and farmhouses provided lodgings for visitors. Resort areas like the towns surrounding Lake Sunapee and Mount Monadnock catered to the upper middle-class tourist. Wealthy tourists sometimes hired a Pullman car which could be drawn onto a side track at a resort depot and stay put for the weekend to take their private passengers back to their homes, perhaps as far as Boston, New York, or

Civil War veterans and others in the Peterborough Coronet Band are, from left to right; George F. Livingston, Wilbur E. Davis, Elijah A. "Bink" Robbins, Harvey Hadley, Clarence E. White, Henry Snow, Harry H. Templeton, John F. Singhi (leader), Henry Preston, Daniel K. Hood, Frank Averill, James M. "Tim" White, Clarence Hardy, Julius Pearl, and Edwin A. Townes. The big drum belongs to the Peterborough Historical Society. The photo is taken in 1866 in front of the Old Town House, before it was renovated in 1886 and became known as the Opera House. The building was lost to fire in 1916. Courtesy of Peterborough Historical Society

even Chicago. The less well-off tourist, nevertheless, found ample accommodations in private homes, on farms, or at camp sites throughout the region. Day trippers of all classes found their way to the more well-known tourist attractions.

If the railroad's extension into the rural and mountainous regions of New Hampshire caused tourism to affect more strongly the social and economic life of the state, when the automobile arrived on the scene at the turn of the century, the entire state opened up to tourism. Enterprising business people built summer hotels around such major attractions as Mount Monadnock and Spofford Lake; farmers opened their homes to summer visitors and groups on day trips to the countryside, always a popular pastime, ventured greater distances to many newly accessible popular sights of the region. Eventually, just about every town in the state entertained visitors at inns or hotels. Until the devastating hurricane of 1938, convenient railway service for passengers and freight operated in every region of New Hampshire, stopping at many towns along the route. After that, roads and highways increasingly served the tourist.

Twentieth-century advances in technology make year-round travel easier. The national lifestyle, with regulated periods of leisure time provided by a calendar of annual vacations and monthly holidays, promotes tourism as a favorite family activity. The region provides recreational facilities that continue to measure up to and keep up with recreational fashions in boating, swimming, water skiing, fishing, hiking, leaf-peeping, hunting and trapping, and myriad snow sports. The consistently beautiful scenery enhances the region's appeal throughout the seasons.

Monadnock

On the reverse of a Monadnock area view (center photo, page 105) is a glowing description:

The Grand Monadnock Mountain is in the southwestern part of New Hampshire, in the towns of Jaffrey, Dublin and Marlboro', and is the most prominent eminence in this part of the state, being 3,750 feet above the sea level, and commands a view of the country around it for fifty miles on every side. The summit is bare rock, but the prospect is one of remarkable beauty and grandeur, in which respects it is not inferior to the famous White Mountain Range. It has many attractions in its wild, romantic scenery, extended view, invigorating air, and is a favorite resort in this region, being annually visited by thousands. From its summit may be seen many beautiful villages, lakes, ponds, etc. presenting a vast panorama sublime and enchanting.

Monadnock is a mountain strong.
Tall and good my kind among

. . . .

Every morn I lift my head,
Gaze o'er New England underspread,
South from St. Lawrence to the Sound.
From Catskill east to the sea-bound.
—Emerson

Monadnock lifting from his night of pines
His rosy forehead to the evening star.
—Whittier

Tourists leaving the Mountain House, passing up and through a fine grove of trees and shrubbery, beyond and above the tree line will find two ways of reaching the summit. The *left*, or western, is the most direct most traveled, and most difficult. The *right*, or eastern, is the better but more obscure.

Many choose to make the ascent by one route, returning by the other. The Mountain House is situated half way between the base and the summit of the mountain, about one mile from the top.

Photographic Views of the Mountain and the magnificent scenery around it, are on sale at the Mountain House, and by J. A. FRENCH, Photographer, Keene, N. H.

Pack Monadnock, situated in Peterborough and Temple, is smaller and less well-known than Mount Monadnock, sometimes referred to as Grand Monadnock to differentiate it from the lesser elevations that have Monadnock in their names. Nevertheless, Pack Monadnock has been an attraction of some importance to the people of the region and to tourists. The term Monadnock is adopted from an American Indian word, applied, at first, specifically to the Grand Monadnock. In current usage, however, the term is applied geologically and refers to mountains of the type described originally by geographer William Morris Davis as "prominent isolated hard rock remnants of a prolonged period of erosion." (Chamberlain, page 120.)

Summer Camp

Tent camps were the forerunner of summer cottages, known as camps locally. In the last quarter of the nineteenth century, they also provided accommodations for the summer encampments of such groups as the Civil War Veterans organization, the Grand Army of the Republic (G.A.R.). The curious "State of N. H." tenting party at Sunapee (top of p. 107) is not otherwise identified in the archives but is probably at a New Hampshire National Guards encampment.

Two different American flags decorate the interior where is set up a table with flowers, a lamp, and what looks like books. The insignia on the uniforms are barely legible although one cap bears what might be a medical first aide symbol. Whether it be of a party of National Guardsmen with their companions or some other occasion, the photo informs us of how highly military service was regarded by local society.

Community involvement with honoring and celebrating the military has a long history. In America, it goes back to the militia musters, which developed into sometimes spectacular events in the decades following independence. Regiments of uniformed soldiers gathered from miles around for inspection and review and to participate in mock campaigns. These central events would be followed by feasts, dancing, and a great variety of festivities. Memorable musters took place in the Sunapee area and elsewhere in the region.

Muster Recipe

Foodways play a significant role in all community festivities. An example is Hanover's Muster Day gingerbread: a "genuine" recipe "and it works,"

1 cup light molasses, 2 large tablespoons butter, 1 teaspoon soda mixed with 3 tablespoons boiling water, 1 teaspoon ginger, 1/2 teaspoon salt, 2 cups flour, kneaded in but not hard. Roll into sheets, mark with fork, and bake quickly. After baking, wet top of sheets with 3 teaspoons molasses while gingerbread is still hot. (Childs, page 89)

Also from nineteenth century Hanover comes this Muster Day rhyme, sung to a fife tune by local militia units on parade:

We've found the way to make ends meet—
Drink STONE WALL and hustle.
[Stone Wall consists of "old cidar" and "new rum" blended in proportions to suit the individual palate and in quantities to match the occasion.] (Childs, pages 88-89)

Tip Top House

According to local history of Coventry-Benton, the finest attribute of the tiny town next to Haverhill is the spectacular view from its highest peak, Mount Moosilauke. "The view from the summit of Moosilauke must be seen to be appreciated. It surpasses that obtained from any other New England peak, since its 5,000 feet of elevation is to a large extent isolated, with nearby neighbors of like elevation." The commentator is neighboring Warren's town historian, William Little, writing in the latter part of the nineteenth century. Little describes the view from Mount Washington to be uninteresting by comparison, offering, as it does, only the presidential range to the eye. Little's description of the panoramic view on a clear day does make the reader wonder at the tourist's neglect of the spot. Benton's own historian, William F. Whitcher mulls over the irony that, despite its spectacular beauty, Benton had not, by the turn of the century, become a tourist mecca. "It is a little difficult to explain why Benton has never become a summer resort town," he says. "It certainly has every natural advantage. It is a mountain town, Moosilauke, Black, Sugar Loaf and Owls Head, or Blueberry mountains covering nearly its entire territory. The beauty and grandeur is unrivaled in the entire mountain region of New Hampshire." The Tip Top Hotel, he notes, "in most seasons is well patronized, but the great mass of tourists pass it by." He soothes himself by concluding that "Benton awaits its discoverer." (Whitcher, pages 278-281)

Before leaving Benton behind, a singular piece of its history is worth noting. Earlier in the nineteenth century, an aptly named justice of the peace, Pardon W. Allen, "magnified his office" and granted a divorce agreement, "according to which . . . the wife promised never to trouble the husband, the cash consideration being

specified. Whitcher speculates that "it is probably the only divorce on record in New Hampshire on the authority of a justice of the peace." (Whitcher, pages 115-116)

Cheshire House

The Cheshire House sat in Keene on the corner of Roxbury and Main streets, site of the Phoenix Hotel which had burned on April 6, 1836. Opened in November 1837, the building used some of the brick walls and the portico left standing from the Phoenix Hotel. (Keene History Committee, page 81) Promotional literature described it as "a noble structure, its rooms airy and convenient, and the internal arrangement in full keeping with the inviting appearance of its external form."

The hotel incorporated the newly introduced Greek revival style of architecture that was to dominate the architecture of commercial and private buildings alike for most of the nineteenth century.

Among the historical occasions held at the Cheshire House was a Union Party banquet for 350 celebrating the election of Abraham Lincoln. In 1885, the hotel served elephant meat after a circus elephant was killed by the Keene Light Guard because of agressive behavior. President Taft spoke from its balcony on October 10, 1912. Dozens of hotel cats are reputed to have kept the food cellars free of vermin. The showplace hotel was closed and demolished in 1934, its fixtures sold at auction, Its name was retained in the Cheshire House Block of stores that were built on part of the site.

The business tenants in the photo on page 112 include M. M. Spaulding who offers "My Mother's Bread," and , in the building to the right, Colonel Wardwell's Auction. The site of the Cheshire had been associated with auctions since early in the century when large cattle auctions took place at the Tavern, the first building to occupy the site. Cheshire Meat Company's delivery wagon waits outside.

Hunting: Historical Note

Hunting has been an important part of the woods economy since settlement, providing pelts and food which, in the eighteenth and nineteenth centuries, were necessary for survival. The settlers of Walpole and Stoddard, like many early pioneers, practiced a strategy of conservation by electing a town deer reeve, the fore-

runner of today's game warden, to enforce deer hunting laws. They recognized the need to maintain the herd of animals which provided the majority of fresh meat for the town. Perhaps they learned the importance of this from the Indians.

An 1897 description of the beaver by the Stoddard town historian reminds us of how observant of wildlife our ancestors were. He says:

> A Beaver was once seen to work on her dam, by one of our citizens, while two young ones were at play a short distance off. She left her work went and caught, first the one, and then the other and gave them a severe flogging with her tail; she then went back to her work, and her idle children followed her. (Gould, pages 72-73)

That her descendents are plentiful in the area today attests to the mother beaver's effective teaching methods. A few years ago, one old-timer from over the mountain pointed out a "beaver's kitchen" on the corner of Route 9 and 123 at Stoddard, where sharpened stumps of a dozen or more trees showed evidence of many beaver meals.

By far the most dramatic hunting stories in the region that have come down to us involve bears and wolves. Some are horrifying and some are told with an ear to entertaining an audience. An example is from Stoddard:

> When Joel Wilson was a young man he encountered a mother bear with two cubs in his woods pasture. He turned back to alert his brothers and neighbors to organize a hunt. Overanxious, the party was soon scattered in the woods where Joel had not gone far before he overtook the bear again. This time the she-bear reared up and stood her ground, then came lumbering toward him. Wilson suddenly realized that all he had for defense was the axe he carried. It seemed inadequate to the situation, and Joel prudently climbed the nearest tree.
>
> But the bear could climb too and proceeded to do so. Fortunately for Joel the tree was small, too small for the bear to get a good grip. Every time the bear lunged upward, Wilson would pull his feet out of reach of her claws. Soon the others heard the commotion and Joel's shouts and, coming up with rifles, shot their bear. The cubs were discovered so far up another tree they had to fell it to capture them. (Stoddard Historical Society, page 32)

The original of this photo bears the stamp of the newspaper, The Milford Cabinet, *and the annotation: "Cantata 'The Haymakers', taken on Town House steps," and "Milford Musical Association,"* Charles N. Merrill, *conductor. The photograph is by S. R. Hanaford, Dunklee Building, Milford, New Hampshire. That the artists are a community group is obvious from the mix of its membership: all ages, men and women, young and not so young. As we have seen, there were numerous opportunities available for amateur music and theater performances in the region throughout its history. Courtesy of New Hampshire Historical Society*

Western New Hampshire supports a great number of community, college, and summer theaters with performances on at least a biweekly basis all year round and more often in the summer. Specializing in musical fare, the New London Players are busy enough at the New London Barn Playhouse to support a full-time box office, funky enough to rent pillows to soften admittedly hard seating, and popular enough to sell out all summer long. Summer theater in New London dates from 1933 when Josephine Ettee Holmes of Mount Holyoke College, at the urging of local supporters, instituted a summer theater with her students as thespians. The curtain went up for the first time on July 11. The next year she found a permanent home in the remodeled 1820 barn of the Robert Knight Farm on Main Street, afterward to be known as the Barn Playhouse. By the late 1940s, a full summer schedule was in effect and the theater, under the able leadership of a number of competent directors, has been a successful summer attraction ever since. Photo by Armand Szainer, 1988

The national agricultural grange organization, begun in 1867 to advance farming, became the heart of rural country social life in the late nineteenth and early twentieth centuries. Organized as a secret society with membership open at first only to farmers and their families, it was unique in that it gave rights and honors to women.

The Peterboro Grange, No. 35, Patrons of Husbandry, was formally chartered September 5, 1874. Samuel H. Vose was elected Master. "The Grange, with a maximum membership of about two hundred, was vital and influential for over fifty years." (Morison, p. 582) The twenty-six charter members of the Peterborough grange No. 35, photographed in 1873, are identified as follows: "1-2, S. W. Vose and Wife; 3-4, F. Field and Wife; 5-6, T. N. Hunt and Wife; 7-8, L. F. Richardson and Wife; 9, Chas. Barber; 10, C. A. Wheeler; 11, Mrs. Chas. Barber; 12, B. F. Smily; 13-14, J. N. Dodge and Wife; 15-16, F. A. Tarbell and Wife; 17, Willard Carey; 18-19, W. F. White and Wife; 20, Geo. W. Marden; 21-22, J.M. Ramsey and Wife; 23-24, D. M. McClenning and Wife; 25, C. W. Hunter; 26, J. A. Hovey." Courtesy of Peterborough Historical Society

Grange investitures were not unlike those of other secret societies such as Masonry. By the turn of the century, membership expanded to the community at large from its initial insistence on active farming as a condition of joining. The Peterborough Ladies Grange Degree Staff presentations were made in March 1906. It is an unfortunate fact that most personal photograph collections are never fully annotated. The identification of the women represented here is incomplete. Back row, left to right: Annie Jellison, Edith Gragin, Jessie Osburn, Mabel Brackett, Leah Baldwin; Second Row: Maria Hadley, ? Rice [?], ? Kendall, ?, and Anna Vinal. Courtesy of Peterborough Historical Society

Heritage commemorative events generated lively festivities and attracted tourists when held at the height of the season, as most were. Decorations and parades were favorite means of celebration. Festive buntings, ribbons, and flowers festooned anything that didn't move and a great many things that did. The original Lancaster Coach Parade was devised as a gala day to enliven the activities of a town that had become quite a tourist center by the gay nineties. Courtesy of New Hampshire Historical Society

Souvenir.
ONE HUNDRED AND FIFTIETH ANNIVERSARY SEMI-CENTENNIAL,
PETERBORO, N. H.

In 1889 the people of Peterborough marked the one hundred and fiftieth anniversary of its founding with parades, parties, and dances. William Knight decorated his milk delivery wagon and posed here on the Main Street Bridge. The house at the right is the Inglestrom House and the Whitney House (in the center) was recently razed. Courtesy of Peterborough Historical Society

Dartmouth College hosted the event but the townspeople participated fully at the Webster Centennial Celebration of 1901. The gaily decorated businesses on Hanover's Bridgeman Block rival the bonfire for spectacle. Many photographs exist of such lavishly garlanded town centers, some going back well over a century. No doubt, the decorative bunting for the 1895 Lancaster Coaching Parade was similarly hung. The practice survives in our time, a reminder of how much we resemble our ancestors in our enthusiasm for "gala days," decorations, and the good times that accompany them. Courtesy of Dartmouth College Library

The arrangement of vehicles, animals, and participants dressed in their finery against the backdrop of an impressive architectural structure imposes a sense of seriousness to what looks like a festive occasion. This stereograph shows Francestown Town Hall on the occasion of its Centennial in 1872. The Town Hall housed the Francestown Academy in the rooms of its second floor and the occasion served as a school reunion, as well.

Francestown Academy, established in 1811, graduated its last student in 1909. Difficulty in getting and keeping teachers and perpetual financial constraints dogged the administration of the Academy through most of its long history. Nevertheless, Academy reunions were frequent occurrences at which the entire community joined the alumni and their families in a day of social-

izing. At the time this anonymous stereograph was taken, Francestown was offering a high school education to all interested grammar school graduates. Courtesy of New Hampshire Historical Society

The excitement is almost palpable at this extraordinary event when Milford celebrates the laying of the cornerstone for the New Town Hall. The crowded scene informs us just how meaningful a milestone such occasions are to those who are the founders and shapers of a community.

The background to the town hall and its own history are interesting. Eagle Hall, the first Milford Meeting House and town hall, was erected in the summer of 1784. THe town supplied "One barrel of rum, two barrels of cider and one quarter of sugar for the raising." (Wright, page 10) The cornerstone for the "New Town House," being celebrated in this stereograph, took place in 1869. The building was dedicated a year later. The building later housed the post office, police station, and town offices. The Paul Revere bell in its tower, the gift of the town's first settled minister, Rev. Humphrey Moore, from his friend, Perkins Nichols of Boston, originally

hung in Eagle Hall. When it hung in the first meeting house, the bell tolled for "Church, joyous occasions, and deaths of noted national and local citizens. The bell [had come] to Milford by ox team." (Wright, page 503)

Milford's bell is one of only twenty-three extant Paul Revere bells and the only one never to have been repaired. The present town hall clock was installed

in 1887 and connected to the bell for stricking the hour. The hour hand is twenty-four inches long and the minute hand is thirty inches. S. R. Hanaford of Milford took this photo and its original bears the stamp of the Milford Cabinet. Courtesy of New Hampshire Historical Society

There are two focal points in this photo, the touring car with its occupants and the festive table handsomely prepared to accept the coming clambake feast. Clambakes are not commonly associated with inland locations like the Monadnock region. However, this photograph, taken at Athol, Massachusetts, (just over the line from Richmond, due south of Keene) and the one at Cunningham Pond, are proof to the contrary. Many area vacationers hail from the Boston region where summer fun can be synonymous with the traditional clambake. The occupants of the touring car, license number 245, are carefully identified on the original photo which implies that the anonymous photographer's intention was to document the "Peterborough Men" rather than the event itself. They are: Butler Jaffrey, G. P. Farrar, Endell Arnold, C. H. Weeks, and Algernon Holt. Courtesy of Peterborough Historical Society

Our Christmas Hunt, Near Littleton. Courtesy of New Hampshire Historical Society

Proud Hunters and Their Prizes, Hanover. Courtesy of Dartmouth College Library

Hunters/trappers and their Cabin in the Woods, Lisbon Area. Courtesy of New Hampshire Historical Society

The traditions of hunting and fishing have maintained a vitality in many of the region's rural communities. Longtime residents and visiting sportsmen, and, increasingly, sportswomen, find recreation and comaraderie in the annual fall deer hunting season. Many towns have Fish and Game Clubs while Game Suppers, an autumn foodways tradition throughout the region, survive now in a dozen or so communities. The New Hampshire Fish and Game Department supervises official hunting and fishing activity statewide, including a recently revived moose hunting season in the North Country. Hunting and fishing stories abound in the region.

Hunters must register their kill with the Fish and Game Department and many communities cooperate by providing weighing stations for the hunters' convenience. These locations also serve as trading posts, providing outlets for the sale of unwanted game to local customers. The Hanover weighing station where the collegians stand next to a rack of dressed game probably displays the kill of several hunters, killed over a period of days. Such are the scenes of hunting season in rural New Hampshire.

This little house hung with hunting and trapping gear appears to be an authentic example of the native New Hampshire woodsman's dwelling. The cabin is plain and practical, giving the impression of a self-sufficient operation.

Diary Entry of Abner Sanger, July 2, 1776: "___ at night, El hears that Eleazer Wilcox is very much hurt with the bear." (page 104)

This bear fight was the talk of the area at the time. Courtesy of New Hampshire Historical Society

Hanover's "Buster" Brown and his handsome catch make a striking photo in 1936. Described as a taxi driver and "alleged former bootlegger," Brown appears here to be worthy of a reputation for being both lucky and easygoing. Had he ever been a bootlegger, one look at this photo would convince the average fisherman that he had probably been a successful one. Pictures of "the catch" are a cliche subject of professional and amateur photographers alike. They provide the perfect counterpart to the proverbial fish stories of "the one that got away." *Courtesy of Dartmouth College Library*

The original of "John's" photograph is but 1½ inches by 1½ inches and inscribed on the back: "To Emily from John: String of Fish Chauncy and I Caught at N[ew] I[pswich]." Dispite the diminutive size, its message is of whopping pride which, together with the simple image, makes a strong visual statement. The very idea of such a "string of fish" lures many an outdoors enthusiast from warm beds into the early morning New Hampshire mist—in our time, as it has for centuries.

In the nineteenth century, fish, including salmon, were so plentiful that commercial catches were common for the individual fisherman. Woodsville, up in the northern reaches of the state, was one place where salmon fishermen congregated. The salmon catches were salted down there and shipped to various markets south and west. Although there are few photographs of women fishing, the sport attracted many female adventurers. One particularly appealing picture included in photographers' catalogs was of a young woman in mutton sleeves standing, fishing rod in hand, line cast well out into the water and titled: "Fisher Girl of the Connecticut Lakes." *Courtesy of New Hampshire Historical Society*

Bullard's Photo Studio, Peterboro', N. H.

Because clambakes require a lot of cooperative labor they were activities that were group sponsored—family reunions, fraternal societies, churches, or civic groups are typical of those that might get together to prepare such a feast. It is interesting that both this clambake at Cunningham Pond, Dr. Keliher's house, and the one in Athol appear to be "Men Only" events. It may be that the pre-site preparations are done by men and women and the actual public cooking and preparations taken care of primarily by the men. The breakdown of labor for community sponsored events is often women in the kitchen and men out of doors. The individuals are not identified although Dr. Keliher is, no doubt, among them. *Courtesy of Peterborough Historical Society.*

103

Bullard's Photo Studio, Peterboro', N. H.

The mock seriousness of these men in their contrived poses reveals a friendly compatibility within the group There can be no doubt about the mutual affection of the poseurs in the Ballard photograph. Perhaps, at these occasions, he was, himself, among the guests. The original photo is enscribed, "Mountain Camp, east of Mountain Pond, Peterborough" and the guests are identified as F. C. Osborne, C. A. Baldwin, David Raymond, E. Davis, Henry Nay, E. Upton, and I. Pratt. Courtesy of Peterborough Historical Society

There is nothing quite like the impression that simple snapshots of the small pleasures and shared experiences make on the viewer. Whether it is a string of fish or a passel of relatives as in this "Family Party at Lithia Springs, Temple, c. 1894," the straightforwardness of the scene commands attention. Such photos reflect the same respect for family gatherings that inspires the creation and upkeep of family photo albums. Birthdays, festivities, holiday trips—all are duly captured for

posterity. The Perry family and friends are pictured here, left to right, George Bain Cummings; Aunt Maria Perry; Mrs. Louise R. Amee; Mother (Mrs. Emma R. Perry); Cousin Elizabeth Perry; Frances Amee; Baby Helen Cummings; in his grandmother's arms (Cousin Angie Cummings); Josie Boyce; and Ruth Amee. (Young man not identified.)

At the end of the last century, Lithia Springs was a featured attraction on Temple's Pack Monadnock. Advertised widely for its therapeutic value, it was also a recreation area and picnic grove. Its advertising read: Lithia Springs contains more Lithium than any other Lithia Spring known, and other valuable constituents. Best remedy for Kidney Trouble and Indigestion." When, after about twenty years of operation, the lithium spring was discovered to be fraudulently enhanced, its owners left town in disgrace and the land was sold to a lumber company which cleared the pine grove. "Lithia Springs," the tourist attraction, faded into memory. Courtesy of New Hampshire Historical Society

This photograph of local people on an outing in the countryside is a fine example of the itinerant photographer's art. The party is on a holiday outing at the Cairn on Pack Monadnock in about 1910. The photographer made the most of the natural setting, grouping the human subjects in a way that sets off the beauty of the natural terrain. Nothing is lost of the group's sociability and much is gained by the aspect of serious fun that the poses lend to the image. Courtesy of Peterborough Historical Society and Dartmouth College Library

The Jotham A. French Studio of Keene takes credit for this set piece, noting O. P. Baston as artist. French was among the earliest working photographers in the region, beginning his business in the 1840s and continuing to work with partners or alone for almost half a century. The advertisement on the back of this photo dates the establishment of his own studio as 1861. Thereon he lists twenty-one views of Monadnock of which he titles this one, The Spring. In the remaining space is contained a concise description of MONADNOCK which brings home to the modern reader how effectively the professional photographer promoted tourism in the region. Courtesy of New Hampshire Historical Society

MONADNOCK MOUNTAIN SCENERY.

Numerous views of tourism were popular items in commercial photographer's catalogs. These examples are typical. This private glimpse of a log cottage or "camp," as upper New Englanders call their seasonal homes, is like an informal visit to a close friend. The woman and child might be competing at doing nothing. The hammock, symbolic of pure vacation idleness, finds its way into many photographs of this era, a few of which are included herein. The setting is Bradford. Courtesy of New Hampshire Historical Society

Two hammocks hang from the porch of Echo Cottage although they'll doubtlessly stay empty until after company leaves. The dress seems rather formal by modern standards but to our turn-of-the-century forebears, would have been appropriate visiting garb for a Sunday outing. Everyone wore hats, adults and children alike, as do those gathered here to play croquet. The cottage overlooks Bradford's Lake Todd. Courtesy of New Hampshire Historical Society

These two photographs are taken a century apart, the first from the eastern shore of Lake Sunapee. The stereograph is identified as "The Landing at Runnel's House, Lake Sunapee." H. J.

Brown, Artist and Publisher, had his Studio in Richard's Block, Newport, New Hampshire. The advertisement on the back includes this as part of his "Newport and Lake Sunapee Series; Unitoga Springs Series," which he claims "comprises Everything of Interest in the Vicinity of Newport, Lake Sunapee and Unitoga Springs." Courtesy of New Hampshire Historical Society

The beach bathing scene is at Lake Mascoma, across the road from the Enfield boat launch at the western end of Shaker Bridge, 1988. Photo by Armand Szainer

Visiting the Boys, Summer Camp, Sunapee. Courtesy of New Hampshire Historical Society

In July, 1896, itinerant photographer W. A. Wright, of Ayer, Massachusetts, made an extensive photographing trip through the Connecticut River Valley area of New Hampshire. This vision of a scrupulously neat campsite, at Camp Fuller in East Westmoreland, captures an itinerant photographer, camera, and tripod at the ready. Is the photographer passing the time by reading a newspaper or studying his map? The tent shelters all his camping and photographing supplies. One cannot help but speculate that this may be a self-portrait. Courtesy of New Hampshire Historical Society

On his trip of July 1896, Wright took this portrait of a quartet of tourists at Camp Sunapee. It effectively balances the scenery and the human figures, maintaining a casualness in their physical attitudes while achieving the still pose necessary for a clear image. The petal quilt adds visual interest. Courtesy of New Hampshire Historical Society

This idealized engraving of "Spafford Lake Looking North from Chesterfield" from the 1885 Gazette of Cheshire County was engraved by L. R. Burleigh and produced by H. B. Halls Sons of New York. A fine example of the engraver's skill, the image is a public relations effort to attract tourists to the Lake Spafford area. Just a few miles from Keene, the lake has always been a popular resort site. Historian Alonzo Fogg, writing in 1875, describes Spafford's Lake as "a beautiful sheet of water. . . remarkably clear and pure, its bed being a white sand. There is a beautiful island in the lake, of an area of six acres, affording a delightful retreat. On its east side issues a stream, called Partridge's Brook, sufficiently large for a number of manufactories. Cat's Bane Brook furnishes many good mill sites." (page 94) Courtesy of Library of Congress, Photograph and Print Division

Photographer J. A. Denison of Keene took these two photographs of people at their summer campsites. At "Old Solitude's Wand," the game old gentlemen pose precariously in the hammock, a spectacle that continues to amuse a century later. Careful scrutiny of the party at "Canadensis Lodge" reveals the same two men among the gathering. Perhaps they are relatives of their camping neighbors. Certainly, similar wit is evident in the tent nameplates. It is interesting to observe the tent set up with what looks like clotheslines stretched across the left side and water bucket handy. Chairs supply comfort for several of the group. The dogs, three of them, are very well behaved. Courtesy of New Hampshire Historical Society

Another of the photos that Wright took on his July, 1896 trip through the region, it rivals the engraving of Spofford Lake for beauty of design. There are two steamboats at the Sunapee Boat Landing and several small boats docked at private landings around the harbor. There is a windmill to the left of the harbor overlooking people who go about their leisurely business. Courtesy of New Hampshire Historical Society

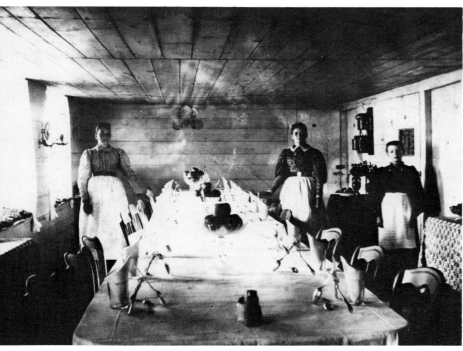

The stone "Tip Top House" or "Summit House" was built atop Benton's Mount Moosilauke in 1860 and later enlarged. In 1896, at the time these photos were taken, the hotel was managed by Dexter Hawkins, third from the left. Hawkins does not appear in the town history as having ever lived in Benton. It is likely he was a summer resident. Descendents of the Foss's identify the others pictured as, left to right, John Foss, Mrs. C[harles] O. Whitcher, Kate Whitcher, her daughter, Hawkins, and Louvia Flanders Foss. John and Louvia Foss were approximately 36 years old when these photos were taken. Courtesy of New Hampshire Historical Society

Tip Top House dining room's plain style and cleanliness would have been a decided attraction to tourists in the nineteenth century. In appointments and settings, the room resembles closely the style that many contemporary country inns try to achieve, suggesting farm fresh fare, authentically New England. Pictured, left to right, Louvia Flanders Foss, Mrs. C[harles] O. Whitcher, and her daughter, Kate. The Whitchers, who lived in nearby Woodsville, were related, probably cousins, to the writer and publisher, William Frederick Whitcher, author of Benton's fascinating, if idiosyncratic, town history: Some Things About Conventry-Benton, New Hampshire.

This portrait of a grand old hotel, the Cheshire House in Keene, is copywritten in 1905 by the Detroit Photograph Company and cannot have been taken before 1900 when the Mason Insurance Agency, visible on the corner of the Bank Block, was formed. Courtesy of Library of Congress, Photograph and Print Division

"Unitoga Springs House" was a comfortable guest hotel at Unity Springs noted for its therapeutic waters, highly charged with iron salts. The hotel provided facilities for invalids and for the general tourist. Perhaps the name "Unitoga" was meant to elicit a connection in the tourist's mind with the era's preeminent spa at Saratoga Springs, New York. Depicted is an admirable accommodation boasting a lively clientele of upper middle-class patrons. The photographer, J. C. Kelley of Newport, offered this stereograph as a scenic view in his catalog. Courtesy of New Hampshire Historical Society.

Before the advent of the automobile, the livery stable was essential for the success of tourism in the region. Every town had one or more stables accessible to the public, very oftren attached to rooming houses and hotels. Considerable activity enlivens this mid-1880s scene at the "City Hotel." Characteristic of many Jotham French photos, figures are everywhere, people, animals and artifacts. An interesting feature is the inclusion of the hotel maids who line the second floor porch and the men with the scaffolding who are in the process of repainting the building, "chang[ing] the white Greek Revival decoration. . . to a darker Victorian color," as they have already done to "the office at the right." (Garvin and Garvin, page 36)

The name "City Hotel" dates to 1874 although the establishment is much older. Located at 109 Main Street, Keene, it was built in the 1830s opening as the "Workingmen's Hotel" and sometimes referred to as "Whitney's Inn" after the proprietor, Elias Whitney. It changed hands several times before L. W. Cummings purchased it and renamed it "City Hotel," the name it carried until 1904. The building has since been replaced by a modern commercial building currently occupied by Rousell's Clothing.

An amusing piece of local history concerning the hotel dates back to January 11, 1837, shortly after it was built. A party of Dublin people using over 50 teams of horses took a sleigh ride to Keene and paraded around the streets before stopping at the hotel for dinner. (Keene History Committee, page 271) The livery stable must have been busy that night. This stereograph of "City Hotel" is from the J. A. French Photography Gallery, Keene. Courtesy of New Hampshire Historical Society

The photos relating to the Hanover/Norwich Station brings home the fact that the concept of border community, brought up the Connecticut River with the first settlers, continued through the centuries and survives today. This tranquil scene by J. A. French could be a transportation metaphor for the history of life in the border region over the past two hundred years or more. The "Iron Horse," riding aloft, seems oblivious to the river (perhaps, the Ashuelot) and the wooden boat. Yet its boisterous appearance permanently altered transportation and the relationship between the river and its people. The figure to the left could be the symbolic Everyman, the objective observer, here representing the river's people—capable, adaptable and accepting. Courtesy of New Hampshire Historical Society

7 TRANSPORTATION AND VEHICLES

Where available, early settlers used Indian paths for their first roads. Their primary concern, however, was keeping in touch with their fellow settlers. An early Sutton resident put it this way:

> The grantees made roads from settler to settler or rather spotted lines, i.e., they marked trees to indicate the course through woods, which answered the purpose of guideboards, not only for men but for oxen also. Mr. Jacob Mastin remembered to have heard the aged people say that the oxen soon became very expert in reading the directions on way-marks thus pointed out. (Worthen)

Oxen guaranteed the clearing of the wilderness and made extraordinary physical tasks manageable. Farmers used oxcarts and larger wagons, often crudely handmade, did most of the hauling. Early market transport was by ox cart.

Charlestown was at the Connecticut River end of the most popular of the three routes that the St. Francis Indians and the Canadian French took when traveling south. The route ended at the river directly across from Number 4 (Charlestown), making the site a frequent target of hostilities.

The usefulness of the riverways for transport was destroyed by the railroads.

A Mr. Nutting is the teamster while Ed Case and Charlie Weeks are the crew of this four-horse team logging sled that is drawn up to M. Keyes' Store at the Peterborough Tavern on a warm day in March 1888. Local youngsters can't resist the temptation to climb the massive log the lumbermen have been hauling. Their coats rest beside Nutting's foot. Fancy handkerchiefs are visible in the "Fine Goods" window visible behind the heads of the second team. Two beautifully matched pairs would be the source of pride to a teamster of this period. Nutting died the year after this anonymous photo was taken. Courtesy of Peterborough Historical Society.

The first farm-to-market road in the state was gradually built between Dover and Little Coos (Haverhill). Known as Old Province Road, it was in use between 1763 and 1820. In 1771, Governor Wentworth built his College Road from Wolfeborough to Hanover, by way of Plymouth, and rode over it to attend the first graduation exercises at Dartmouth College.

Our ancestors used the fullness of their ancient wisdom in converting the wilderness to roads. Their knowledge of trees, soil, and construction led them to rely on traditional methods of road building that had served them well in their homelands. For example, we learn that

> [f]ormerly on the long turnpike routes the willow most effectually served the road-makers. They planted willows on both sides of every piece of road built through boggy land, to help support the roadbed and keep it in place. It is needless to remark that the trees always proved faithful to duty, and, strange to say, never seemed to die or grow old. (Worthen, page 568)

In 1905, the State Aid Road Law entitled towns and counties to receive funds from the state to build roads. Ten years later, the Federal Aid Road Act, by contributing 50 percent toward the building of roads, added greatly to the impetus for road building throughout the nation.

The history of the region's transportation is one of steady change. At first, besides walking, there were canoes and beasts of burden. Later, came walking, rowing, oxen,

and horses; then walking, horses, and steam engines (railroads, steam boats); then walking, horses, and railroads; then walking, horses, electric trolleys and automobiles (bicycles, too); then automobiles, bicycles, autobuses, and railroads; and finally, buses and automobiles. Today, the automobile rules the road—although walking (running) and bicycling are again finding advocates in the adult population, for recreation rather than transportation.

Occasionally, some idiosyncratic mode of transportation turns up in the region's history. Early in nineteenth-century Keene, e.g., the

> course of the Town Brook in Keene was altered to flow into Beaver Brook rather than across Main Street at the old causeway, and the work of covering it commenced. Still, at about this time, Harry Willard, riding in a huge potash kettle, could paddle across Main Street . . . . (Keene History Committee, pages 46-47)

The Stagecoach

In the early nineteenth century stagecoaches provided the isolated communities scattered throughout the western region of New Hampshire with a lifeline to the world. Several lively reminiscences of the stages survive. Roswell T. Smith's colorful note about stagecoach travel in his youth is a good example:

> In addition to the regular Hanover-Haverhill line, a

mail coach carrying six passengers ran daily where the River Road now is, until it struck the county road for Lyme. . . . It was called "The Telegraph Line" and ran with great regularity and speed, regardless of the state of the roads. The six splendid horses, seldom broke their trot except as they passed over the crest of a hill, down which and across the valley they would go upon the run. (Childs, page 46)

Augusta Worthen's insightful commentary on the impact of the stagecoach to towns like Sutton is vivid and informative:

The introduction [in 1832] of stages making regular trips through this town was of very great importance to the people. Not only did the stages transport passengers and their baggage, but the mails as well, so that when they came the post-rider disappeared.

The girls began to go to work in the cotton factories of Nashua and Lowell. It was an all-day ride, but that was nothing to be dreaded. It gave them a chance to behold other towns and places, and see more of the world than the most of the generation had ever been able to see. They went in their plain, country-made clothes, and, after working several months, would come home for a visit, or perhaps to be married, in their tasteful city dresses, and with more money in their pockets than they had ever owned before.

The students from Dartmouth college also availed themselves of the stage for making their transits through this section, and their coming was looked for with much interest by many of the people on the road, who were by no means averse to exchanging jokes with them, even though these young men were sometimes a little saucy. Not unfrequently, however, they found their match for impudence in the farm lads they hailed, as they looked down upon them from their lofty stations on the top of the stage. (pages 192-193)

There is no mention of Fred Keyser among those who kept store in Sutton before 1890 although Keysers are found among the early settlers (Ebenezer Keyser was Sutton's first blacksmith.) The "Cold Soda" and "Post Office" signs imply a typical, all-purpose country store. The college boys waiting at Keyser's for the stage show no sign of sauciness. (page 119)

A coach sleigh traveled the upper Connecticut River Valley, as described by a local historian:

There was also a larger four-horse stage with an extra and somewhat hazardous seat on top. This seat and its occupant teetered up and down over the baggage rack, the only consolation being the passenger's ticket which cost but twenty-five cents for two rides. And there remained that fearful and wonderful winter vehicle known locally as "the street car." Long and low, it ran on sledlike runners,

Young steers and heifers were customarily used to pull loads on the farm but less frequently on the public road. The lovely proportions of the milk wagon/sleigh next to the placid animal with his rakish look makes this an entirely charming image. The strap of sleighbells hints at equally pleasing sound effects. The pedestrians in Pentwater take it all for granted. The sign on the milk wagon reads: Milk And Cream. Courtesy Dartmouth College Library

had three doors to a side and running-boards. It met all trains, and the town kids watched surreptitiously for a chance to hook their sleds onto the baggage rack at the back. (Childs, page 50)

Col. Whitcomb French opened the Peterborough Tavern after running the Keene to Boston stage for a few years beginning in 1830. A gifted businessman, he called it The Safety and Dispatch Line.

These stages carried eight passengers the ninety-odd miles from Keene to Boston through Peterboro in twelve hours, the fare being $3 a passenger. (Morison, pages 298, 299)

The stagecoach drivers come alive in the reminiscence of Amos Tarleton, Haverhill landowner, whose "vivid description of stage-drivers on the Hanover-Haverhill line" is quoted by Armstrong Sperry:

The winter dress of these old drivers was nearly all alike. Their clothing was of heavy homespun, calfskin boots, thick trousers tucked inside the boots. Over all these were worn Canadian hand-knit stockings, very heavy and thick, colored bright red, which came up nearly to the thighs, and still over that a light leather shoe. For hand protection they wore double-pegged mittens, leather gauntlets, fur gloves, wristlets and muffettees. Their coats were generally fur or buffalo skin, with fur caps and ear protectors, wool or fur tippets. Also a red silk sash

that went around the body and tied on the left side with a double bow with tassels. (Childs, page 48)

Sleighs

Sleighing parties were a favorite winter entertainment before the automobile chased the snow and horse-drawn vehicles from the roads. The parade of fifty sleighs from Dublin in 1835, mentioned elsewhere, was not a singular event. Keene records two others in the same period:

About a hundred years ago on evenings when the winter weather was clear and bright, and the snow in the roads had been smoothed and hardened by the great rollers that were used then to roll it down, it was the custom to have "sleighing parties."

On January 7, 1836, there were two parties, one of 25 sleighs from Sullivan to Keene, the other of 40 sleighs from Dublin to Keene. "In the center of the latter party was an omnibus well filled with a band for music."

On January 15, 1836, 72 sleighs with about 150 people rode from Keene to Walpole. (Keene History Committee, page 591)

Our ancestors certainly knew how to organize themselves for fun, but those Dubliners knew how to put the icing on the cake. This mention of snow rollers runs contrary to what has been previously documented about these machines. Prior to the 1880s, snow would have been

packed down by teams of oxen or work horses dragging large logs. In earlier years, the farmer farthest from town would hitch his teams and, with the log drag, pack the snow between his house and his nearest neighbor who would do the same between his house and the next neighbor. By this chain method, a way would be made through the town. The mention of snow rollers in Keene in the mid-1830s is probably an oversight, not to be taken at face value.

The Railroads

Starting in 1838 with the chartering of railroads that soon reached throughout the state, a period of great commercial development began that had a tremendous impact on the western regions of the state.

To cover the section between Concord and White River Junction, Vermont, the Northern Railroad was chartered in 1844. Trains first crossed the Connecticut River at West Lebanon in June 1848 and Woodsville in 1853.

A Charter was granted in July 1846 to the Sullivan Railroad to operate from the Massachusetts to the Vermont State Lines through Keene, and the road was opened in February 1849. The line suffered repeated business failures by various companies until it finally became part of the Boston and Maine Railroad in 1893.

In New Hampshire's eagerness to be in the forefront of progress that the development of the railroad symbolized to many, early railroad licenses in the state were chartered almost willy-nilly, resulting in severe financial strain for many of the smaller community operations.

Merger after merger gradually consolidated multiple small lines into larger conglomerates. Thriving commercial lines into which smaller lines fed often floated bonds or otherwise invested in such mergers as a means of expanding their trade and assuring a competitive advantage for their own well-established routes. In 1873, the Northern Railroad, as a case in point, made generous bond guarantees to the Concord and Claremont Railroad, formerly the separate corporations of the Concord and Claremont, Sugar River and Contoocook River Railroads. By century's end, various manipulations and entrepreneurial efforts wrested control of the local lines to a corporation controlled by Boston bankers.

Train crews became part of the social life of the western region. Able to keep regulated schedules, they grew to know personally the people who worked at stations along the route. Sometimes they'd have an hour stopover, as in Claremont when waiting for the daily noon debarkation to Concord necessitated by regional train connections. Friendships developed and the people of the region took a proprietary interest in the doings of the railroads and in the workers they came to know on a daily or weekly basis. Their neighbors had built the railroads and worked on them. Friendly regulars from stations up and down the lines brought convivial conversation about their diverse and sometimes slightly less provincial world to the small inland towns. Locals saw to their travel comforts. The situation was a natural outgrowth of the camaraderie that area residents had felt with the forerunners of the railroad crew, the coach and wagon drivers who had actually lived in their own communities or

The stage adapted itself to all kinds of weather and as with every transport vehicle in use, a stagecoach on runners was normal for the winter months in the region. Here we have a stagecoach sleigh far simpler in design than the Abbott and Downing coaches common on local roads in the dry season.

The groups of onlookers standing outside of the Peterborough Tavern are, perhaps, bidding farewell to friends and family. The photograph appears to be the work of an amateur photographer since the image is poorly focused. The Peterborough Tavern was torn down in 1963; Peterborough Savings Bank occupies the location today. The faded photograph was found in the Townsend House and donated to the Peterborough Historical Society by William L. Bauhan, publisher, of Dublin. Courtesy of Peterborough Historical Society

nearby.

Long beyond their heyday before the Second World War, the railroad effectively supplemented other forms of travel and, at times, such as in periods of sub-zero temperatures or during gas rationing days, served as the primary mode of transport for most citizens in need of long distance travel. However, the devastating floods of 1927 and 1936, and the hurricane two years later, ruined rail travel for several regional towns and greatly diminished railroad travel everywhere. The demise of the flexible passenger railroad service to the small communities in western New Hampshire and elsewhere is attributable to lax maintenance, competition with the major rail lines, and the emerging supremacy of the asphalt highway. The last east-west passenger service in western New Hampshire was in 1955. There has been sporadic north-south service since, but none at present. There is talk in the air once again about a Boston-Montreal train, however. If rumor reaches reality, the train would again wend its way through this once familiar territory.

At one time, the train took about three hours to go from Concord to Claremont and longer to Hanover or Lebanon and points beyond. With better equipment and fewer stops, the train reached Claremont in two-thirds the time. When one considers that by automobile in the 1980s, riding over interstate highways, it takes just about an hour to make the same distance for those familiar with the roads, the railroad, with its frequent stops, kept to a fairly efficient schedule.

Local Inventions

The town of Hancock claims the original "snowmobile" as a 1923 invention of two local residents.

Ron Perry retired from the Navy, returned home and went into business as a blacksmith, renting the second floor of the garage building owned by his brother-in-law, Bill Hanson. While Bessie, Bill's wife and Ron's sister, manned the gasoline pumps, the two men collaborated in making the forerunner of today's snowmobiles. In the garage Bill stripped down Model T Fords, making them eighteen inches narrower so that iron runners which would fit sleigh tracks could be welded to them. On the backs were attached belt rigs with cleats. One of these strange appearing and noisy vehicles went with Commander Byrd to the North Pole. Others were purchased by doctors and one by the Public Service Company.

Riding in one of these unwieldy machines was apparently not exactly relaxing. It is reported that at least one old-timer, accepting a lift to Peterborough, spurned the return offer and returned by train. (Hancock History Committee, page 62)

Like Hancock with its early snowmobile mechanics, Antrim had an automobile tinkerer. Old Bussie Thompson was known locally as an inventor. In his shed he kept one of the memorable products of his tinkering,

a fantastic automobile. It had a regular front seat, but the rear seat was round like a large tub with a beautifully upholstered seat following the contour. There was no top, and the only entry to the back seat was from the rear by a step and a small latched door. Once aboard, the four passengers had a choice of riding forward, backward, or sideways. During one [town] gala day, Ed [Thompson, Bussie's brother], who owned the vehicle, managed to get it going a short distance in the parade. About that time it was

This photograph of the Dartmouth Stage gives a clear sight of the rear trunk rack of the standard stagecoach. Something of the social ambience can be discerned in the head sticking out the window as if to watch what's getting thrown onto the trunk rack, and by whom. The bare branched trees shadowed across the street place the season in the fall, before the snows. E. H. Marshall's Sweet Milk Cream delivery wagon is at curbside. The driver resembles Ira Allen but certain identification is not available. By the end of the stagecoach era, these vehicles, so romantic in the contemporary imagination, were being called "hacks," a decidedly inelegant term. Courtesy of Dartmouth College Library

Somewhat more elegant than the coach sleigh at the Peterborough Tavern, Howe's Livery Stable coach sleigh met the trains at Hanover/Norwich Railroad Station. The driver standing beside the recently painted sleigh is unidentified in this striking photo from the turn of the century. The 1840s mark the heyday of the large stables in Hanover "when sometimes as many as eight and even ten horses dragged huge loads of freight over the turnpikes." (Childs, page 128) But the stage and other horse-drawn public transport continued in active operation into the twentieth century.

"Hamp" Howe of Howe's Livery took over the stage from Ira Allen when he became too old to continue, probably around 1880. "Crotchety and sharp-tongue, but witty and kindly as well, Howe was well liked and called 'Jason' and 'Uncle Dud' by townspeople and students alike." (Childs, page 146) The Hanover/Norwich Station was in business from 1847 to the end of 1959. Courtesy of Dartmouth College Library

By 1929, when these sleighs lined up across the Green from College Row waiting for Winter Carnival passengers to the ski jump, they had become special-event transport for most people. It is prophetic that their ranks are broken here by an automobile. The stately "Dartmouth Elms," most of which have succumbed to Dutch elm disease, are healthy overseers of the ice sculptures dotting the Green. Human figures, including the bodiless one in the right foreground pausing to read the Carnival sign, keep the image in scale. Courtesy of Dartmouth College Library

said to have been bought for the Ford museum, and was never seen again. (Antrim History Committee, page 70)

Road Maintenance Vehicles

Dirt roads required constant upkeep and the use of a variety of machines to accomplish the seasonal tasks of the road crews. In parts of New England, landowners would join their neighbors to make up a road servicing crew to work on the roads abutting their properties. Some communities allowed property owners to work off part of their road taxes in this way.

Among the more dramatic examples of road working machines are the massive wooden snow rollers that appeared on town road maintenance records at the end of the nineteenth century. The large, wooden cylinders would compact the snow for ease of travel on sleighs and other vehicles with snow runners. Pulled by teams of workhorses, the snow rollers traversed the towns and outlying farms. After a heavy snow, the work often took a couple of days to complete necessitating frequent stops for refreshment—of man and beast. The rollers used by the town of Sunapee beginning in 1897 were eight feet high and ten feet long and required three teams of horses. They were made in Georges Mills by the Holmes brothers. According to a reminiscence of Charles Hill, in Sutton, it was often the older men who drove the teams, bundled in buffalo robes. The younger men "would walk to keep warm." He recalls old Jack Rowell.

[Jack] was unable to walk without canes, but he could drive a six horse hitch without help. He had a very heavy voice that carried half a mile. He would holler to Harry Sewell or George, whoever lived on the farm, "Do you have any cider?" If the answer was "No," Jack would holler "Git up" to his team and

leave the barnyard unrolled. (Rowell account recounted in Sunapee Bicentennial (1769-1968) commemorative booklet, pages 39-40)

Perhaps the star of this story is a Rowell of "Rowell's Mill," the remains of which were documented for the WPA Historic Buildings Survey in the 1930s. The neighboring town of Sutton has preserved its old snow roller.

Steamboats

The original images of *Lady Woodsum* and *Armenia White* are blueprints, probably artists proofs, taken between 1910 and 1915. (page 128) This explains the softness of tone in the reproduced photographs.

Steamboats appeared on Lake Sunapee, the highest large lake in New Hampshire, as early as 1859 and by the end of the century there was a virtual fleet of them. The Woodsum Steamboat Company, owned and operated by brothers Frank, Daniel, and Elias Woodsum, floated four steamers. They started their business with the 50-foot *Lady Woodsum*, built in 1876 that provided a barge for freight. Its three-man crew, captain, purser, and fireman, served as many as seventy-five passengers. The most admired of the Woodsum fleet was the SS *Armenia White*, named after a leading citizen of Concord who was a mover and shaker in the areas of temperance, women's rights and the care of the elderly. It was the largest steamer ever to sail Lake Sunapee. At 101 feet long and 23 feet in the beam with a 650 passenger capacity, she was the flagship of the Woodsum fleet, built in 1887 at a cost of seventeen thousand dollars. The steamboats served both as pleasure crafts and as important links in the transportation network connecting the small communities around the lake to each other. They also connected them to the railroad depot. It took about 3 hours to make the trip around the lake with stops at the major landings

of Sunapee Harbor, Georges Mills, Lakeside, Blodgett, Brightwood, Pine Cliff, Lake Station, Soo-Nipi, Burkehaven, and Granliden. The steamboat era on Lake Sunapee lasted into the 1920s. It is still possible to sail majestically around Lake Sunapee. MV *Mt. Sunapee,* a handsome double decker, was launched April 21, 1966 as a summer attraction.

Interestingly, tourists found entertainment in both watching the steamboats and watching the trains, often hopping a boat to the depot where they could observe trains lingering at the station to take on needed water. Four regular daily trains came into Sunapee Station year-round. At times, freight and seasonal traffic swelled this number considerably.

The "Paper Train" that arrived from Boston at 11:32 a.m. conceivably established an early noon hour schedule for Sunapee residents eager to get news from the city. Cargo handlers marked their respect for the time-honored priority of print journalism by unloading the newspapers first.

Local history credits Capt. Frank Woodsum with prophesying the end of the steamboat era. B. A. "Bud" Hoban, purser on the *Armenia White* at the time, wrote a reminiscence of the prophesy.

Vitality emanates from this late 1930s Adrian Bouchard photograph of assorted Hanoverites and Dartmouth students waiting for the train to bring their Carnival dates. Courtesy of Dartmouth College Library

On a beautiful July morning in 1910, as the steamboat "Armenia White" was swinging into Sunapee Harbor, Captain Frank Woodsum blew the whistle signal from the pilot house...the whistle meant that [he] wanted to see me in the pilot house.

As I entered the door, the Captain said: "Do you see what I see there at the dock?" I took the glasses and looked, and there at the landing stood the first Model-T Ford we had seen in Sunapee. Captain Frank, arms folded and steering the ship with feet and knees, as he so often did, said solemnly, "There, my boy, is the end of the

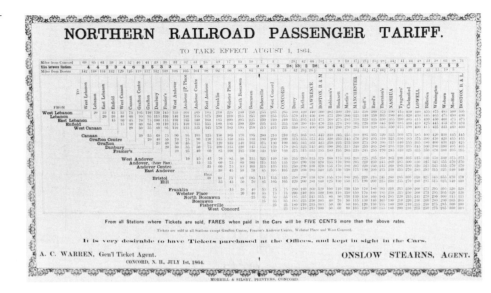

*Northern Railroad Passenger Tariff.
Courtesy of New Hampshire Historical
Society*

*The motif of the horseless carriage,
requiring real horsepower to move it
along, is a favorite one in photographs
and anecdotes from the automobile's
early years such as this one from 1910
to 1912. No less funny to the modern
viewer, it well earns its enduring
popularity. Few old-timers haven't heard
an anecdote that elaborates such a
situation. Courtesy of Peterborough
Historical Society*

steamboat." How right he was . . . . (Squires, page 576)

Hoban goes on to report that the *Lady Woodsum* burned and sank "in that year, 1910. . .the 'Armenia White,' the queen of the Lake, was decommissioned. . .and a few years later sold for scrap." By 1933, the entire fleet was gone. Squires does not cite his source for Hoban's account.

New Hampshire and Vermont both sought ways to promote the use of the Connecticut River for commerce and transportation beginning early in the nineteenth century. Steamboats serviced most of the stretch of the border and towns along the river had one or more boat landings to serve the needs of the communities. The railroads made inroads into freight transport by water and

the automobile hastened the demise of passenger travel by boat.

"It took the "Water Witch" 40 minutes to go downstream on her first commercial voyage to South Charlestown, July 21, 1884, and 45 minutes to return upstream. The 30 passenger steamer had regular service to Bellows Falls and rented out for excursions in the summers. The fare to South Charlestown was 25 cents, to Commissary Brook 10 cents. . .Manufactured in Portland, Me., the boat drew 2 1/2 feet of water." (Frizzell et al., page 117)

An attempt some years later to move the steamer to Dublin Lake was thwarted by the weather at the embarkation point and the residents of the lake at the debarkation point. It eventually rotted away in a Dublin pasture.

Rural school buses are often owned by private citizens who contract with the schools to provide bus service. "Mr. Wilder and School Bus" were the daily companions of a generation of area school children at mid-century. "That's the Hancock school bus!" an area resident exclaimed when he saw it. Fred Wilder, who also provided garage, taxi, and mail service at the time, began to run the Hancock school bus in 1926. He purchased the first motorized bus in the area that fall. The undated photograph is of Otis Wilder. Courtesy of Peterborough Historical Society

The name of the express company is not discernible behind the wheel spokes of this early express wagon. Rags were a valuable commodity through the Second World War after which rag collection ceased abruptly. The location is the Alley behind Main Street, Peterborough. Courtesy of Peterborough Historical Society

A cleverly homemade carrier sled, the drag on skis accommodated the hauling needs of this Mount Mooselauke area household. The row of skis, looking like regimented saplings, are stored where they are most handy. The platform of the carrier is capable of a heavy load. The snapshot was taken by Ralph Sanborn. Courtesy of Dartmouth College Library

125

There was a market in the North Country for winterized automobiles, most of which, apparently, were adapted to travel in the snow by having skis fitted under the front wheels as seen in this touring car. One area old-timer recalls that an automobile dealership in Ossipee adapted Model Ts for winter use. (Blaisdell, One, page 178)

The mechanic who adapted the one pictured here also courageously removed the wheels altogether and replaced them with ingenious ski contraptions in a way similar to the Perry-Hanson model described in the text. Understandably the object of curiosity on Hanover's Main Street, the primitive skimobile was caught by the lens of an anonymous photographer sometime in the 1920s. Courtesy of Dartmouth College Library

Charlie Hall and his absolutely unique "Grass-cutting Rig" must have turned heads in Hanover wherever he mowed. It boggles the imagination to try to figure out what all Hall has patched together to create this amazing one-horsepower machine. The image is the quintessential example of just how gradual was the regional adaptation to the machine age. Dartmouth's Crosby Hall is in the background as the college maintenance man goes about trimming the lawns. Unfortunately, the original photograph is undated. Courtesy of Dartmouth College Library

The Hanover snow roller pauses for the photographer by the Green across from Dartmouth's Webster Hall. The age of the snow roller was short-lived, replaced by the snowplow once the automobile created the need for clearing snow from the roads. Courtesy of Dartmouth College Library

The old dirt road sprinkler has a contemporary counterpart in the street cleaning trucks that groom city streets throughout the country. The massive wooden water reservoir riding on spoked wheels behind a team of snow white horses presents a formidable appearance in this 1885 photo. Alvin Townsend, stopping here at the corner of Grove and School streets, Peterborough, was on contract with the village to help lay the dust in the dry season. The sprinkler makes its rounds of the main streets on a dry August day, spreading the water behind it as it travels.

Milford records that the town's road sprinkler drew three hundred gallons of water from the river to fill its tanks. It used between forty and fifty tanks a day to lay the dust in the town square area alone in the dry season. (Wright,

page 452)

Townsend operated a livery stable in Peterborough starting in 1870 and is remembered for owning the first car on

record in that town: a Knox gasoline-engined and air-cooled automobile he bought in 1901. Courtesy of Peterborough Historical Society

Fred J. Ames, one of Peterborough's leading citizens, stands to the left of the road crew as they take a rest while rebuilding Concord Street. The road roller looks like a steam driven machine. The photo was probably taken in the 1920s. Ames had a house north of

Happy Valley (originally, the Melvin House), on the corner of Greenfield and Burke roads. His was one of several local families who took in boarders during the tourist season. Courtesy of Peterborough Historical Society

Lady Woodsum, *Lake Sunapee. Courtesy of Library of Congress Photograph and Print Division*

SS Armenia White, *Lake Sunapee. Courtesy of Library of Congress Photograph and Print Division*

The Ashley Ferry at Claremont was one of the subjects that W. A. Wright took when he was traveling throughout the region in July 1896. Wright had a marvelous eye for memorable pictures and an unerring instinct for documentation. Ashley's is a simple, serviceable ferry, little more than a raft with a small shelter from the elements, a long bench for the comfort of patrons and a simple crossbar to keep everything on board. The enclosed carriage bears a close resemblance to the carriage in **Wright's photograph at Camp Fuller (p. 107). One is tempted to speculate that it is the photographer's own.** *Of the seventy original proprietors of Claremont, only two families by the name of Ashley actually took up residence there. In 1767, two Samuel Ashleys, father and son, and an Oliver Ashley became settlers in Claremont.*

A local anecdote set at the Ashley Ferry gives some insight into the down-to-earth practicality and resourcefulness of some of our ancestors: "A favorite drive of the

summer people was up one side of the river, crossing at Ashley's Ferry in Claremont and returning south on the other side of the river. Many of those who hired rigs drove for themselves. The story is told of one party of women who were out riding in company with George

Olcott when a part of the harness broke. While he obligingly turned his back one of the women tore from her petticoat strings pieces with which to tie up the harness. (Frizzell et al., page 281) Courtesy of New Hampshire Historical Society

128

Lakes Sunapee and Winnepesaukee, while renowned for their steamboats, were not alone in carrying proud vessels across their surfaces. A small steamboat, the Myra, sailed on Highland Lake in Stoddard. The steamboat Helena is said to have traveled the five-mile length of Enfield's Lake Mascoma.

There seems to be no vehicle that does not attract the artist's attention and few subjects that exceed transportation in the affections of those who chronicle our past. Courtesy of New Hampshire Historical Society

Besides the G.A.R., there were numerous small veterans' organizations in towns scattered throughout the state. One such group was Peterborough's "Cannon Club." An unidentified clipping, probably from the Peterborough Transcript, attached to the original photograph, provides documentation: "In August, 1901, the old Wallace Scott cannon which gave the morning salute for Old Home Day, was photographed together with ten of our boys who had manned this old cannon on various occasions, and in the death of Frank E. Russell this chain of old friends is broken for the first time. This picture comprises the following gentlemen: John F. Wilder, Charles G. Rourke, Herman A. White, Clarence E. White, James M. White, Albert Shattuck, Fred G. Robbe, James F. Brennan, Harry H. Templeton, and the

8

HERITAGE AND PERSONALITIES

Town Meetings

T own meetings were regulated by the legislature in 1791. Originally the third Tuesday of March, they have since moved to the second Tuesday and can run over to a second day, if town business so demands. In recent years, many towns separate school budget meetings from the regular town meeting day, although, technically, they operate within the town meeting structure. Towns post warrants at least two weeks in advance of town meeting in order to give citizens a chance to study the questions being raised. Election of town officials, originally a town meeting agenda item, has been moved from town meeting to an election day that occurs in November. With due notice, special town meetings and elections may be called at the discretion of town officers or by citizen petition.

In the nineteenth century, Lyme's town meetings had become "smoky affairs" but Fitzwilliam did not allow smoking. Chewing tobacco was permitted, however, and sawdust was spread on the floor to accommodate those with the habit.

The town of Sutton celebrated its centennial year in 1984. As part of its observance, local officials wrote articles into the warrant for the March 14th town meeting that were really small enactments of the town's heritage.

All officers were duly nominated including twelve nominations for Hogreeve. When asked to explain the duties of the office of Hogreeve, town Selectman, Robert Bristol, who was among the principal designers of the bicentennial warrant, "explained that they round up stray hogs and take them to the custody of the Pound Keeper." All nominees were elected to their respective office. A little later,

Article 13 was read by the Moderator:
　　Thirteenthly to see what the Town will provide for the militia; and the furnishing of the provisions to be put at vendue and struck off to the person who will furnish the same for the least sum.
George West made the following motion:
　　Move that each noncommissioned officer and private soldier belonging to this town and bearing firearms at the next General Muster be furnished with one pound of good boiled beef, one pound of fine bread, one gill of West Indian rum and one quarter of a pound of powder and one barrel of good cider for the whole, all which to be furnished on the field of parade excepting the powder which shall be ready for delivery to the several commanding officers at least one week prior to the said day of Muster provided nevertheless that musicians shall draw no powder unless equipped, uniformed, and bearing firearms. And that the furnishing of the aforementioned provision be put up at vendue and struck off to the person who will furnish the same for the least sum.
　　The motion was seconded by Phillip Thompson and briefly discussed.
　　On a voice vote, the Moderator declared Article 13 adopted. (Sutton's *200th Annual Report,* pages 25-26)

Obviously, an entire town enjoyed the event to the utmost. Other commemorative events through the year included the construction of a town quilt, a tradition in the area. Sutton's *1984 Annual Report,* designed as a historic document, placed a color photograph of the quilt on its cover.

March 12, 1839, diary entry of Denison Gould, Hillsborough:

　　Clear and coolish. Town meeting throughout the state of New Hampshire today. Whigs crazy and saucy as hell. Paige for Governor got 220 votes,

Wilson a Tory, 86 votes. [The Whig party had formed about five years earlier in opposition to the Democratic party. The Tories were British royalists.]

Near the time of the Revolutionary War, Patriot and Tory loyalists became an issue in western New Hampshire, as elsewhere. The Sangers, for example, were a Tory family. Abner was incarcerated at the Fort in No. 4 for several months and his brother, El, relocated with his wife and children to New Brunswick, the destination of many New England Tories. Several accounts of inquisitions appear in town records. From the distance of time, it is not always possible to determine whether or not the individuals in question were really anti-loyalist or were, perhaps, scapegoats to the private interests of their neighbors. In Stoddard, the Committee of Safety took action, some not approved by the town, against suspected Tories. One of these was Oliver Parker, called by the Committee to

answer charges of being "inimical to America and its liberties" and "notoriously disaffected to the American cause." The committee sought to disarm him and place him under house arrest in June, and warned all persons to avoid him and refuse dealings with their allegedly disloyal neighbor.

Parker protested in a petition of his own on June 18 [1776] that the committee had no proof of his disloyalty, but were in fact motivated by malice. He offered a challenge to anyone to prove anything against him, and no less than 20 of his neighbors joined in support of his "good disposition" and even support of the war as a military officer and inferred that the proceedings against him were being pursued in an irregular fashion.

Not only did Parker refuse to appear and answer the charges, but he was accused of writing a satirical "Receipt [recipe] to make a Whig which ran as follows: "A Receipt to make a Whig—Take of conspiracy and the root of pride three handfulls two of ambition and vain glory, pound them in the mortar of faction and discord, boil it in 2 quarts of dissembling tears and a little New England rum over the fire of Sedition till you find the scum of folly wood to rise on the top, then strain it through the cloths of Rebellion, put it into the bottle of envy, stop it with the cork of malice, then make it into pills called Conspiracy of which take nine when going to bed say over your hypocritical prayer, and curse your honest neighbor in your bed chamber and then go

Few photographs announce themselves to be the embodiment of heritage as does this superb example from Brookline. As noted along the bottom, the figures are those Brookline citizens (the men, that is) who were born before 1840. The individual images, taken together, demonstrate the development of photographic portraiture style in the region from approximately the 1860s to the 1920s. Clarence R. Russell collected and effectively arranged the pictorial documents (notice the vertical placement of the horizontal picture in the upper right corner—a charming touch.) Clarence and Charles C. Russell, presented the *visual* tour de force *to their fellow residents, March 11, 1930. Courtesy of New Hampshire Historical Society*

"C. Breneu, Mexican War Veteran," reads the identification on the original photograph. A second hand notes that the subject is probably Charles Burrell, a well-known Hanover resident. Photographer H. O. Bly arranges Burrell, nostalgically attired in antique homespun trousers (trews) and short piped jacket, leaning on a rustic tree trunk, against a painted backdrop, standing on a platform liberally strewn with hay. Such stage sets were standard props of the professional artist's studio. Certainly Bly's studio has ample space for such an arrangement. A drawing of Bly's studio appears later, in the photographers section. Sometimes, photographers would transport such set-ups to local fairs and festivals, taking their cameras to where customers might be in a spending mood. That Burrell's claim to his community's memory is his role in the Mexican War, reflects the high value placed on military service in civic life, a value that eventually led to numerous entitlement programs for the nation's military veterans.

Hillsboro's Gen. Franklin Pierce, later to become president, and Abemarle Cody of Keene were heroes of the Mexican War. Gen. Leonard Wood of Winchester not only served with distinction in the Spanish American War but he administered Cuba during its postwar reconstruction. *Courtesy of Dartmouth College Library*

to sleep if you can, it will have so good an effect that all the next day you will be thinking how to cozzen cheat lie and get drunk abuse the ministers of the Gospel, cut the throats of all honest men and plunder the Nation." (Stoddard Historical Society, page 25)

The satire is a conventional parody common in the tradition of European cultures. Parker was jailed in Exeter in 1778 and his movements restricted in 1782. He, too, eventually went to New Brunswick.

Revolutionary Patriot, Gov. Josiah Bartlett, a signer of the Declaration of Independence, was a proprietor of Perrystown, later Sutton, by virtue of having purchased a right from the Masonian proprietors who were among his associates and peers. He, his brother, Maj. Enoch Bartlett, and two others acted on behalf of the town in renewing the charter of the town in 1773. The settlers had been unable to fulfill the terms of the original charter and were vulnerable to excessive renewal costs or loss of their charter or both. The Bartlett brothers were successful in the matter.

Enoch Bartlett has yet another claim to fame. To him

we are indebted for the Bartlett pear. He discovered its merits [through grafting], and took pains to introduce it in various parts of the country, giving his name to it.....

It appears...that to Major Caleb Stark, eldest son of Gen. John Stark, born in Dunbarton, 1759, we are indebted for the introduction into this region of the practice of grafting and budding fruit-trees. he visited every section of Massachusetts where he heard of choice fruit, and obtained scions for his trees, and with his own hands he set grafts and buds in his own orchards and in those of his nearest townsmen who were sufficiently credulous to consider the strange experiment worth trying. In a few years a plentiful supply of fruit more than realized their expectations. (Worthen, Pages 567-568)

Turn-of-the-Century Benton

Small town politics sometimes had their own structure. Benton's town historian, having the advantage of one who had been raised in a family traditionally active in town politics, suggests one political model that must

have been familiar to the residents of rural New Hampshire. He tells us that Benton,

almost from the beginning of its history made much of its town meetings, and its citizens were pronounced in the expression of their political opinions. In the early days they were for the most part Federalists, but later, when the north part of the town came to be settled, the residents of that sections were Jeffersonian Democrats, and, in the days of Andrew Jackson the town became unanimously Democratic. It remained pretty nearly so for years, and even after the organization of the Republican party, and the transference of New Hampshire from the Democratic column to the Republican column of states, Benton always remained faithful to its Democratic allegiance....

In the days, however, when the town was unanimously or nearly unanimously Democratic, there were bitter contests for the town offices and for the office of representative, all the more bitter perhaps, since nearly all parties to the contests were Democrats. For many years there were three parties: the Page party, led by James J. and Daniel D. Page, and having their adherents for the most part in the Page district, the Meadows and at High Street; the Wells party, of which Capt. Enos Wells was the head, with his sons for lieutenants, and the Whitcher party, of which William Whitcher, and later his sons, were the head. Neither of these parties or factions was ever quite able to control a majority of the voters and so the way was opened for alliances, offensive and defensive, for bargains and deals, and the opportunity was improved and there were alliances, bargains and deals, and Benton political campaigns lasted all the year round. It was a dull boy, brought up in Benton, who had not become a pretty well trained politician by the time he reached his majority. (Whitcher, pages 143-144)

Town meeting form of government prevails in most communities in the western regions to this day.

Suffragettes

The *Franklin Journal-Transcript* of November 16, 1906, reported that a

Woman's Suffrage meeting was held at Clara

The Peterborough Chapter of the Daughters of the American Revolution pose by the memorial tablet to Catharine Putnam at the dedication ceremonies of Putnam Grove, August 24, 1915. A warm personal reminiscence, delivered by a Putnam family representative, was followed by a formal address by the Honorable Ezra M. Smith.

Catharine Putnam had given the land to the town in her lifetime and the town formally accepted the gift in 1862, by payment of the symbolic dollar required by the terms of the deed. The land of Putnam Grove had been part of the acreage of Morison's original Mill Farm, Lot No. 112. She spelled out the precise use the town could make of the land: "... the said described premises shall forever be held by said town for the purpose of Public exhibitions, public meetings, public or private walks, picnics, private parties, or other exhibitions and amusements in which the public take an interest. ... No society or class have exclusive rights to its enjoyments or control. The rich and the poor, the cultured and the unlettered may here enjoy the same privileges and have the same rights. It was set aside for pleasure and not for profit. ... (Peterborough Historical Society, page 228) Courtesy of Peterborough Historical Society

The Grand Old Army's Civil War Monument predated the Catharine Putnam tablet by almost twenty years. In this circa 1897 photograph, it is evident that the town respects the donor's conditions of use. What looks like a ceremony of some kind takes place around the statue. The band is at ease and the crowd's attention is not particularly focused. The young couple behind the tree at the far left, heads leaning on hands, look decidedly bored. In general, a pleasant mood prevails. The man entering from the right hand corner of the photograph carries a picnic basket in hand.

Among Revolutionary War heroes from the western regions are Generals John McNeil of Hillsboro and Eleazer W. Ripley of Hanover. Many Civil War heroes also came from the region, notably such commanders of New Hampshire regiments as Haldimand

S. Putnam of Cornish, Louis Bell of Chester, and Everett E. Cross of Lancaster. Courtesy of Peterborough Historical Society

Registration for the draft in 1942 took place all over the country. Adrian Bouchard caught the historic scene in Hanover. After the young men complete their registration forms, a typist prepares their draft cards. The die is cast. A town historian wrote: "In the period immediately before our country entered World War II this community was not united in its opinion of the proper course of action. In traditional manner Hanover debated the issues pro and con but it became apparent before Pearl Harbor that the trend favored acceptance of the obligations as well as the privileges of freedom. The college

introduced defense courses in 1941 and the 'accelerated program' involved the Town as well as the College in a vigorous and unifying effort which led to Civilian Pilot Training, Indoctrination Schools, the Navy V-12 College Training Program, and other activities essential to ultimate victory." (Childs, page 87-88) Courtesy of Dartmouth College Library

Currier's. Miss Mary N. Chase (of Andover) has been able to cause fourteen clubs to be formed in the last four years. $100 was sent to Oregon, $70 to the National Club, and $100 remains in the treasury.

The History of Andover, when citing this entry, added the following, in parentheses:

> Women received the right to vote in 1921 under the 19th Amendment. Because of her activity in the cause Miss Chase earned the nickname among the younger groups of "Suffering Mary." (page 211)

No further mention was made of the capable group's formidable fundraising.

First Presidential Ballots, 1940

November 5, 1940, the town of Sharon cast the first votes in the nation: twenty-four votes for Wendell Wilkie, seven for Franklin Roosevelt. It was the first time in history that every one of Sharon's voters exercised their voting privileges. A chicken-pie supper, including rolls, doughnuts and coffee, was eaten at the desks of the schoolhouse from 10:30 to 11:00 p.m. for early arrivals, many of whom had walked the distance to the polls.

Uncle Sam

What more appropriate figure to celebrate regional heritage than Uncle Sam? The original "Uncle Sam" is alleged to have been Samuel Wilson who moved to Mason in 1780 at fourteen and lived there with his family until 1804 when he and a brother moved to Troy, New York. They became meat suppliers to the Army in the War of 1812. According to legend:

> He had been for a long time known as "Uncle Sam," to distinguish him from his brother Edward, who was called by everybody "Uncle Ned." The brand upon his barrels carried the appropriate initial

of the Government, "U.S." It is related by Lucius E. Wilson, Samuel's grand-nephew, that "Uncle Sam" once told him that "one day, when a large consignment of beef and pork in casks and packages was on the wharf at Ferry Street . . . [a ferry passenger] inquired of the watchman . . . what the letters on the packages stood for. 'I dunno,' he replied, 'unless it means they belong to Mr. Anderson and Uncle Sam.' 'Uncle Sam who?' was asked. 'Why, don't you know? Uncle Sam Wilson, of course. He owns near all about here and he's feeding the Army.'" This was soon passed around and the transition from the "United States" to "Uncle Sam" was easy. Files of old newspapers show that the term "Uncle Sam" as applied to the United States, appeared in print as early as 1813. Samuel Wilson died at Troy, New York, July 31, 1854 aged 88. (*WPA Guide,* page 502) "Uncle Sam's " historic house still stands in Mason.

Other famous Masonites include Jonas Chickering who invented and patented the first upright piano in 1837 and Henry Dunster, first president of Harvard College.

Remembrances of War

Walpole

In the years leading up to the War of Independence, Walpole was a center of patriot sentiments. Several of its men served with distinction in the Revolution and the town provided for their families, through self-taxation, while the breadwinners were away at war.

March 4, 1835 diary entry of Denison Gould, Hillsborough:

> This is the day that the old Revolution soldiers have to swear that they are alive so as to get their pensions. But it is so cold that I don't think their swears will reach more than two rods in the sunshine.

From the 1840 *Annals* of the town of Peterborough:

1840, July 4th. A procession was formed from Col. French's tavern to the church. Exercises were introduced by an anthem by the choir, vocal, instrumental, a prayer by Dr. Abbott, a hymn, Declaration of Independence, read by Dr. A. Smith, music, an oration by James Smith, a senior member of Yale College, music. Procession from the church to Col. French's hall, where more than 150 ladies and gentlemen sat down to a cold collation. No ardent spirits. Good humor and social feeling prevailed through the whole. Nothing of party politics disturbed the harmony and cheerfulness of the festival. Mr. Smith was requested to deposit a copy of his oration in the Ministerial Library, but declined the request. In the evening, there was a display of fireworks from the hill. No occurrence took place during the day or evening, unfavorable to the joys of the day.

The toasts given at the festive luncheon were deposited in the town's annual records for that year; a sample follows:

No. 1. THE DAY WE CELEBRATE, Emphatically the Birthday of Civil Liberty, whose sun shed a cheering ray upon our Fathers of Seventy-six like to the natural sun upon the Tempest-tost mariner, and as it rises toward meridian splendor, we'll shed a glorious effulgence over the benighted regions of the other climes.

No. 3. THE STAMP ACT. The signal gun for the Revolution. It has taught the Mother Country a lesson she never can forget.

No. 6. THE CONSTITUTION. The Temple of our Liberties. Should any Sampson in his blindness wish to pull down any of its pillars, may it fall on him and crush him to powder.

No. 7 NEW HAMPSHIRE. The great manufactory of heroes, statesmen and patriots. Whence other states derive their supplies.

No. 13. WOMAN. Formed by the hand of Providence to share with man the excellencies and frailities of human nature, and as she sympathizes in his toils and sufferings, may it ever be deemed right that she should join with him in his festivities. [final toast] (Peterborough Historical Society, pages 175-176)

Cannon Clubs were not uncommon for on the Fourth of July towns fired their Revolutionary War cannons to mark the occasion. Cannon kidnapping is an old prank that appears in the historical literature of many American towns. A fine example appears in the history of western New Hampshire.

When several of Keene's "gay blades" stole one of the historic cannon of colonial days from Walpole's Main street in the spring of 1807, it raised the indignation of that town against Keene, and the affair was followed by all with avid interest. As only Chesterfield, Westmoreland, Walpole, and Charleston could boast such ordnance and fired them triumphantly on days of public rejoicing such as the Fourth of July, inhabitants of nearby towns which had no such relics were jealous of this privilege. Return of the cannon was demanded by court action. Attempts to arrest the culprits proved unsuccessful and only added to the general excitement. One of the Walpole citizens aiding the sheriff had a good idea of the identity of the person for whom he was looking, and concealed himself to await his quarry's return. Dr. Daniel Adams, a respected physician, noticed the hidden watcher, and discovering that he himself had been seen but not recognized, led the pursuer a merry chase through woods and swampland to his own doorstep, thus preventing the real culprit from being captured. In the end several of the gulity were arrested and brought to court, but the judge ruled that the cannon was not the exclusive property of Walpole, and set the defendants free. The cannon was immediately drawn up before the Court House

and fired. "May it please your honors," Lawyer-for-the-defence Vose said as the echoes reverberated through Keene Valley, "the case is already reported." *(Keene History Committee, page 48)*

The Walpole men recovered the cannon in a daring raid on the night of July 4, 1909, delivering it home at daybreak to the sounds of church bells.

Thanksgiving

The "Avery mowing" was the finest mowing in Temple in 1850; it was about two hundred acres in size and lay at about sixteen hundred feet above sea level, which gave it a commanding view of the surrounding landscape. In 1866, with the conclusion of the Civil war, the Temple folk gathered on this mowing for their Thanksgiving Day dinner. It is said that 610 people sat down for dinner that day; horses and oxen with attendant carts and carriages were tied up along the road for over two miles. (Historical Society of Temple, page 482)

Jaffrey Memorial

Jaffrey's Second World War Memorial was erected in 1950. An earlier proposal for the World War II memorial met with some opposition from returning veterans who thought it "a personal tribute rather than historical and dedicatory" and wanted something "more proper and fitting." After polling veterans organizations and the families of the deceased soldiers, the town passed a

resolution at its town meeting of 1949 unanimously in favor of erecting Brandt-Erichsen's monument, the money to be raised by means "other than taxation." Perhaps for lack of funds, the intended monument was never completed and the artist moved to California with his family a few years later. Before he left, however, he completed this "smaller and more modest memorial" to the memory of Jaffrey's war dead, named thereon. Edward Allord, Donald Brooks, Adelord Caron, Eric H. Hamilton, Clifton Hurd, Raymond LaFreniere, Edward Morris, Richard Patterson, and Arthur Sirois represent the village's great sacrifice to the war effort. The United Nations of names reflect the changing population in the region during the late nineteenth and twentieth centuries.

Jaffrey's memorials to the Korean War and Vietnam War are two pillars set in a memorial park designed for meditiation and reflection. The park is located on River Street, across from the Police Station.

Towns in western New Hampshire honor their war dead in many ways, most publicly, of course, by placing substantial memorial monuments. Commonly, citizens bequeath monies for these or they are put forth as articles on the town warrant. Other types of memorials include the planting of trees. Temple replaced such a memorial in 1972, planted in front of the church in memory of three soldiers who lost their lives in the Second World War. Albert Quinn, brother of one of the slain soldiers, made these remarks at the rededication:

On June 6, 1944, the people of Temple gathered at a spot in front of the church to dedicate a Memorial tree to the memory of David Quinn and Leon Blood,

This brightly painted Second World War Memorial stands near the bandstand on Jaffrey's Village Green. Erected around 1950, it was presented to the town by its artist, Danish sculptor and local resident Viggo Brandt-Erichsen. Models were Lillian La Freniere and Hilma Suuspakka (Mrs. Antti) Brooks. Brandt-Erichsen also designed the more well-known "Buddies Monument" dedicated on Armistice Day, November 11, 1930, as the town's memorial to World War I. Of Jaffrey granite, the massive work depicts a soldier carrying his wounded companion. The sculptor had come to Jaffrey in 1928 for the interment of his American wife's ashes in a mausoleum he designed in Jaffrey where she had wished to be buried. Photo by the author

Town business districts are apt to decorate their shops with bunting in this characteristic manner achieving displays conspicuous for their gaiety. Period photographs of businesses and streets decorated in the manner of the "Peterboro House" are plentiful. This one shows the hotel, hitching posts neatly lined up in front, and its neighboring buildings of the Riley Goodridge Block, upper Main Street, dressed up for an unspecified occasion. The banner reads: "The Home of Peterborough Grange/Patrons Welcome." A Meat Market sign juts out from the near corner of the hotel's porch. Courtesy of Peterborough Historical Society

A roving reporter no doubt took this photograph of Troy's proud Mr. Johnson and his Boy Scout Troop. It is credited to E. A. Stolba of Fitchburg, Massachusetts and was taken at a Fire Companies Muster in Winchester, Massachusetts. Undated, it appears to be from the late nineteen forties or early fifties. The Hand Tub was made in 1828 and found in a local barn. Mr. Johnson traveled with his Scout Troop all over the region demonstrating the vintage piece of firefighting equipment. Courtesy of New Hampshire Historical Society

who died in the service of their country during World War II. Later the name of Murray Day was added to that sacred Roll of Honor. On that day the mood of the town was a somber one. At the Town Meeting in March a Memorial tree had been voted to honor one son, and now it must be dedicated in memory of two [Quinn and Blood, Day died later] . . . .

Today we are dedicating this tree that there may be a little more beauty in the village of Temple. It is a symbol of our love and the hope that springs eternal in the human heart. We are dedicating this tree as a living memorial to these, our beloved and honored dead. . . . We can do no less than dedicate our lives to the making of a better world—a world without war, pestilence, or strife—a world of peace without end. (Historical Society of Temple, page 18)

A 1952 addition to Temple's town library honors the veterans of that war.

Outlanders

Incursions by "outsiders," tourists, summer people and retirees, into the rural hinterlands of New Hampshire go back to the middle of the last century. In his history of Cornish, William Child identifies such new residents, unrelated to the older families in town, as "City Folks." Child, when he was compiling the town history, invited one of their number, Homer Saint-Gaudens, son of the renowned artist, to contribute a chapter detailing their membership and commenting on their place in the community.

Saint-Gaudens' account is comprehensive and informative. The tone and attitude of his essay reflect the place that the "outsider" has on the fringes of rural community life. In general, his brief descriptions emphasize the prestigious achievements due two generations of individuals who collectively enjoy fame, even to this day, as members of the Cornish Artists's Colony. He describes Stephen Parrish, a Philadelphian, as "the only man to build a house on the north slope of a hill, out of sight of the much-prized mountain [Ascutney] purchasing his property from Mr. S. A. Tracy." Tracy was a local farmer active in town affairs. One can imagine the gossip that must have surrounded the sale—Tracy, the clever trader, gets the gullible city slicker.

Of Maxfield Parrish's friend, Charles A. Platt, a landscape painter and etcher-turned-architect, Saint-Gaudens observes that he saw fit "to decorate Cornish slopes with pseudo-Italian buildings and to crop the heads of our native white pines that they might pathetically imitate the fashion of the trees in southern Europe." (William H. Child, page 223)

Saint-Gaudens obviously shares many of the countrymen's views and his desire for their acceptance reflects the hopefulness of many newcomers to the region, down to the present day.

Despite Saint-Gaudens optimism no timely blending of the two groups has occurred during the intervening years. There continue to be shared interests but there remains, as well, the typical country dweller's distrust of the outsider. Nevertheless there are also the companionable moments such as occur when rebuilding a neighbor's barn destroyed by wind or lightning or co-sponsoring charitable events when all neighbors, new and old, join in the effort.

A local resident of Cornish, updating the town history in 1974, is similarly optimistic to his predecessor in this assessment of the situation. He says of late twentieth-century newcomers, many of them academics and writers: "The newcomers enjoy country life of a simpler and more practical sort, and rejoice as did their predecessors in freedom to go their own way without interference." (Wade, page 94) Wade's words might apply, in fact, to the broad population of the western regions, so large an incursion of "outsiders" has continued in recent decades.

The mobility that the coming of the railroad gave to Americans greatly changed the population base of the small towns in the region. An Andover historian comments:

Before the railroad many of the descendants of the early families had little direct connection with the outside world. They intermarried and increased in numbers until there were Cilleys, Emerys, Fellows, Browns, Weares, Tiltons, Rowes and many others living in all parts of the town. Today not a single male direct descendant of any of those families mentioned is resident in Andover. The genealogical section of the Eastman History lists nearly 250 families who lived in Andover at some time prior to 1900. Of them all only about thirty of the same name are found here in 1965, and of this thirty only a dozen individuals can claim direct descent from the early families of their name. (Chaffee, page 9)

The high stepping "Uncle Sam" pictured here entertains the crowds at the Shriner's Parade in Hanover sometime in the 1970s. The parade heralds a traditional sports rivalry known as "The Shrine Bowl," a charitable fundraiser, at which New Hampshire high school seniors combat Vermont high school seniors in a pre-season football game every August. Courtesy of Dartmouth College Library

Photo Collage: Daniel Webster. Courtesy of Dartmouth College Library.

The situation is typical. Many of western New Hampshire's old homes and farmhouses serve as summer residences for out-ot-towners or have been adapted as commercial offices for upscale businesses.

Old Home Week

The enduring traditional community celebrations that come down to us from our ancestors invariably have a patriotic focus. Even such relatively recent celebrations as Old Home Week find their justification in a pride in the past with patriotic overtones. Of the turn-of-the-twentieth century vintage, Old Home Week was proposed "to draw people back to the Granite State in the third week of August each summer, and to revive and stimulate love for and interest in the past of each town." Although not explicitly stated, another purpose was to promote tourism in the state. (Squires, page 411)

Significantly, the operational office of the Old Home Week Association was in the Department of Agriculture and fostered through local granges statewide. Old Home Week continued unabated in many communities since its first official observance in August 1899. There may well have been local Old Home Days that predate 1899 and inspired its formal promotion. Andover records an Old Home Day in 1898, for example.

The Old Home Day concept was an idea waiting to be born. It fulfilled a previously unrecognized need in small town New Hampshire at the time. The wave of western movement left lonesome friends and family eager for continued contact with former residents, men and woman still vivid in local memory and who, in turn, identified very strongly with their New Hampshire roots. While only a very few who had moved great distances returned for the celebration, many did send letters and telegrams which were shared with the community. Those who lived in more proximate locations returned home in droves. From the very beginning, regional town records reveal that Old Home Days became the occasion for honoring town heritage, often by the dedication of historic monuments. Previous commemorative holidays, such as the Fourth of July and Memorial Day, were in and of themselves specific in their intention and their observances well proscribed. In some communities, Old Home Day became the most festive occasion of the summer.

There was a revival of Old Home Days following World War II and another more recent revival dating from about the late 1970s. Adapted to contemporary lifestyles, Old Home Days may vary from community to community; they may be held for one day, a weekend, or longer. The emphasis on encouraging the return to the state of natives is no longer a cornerstone of the event although many family and school reunions occur around local Old Home Day observances. In most towns, they are

tourist attractions and during election year, Old Home Days offer an opportunity for statewide and national office seekers to shake the hands and kiss the babies of their current or prospective constituents.

Lyme is one town that revived Old Home Days in the late nineteen forties that continued for a decade or more. There,

> . . . activities at Old Home Day included a combination of the following: a parade with prizes for entries, one and sometimes two band concerts by McLure's Student Band, a speaker, an auction, exhibits and sales, horseback riding and games for children, an old-fashioned sing, an amateur hour, and an evening dance at the Academy Hall. The first year's basket lunch and supper soon evolved into a large noon dinner of chicken pie or ham or roast beef. At one time dinner was served from Pearl Dimick's window and everyone sat in chairs in the yard. The potatoes for these dinners would be peeled out of doors, put in milk cans full of cold water, and then cooked in large canners. Receipts for 1955 list $5.00 paid for 28 1/2 dozen rolls, all made by Ruth Elder (Mrs. Kenneth) who also baked 150 cupcakes for the band! (Cole, page 294)

New Hampshirites take historical anniversaries seriously, using them both as an excuse for richly varied festive commemorations and as an opportunity for public reflection of the eventful heritage of the state region, community, or institution being remembered.

Personalities

Many illustrious historical figures made their way to the western regions of New Hampshire. These photos illustrate the high regard and hospitality that the local population often lavished on visitors from such imposing arenas as politics or the arts. They represent a vast number of similarly important people who visited or lived in the region over the past centuries.

Another class of personality that garners the high regard of local people is the "town character," that unique individual whose personality embodies the community's sense of itself. A representative "town character" appears here as well.

Accompanying these photographs are anecdotes or commentaries about well-known figures who made an impact on the region or who have carried something of the region with them to the outside world.

Carl Sandburg's poem, "New Hampshire Again," from *Good Morning America*, includes the following lines,

I remember black winter waters,
I remember thin white birches,
I remember sleepy twilight hills,
I remember riding across New Hampshire
    lengthways.
I remember a station named "HALCYON,"
    a brakeman calling to passengers
    "HALCYON!! HALCYON!!"

Halcyon is an Andover place name. Halcyon Island sat in Highland Lake and the Halcyon Hills Farm, a flourishing farm and orchard a hundred years ago, was a local showplace. Beginning in 1908, railroad policy required that "for reasons of safety" no local station could carry a compound name. It seems that an accident in Haverhill that year had resulted from a communications error when the prefix "East" had been left off a train order. East Andover's passenger station was renamed Halcyon. (Chaffee, page 140)

Joyce Kilmer composed the famous poem, "Trees," during one of his many visits to the Holbrook farm on Winch Hill in Swanzy. So popular was it that it eventually became one of the most parodied of all American poems. But this was not before it had made its author one of the most beloved American poets.

Nobel Prize winning author, Rudyard Kipling resided for a few years in Dummerston, Vermont, within sight of Mount Monadnock. Through an ingenious private joke between Kipling and his knowing readers, he worked southwestern New Hampshire place names into his story, "How the Whale Got His Throat."

Mark Twain (Samuel Langhorne Clemens) was one of dozens of notables who summered at one time or another in Dublin. In one interview with reporters, he mentioned that beyond the beauty of the view and the fine country air, the major attraction of the town was the variety of interesting neighbors, artists, writers, and scholars he lived among.

Another way that communities acknowledge their personal affection for public personalities is through creating place names in their honor. Some of Keene's streets provide examples of this. Cobb Street and others in its neighborhood were names after well-known baseball players. Douglass Street may have been named after ex-slave Frederick Douglass, who made two speaking engagements in the town, where he was received with great enthusiasm, 1865 and 1866, the very year the street was named. And Roosevelt Street was named after Theodore Roosevelt, president at the time it was laid out.

So associated is the name of Daniel Webster (1782-1852) with the heritage of the nation, it is not to be wondered at that many New England institutions and communities make some proprietary claim to Webster's memory. Hanover's claim to Webster cannot be challenged. Not only was he a graduate of Dartmouth

READY FOR MOVING
The Webster House, with Front Porch Removed, Ready for its Last Journey

"Miss McMurphy's House"

While not nearly as famous as his birthplace in Salisbury, the cottage Webster lived in during his student days is a Hanover landmark and today houses the town Historical Society's collections. Pictured here is one of several 1928 photos documenting the move of Webster Cottage to its present location. A photo of the building as it looks today is located among the color plates herein.

Time has a way of exaggerating memorials. In fact, Webster merely roomed in this small farmhouse for the year 1801 to 1802. He reached the tiny south chamber under the roof by way of a steep stairway of twelve steps with a sharp turn in it. Courtesy of Dartmouth College Library

College but he also led a masterful defense of the College's sovereignty before the bench of the Supreme Court and won a momentous victory that has gone down in the annals of American law.

As a favorite native son, Webster was invited aboard the first train running between Concord and Lebanon, November 17, 1847. His remarks on the occasion must have echoed the thoughts of many of his fellow-citizens:

> . . . everybody knows that the age is remarkable for scientific research. . . . The ancients saw nothing like it. The moderns have seen nothing like it till the present generation. (Childs, page 49)

When Dartmouth College hosted Webster commemorative events throughout its history, the town of Hanover entered into the celebrations wholeheartedly. For example, for the 1901 "Webster Centennial at Dartmouth," the town's businesses decorated lavishly with patriotic bunting. The date coincided with the centennial of Webster's graduation from the College.

H. H. H. Langill, Hanover photographer, published a group of photographs of Webster and artifacts associated with him as souvenirs of the occasion, all twenty-nine of which are arranged in the collage on page 141. Only two were actually of sites in Hanover. No. 7 "Dartmouth College in 1801" is a reproduction of a watercolor executed by George Ticknor in 1803 when he was a Dartmouth sophomore.

The artifacts and the public's treatment of them exhibit a facet of mythmaking that surrounds the persona of the truly famous personality. The many stories about Webster also help to define him in the popular imagination. While he was a man of mythic proportions in his own lifetime the stories about him tend to emphasize the down-to-earth qualities that keep the hero on a level that ordinary folks can identify with.

A charming anecdote about Webster is found in the 1840 town Annals of Peterborough:

> Daniel Webster, passing through this town on his way from Keene to Nashua, made a few remarks to such of the citizens as were hastily assembled at Col. French's tavern. An incident occurred to him after his departure from this town which may be worth mentioning. In passing through Temple, his horse began to fail, and meeting with an elderly man (Mr. Boynton) with a spirited horse, he engaged him to carry him to Wilton. During the ride, they entered into conversation which, naturally enough, turned upon politics, and among other things the name of Daniel Webster was mentioned. Mr. W. asked the other if he had ever seen Daniel Webster. He said he had once, many years ago. He then asked him if he should know him if he saw him again, to which he replied that he thought he would. Mr. W. then raised

his hat, and, looking him in the face, said, "Did you ever see me before?" The other, observing him for a moment, exclaimed, "I declare, I believe you are the very critter." (Peterborough Historical Society, 1958)

Dartmouth College Case

In 1815 the celebrated Dartmouth College controversy arose. This case forms an important part of the history of New Hampshire because of its bearing upon the rights of educational institutions and the inviolability of contracts. The case was argued and won by Daniel Webster. . . . (*WPA Guide,* page 44)

In contemporary jargon, the Dartmouth College Case came about in Dartmouth College's intense desire to fend off an unfriendly takeover attempt by a newly Republican state government. James Duane Squires speculates that sentiment against Dartmouth College stemmed from the perception that the College leaders had been behind the secessionist movement of the 1780s and from the objections that some of the Dartmouth Board of Trustees had to the authoritarian presidency of John Wheelock who inherited the presidency at the death of his father, the founder. Be that as it may, in a strictly partisan move, the New Hampshire legislature, at the instigation of newly elected Governor William Plumer

> passed a bill changing the institution at Hanover to Dartmouth University, increasing the number of trustees from twelve to twenty-one, and authorizing a new. . . Board of Overseers. . . of twenty five members, appointed by the governor and the Council, and entrusted with veto power over all actions by the trustees of the University. (Squires, page 190)

The Board of Trustees boycotted all meetings, thus preventing a legal quorum; however, the single Trustee who defected to the University side was William H. Woodward who, as

> secretary and treasurer of the board, . . . [carried] with him the seal of the College, the records, and the title to the property. . . . [T]he subsequent legal action by the College to recover its property carried his name [Dartmouth College v. Woodward]. (Squires, page 190)

The case was heard at the state court in Exeter with Jeremiah Smith, Jeremiah Mason, and Daniel Webster as defense attorneys. The judgment of November 6, 1817, went against the College. Webster himself later argued the case before the Supreme Court, in the process earning the reputation of a brilliant orator. His most famous lines greatly affected the Justices. He said,

> It is, sir, as I have said, a small college,—and yet there are those who love it . . . . Sir, I know not how others may feel, but, for myself, when I see my alma mater surrounded, like Caesar in the senate house, by those who are reiterating stab upon stab, I would not, for this right hand, have her turn to me and say,—*et tu quoque, mi fili,*—"and thou too, my son." (Quoted in Squires, pages 191-192)

The case was settled in 1819 and was really an extraordinary legal decision. The decision proved to be far reaching. To quote Squires,

> The decision by the U. S. Supreme Court freed existing corporations from control by the states which had created them, and thereby became a bulwark to the nineteenth century theories of laissez faire.

Squires goes on to quote Chancellor Kent's *Commentaries:*

> It . . . did more than any other single act...to give solidity and inviolability to the literary, charitable, religious and commercial institutions of our country.

Webster immediately wrote the news home to his brother, Ezekiel Webster. The text of his letter reads:

Washington Feby. 2, 1819

My Dear E.

All is safe. Judgt. was rendered this morning, reversing the Judgt in N. Hampshire Present, [?] Marshall, Washington, Livingstone, Johnson, Duval & Storey—All concuring but Duval, & he giving no reason to the contrary—The opinion was delivered by the Chief Justice—it was very able and very elaborate.—It goes the whole length—& leaves not an inch for the University to stand on.

Yrs affectionately
D. Webster
in Court

By his eloquence and acumen, Webster earned the everlasting gratitude of Dartmouth College and the respect of a nation.

The College took charge of its property within the month. Webster's co-defender, Joseph Hopkinson, in a letter to Dartmouth President Brown wrote:

> I would have an inscription over the door of your building. "Founded by Eleazar Wheelock, Refounded by Daniel Webster."

Letter from Daniel Webster to his Brother. Courtesy of Dartmouth College Library

In the upper Connecticut River Valley, the news was received with joy and revelry. In writing about the history of relationships between Dartmouth College and its surrounding towns, Prof. Francis Lane Childs refers to this incident as an illustration of the generally amicable state of communion that has prevailed there throughout a lengthy history. He writes:

> . . .cooperation has always exceeded disagreement. The unifying factor has been the natural love of place that most men feel for the town in which their lives are cast, combined here with the pride that all have felt for Dartmouth College, even when disagreeing strongly with some of its policies and actions. In days of crisis for the institution, the townspeople as a whole have stood loyally by it. When, for example, the news of the great decision of the Supreme Court in 1819 reached Hanover, an undergraduate wrote home: "The expressions of joy are excessive. The officers entreated the inhabitants to desist, but to no purpose. In Norwich the shoutings were very great, and in most of the towns in the vicinity." (Childs, page 273.)

Webster's sagacity is credited with another legal decision of great importance to the state of New Hampshire, this one the Webster-Ashburton Treaty in 1842 in which the northwesternmost reach of the Connecticut River was established at Halls Stream. The location thereafter marked the border between Canada and New Hampshire and the decision laid to rest an old controversy. The territory had been in such dispute that the citizens of the region had seceded in 1832 and defended their independent nation of Indian Stream until it was formally incorporated as Pittsburgh, New Hampshire in 1840.

There are countless tributes to Webster's memory in western New Hampshire and elsewhere expressed in such place names as the town of Webster and Lake Webster and in names or nicknames for numerous local organizations. A major north-south artery, the Daniel Webster Highway, called locally, "the D W Highway," also bears his name.

Before the institution of New Hampshire's "first-in-the nation" primary status, the visit to the state by a sitting president was a momentous occasion, certain to attract local crowds to public appearances that were part of the itinerary. Today, New Hampshirites, respectful as ever, take it almost as their right to entertain presidents and would-be presidents in the period leading up to presidential elections.

Owing to his frequent visits to relatives who lived in the upper Connecticut River Valley, Pres. William Howard Taft made numerous appearances in the western regions of New Hampshire throughout his presidency. There are

many accounts and a number of photographs documenting President Taft's occasional stops at towns along or near the Connecticut River. He motored through the area several times on family trips stopping in Dublin, Keene, Claremont, Hanover, and other towns along the way for formal or informal visits. Several photographs exist of his October 10 to 12 visit to Lebanon, Claremont, Hanover, and surrounding communities while on an extended tour of New Hampshire. He visited Hanover, at the invitation of the president of Dartmouth College, between visits to Bretton Woods and Keene. The First Lady accompanied him and Col. F. C. Churchill was his chauffeur for this tour. He made another formal visit to Dartmouth College on March 12, 1915, and several informal visits to the Monadnock region. Several town histories of the region acknowledge one or more stops that Taft made on his New Hampshire excursions.

The visit of a president was a big thing to the people of these towns in the years prior to the state's acquiring the "First Primary." For example, Taft was only the second president ever to have visited Dartmouth College. Taft often spoke to the people from his open touring car, as he does in this photo on page 149, an efficient plan, surely, providing him the potential for quick leave-taking if his schedule was tight. The crowd gathered to hear him in Lebanon are typical—small American flags in hand, local Boy Scout troops in their knickerbocker uniforms a proud legion of honor. Security forces seem to be made up of professional bodyguards (secret service) and local police.

During President Monroe's visit to Hanover a century earlier, which happened to coincide with the political turmoil that led to the Dartmouth College Case, he called on

> Madame Wheelock, widow of John Wheelock [son of the founder, Eleazar], the second president of Dartmouth College. Dr. John Wheelock had been dead about three months at the time of the President's visit. There was a bit of romance connected with the meeting, for Mrs. Wheelock many years before, had nursed the President, then a lieutenant in the Revolutionary army, when he had been severely wounded in a foray in eastern Pennsylvania. (*DAM,* 1912, pages 15-16)

The president's Hanover itinerary diplomatically circumvented the tensions of the political situation.

> The arrival of the President was announced by a salute of the artillery, paraded for the purpose. . . . In the evening, calls were made upon President Francis Brown, of Dartmouth University, as his visit was made during the double occupation preceding the settlement of the Dartmouth College Case. (*DAM,* 1912, page 15)

Monroe visited as many places as he could fit into his

itinerary, including the Copper Mines in Strafford. Claremont, too, recorded the affects of Monroe's visit on the area with equal discretion in reference to the affairs of Dartmouth.

> In the summer of this year (1817) the people of this vicinity had their first sight of a president of the United States. President Monroe entered the state and proceeded as far north as Hanover.... [He stopped at Shaker Village, Enfield.]
>
> He passed from thence through Lebanon to Hanover, where he unexpectedly met an old acquaintance in the widow of the late revered and lamented President Wheelock. This lady was a native of New Jersey, was at Trenton at the time of the battle in which he was a lieutenant of a company. He was wounded in the battle and she dressed his wound after he was conveyed to the house where she then was. The president did not remember her at first, but as the past came to his mind the interview became peculiarly affecting to the two individuals and highly interesting to the large circle of ladies and gentlemen. In a letter from Hanover it was said: "We were delighted with the short visit of the president. For his sake the hatchet was buried for at least twenty-four hours; a short truce, but a merry one." This was said in view of the bitterness existing between the political parties of the day. (*Downs*, pages 232-233)

That the facts of the case are so explicitly known to Hanover's neighbors, however, suggests a strong local interest in the affair, fed, no doubt, not only by the letter cited, but by considerable gossip as well. The discrepency in the location of battle at which Monroe was wounded is trivial. Trenton sits on the Delaware River, the boundary between the two states mentioned.

The Dartmouth chronicler of Taft's visit bemoans the difference between the pace of President Monroe's 1817 visit, by carriage and on horseback, and the motorized visit of President Taft. "In these less leisurely times the President rushes in by motor; allows a bare half hour for luncheon, speaks from his briefly halted car, and speeds on." To the wistful contemporary onlooker of presidential politics, the remarks seem ironic. Television appearances and intense security at public appearances deny the public the intimacy still to be found in this early twentieth-century scene. Perhaps it is a desire to maintain something of this personal link between the people and their leaders enjoyed by our ancestors that motivates New Hampshire residents to insist on its first-in-the-nation primary status.

In the Dartmouth College Photo Archives, a small portrait, probably the work of H. H. Langill's studio, carries a brief biographical note: "Ira Allen lived in Allen's Lane opposite his livery stable, where now [1953] is the Inn Garage (photo p. 150). The stable stood about where the Travel Bureau & Gazette office is now. And Mr. Allen sat outside his door watching the children going to & from school during the 1880s." An additional note gives his dates as 1815 to 1890. The Inn Garage is no longer, but Allen Street is still in the very hub of Hanover's downtown commercial district.

Among the more colorful local residents, Ira Allen was a familiar face throughout the upper Connecticut River Valley. As a livery stable operator and stagecoach driver of many years' experience, he would have been known to a wide community. He is to be seen atop his stage in one of the photographs depicting the history of transportation in the region. Among many delightful anecdotes about him is one retold by William Randall Waterman in the town's bicentennial history. The incident occurred in the middle of the nineteenth century, when the Ledyard Bridge proprietors were the object of much resentment in the local community. The *Dartmouth Advertiser* reported the story. Ira Allen is its hero.

> A short time ago three of the owners happened to be on the stage together. With a spice of the waggish the driver laid on the strings, the bridge swayed and shook so that they were really alarmed for their safety, and called out for him to stop. "Oh! safe enough! no danger! got the *owners* aboard! get up along!" was the reply. (Childs, page 36)

Francis Lane Childs also relates a couple of oft told tales about the lively coachman:

> Allen was the first regular driver of the stage from the Lewiston [Hanover/Norwich] station to the village, and used always to stop the coach as soon as it crossed the bridge and collect the fares, in order to prevent students from jumping off the vehicle before it reached the hotel, thus winning a free ride. Many anecdotes have been told about Ira, the one most often quoted preserves his remark when the authorities proposed putting up a sign forbidding persons to drive on the newly laid asphalt sidewalks: "It won't do no good; horses can't read and asses won't."

Our forebears were self-consciously aware of a sense of New Hampshire's importance to the nation at large. In a 1921 address attended by the governor, secretary of state, and other dignitaries, Henry Harrison Metcalf forthrightly asserted that "[m]ore men and women, who have made a marked impress for good upon the life of the nation at large, have been born in New Hampshire than in any other State in the Union, in proportion to population, and it would almost be safe to say it without the qualifications to population." (Metcalf, pages 7-8) Of course, western New Hampshire claims its fair share of them. Metcalf pays tribute to numerous New Hampshire natives who succeeded in meaningful ways. Of the regional celebrities listed below, some are names familiar to a wide public, while others are proudly remembered primarily in their local communities. A number have drifted into the realms of forgotten history.

Important names in music cited by Metcalf include Amy Marcy Cheney Beach of Henniker, world renowned pianist and composer who continues to enjoy a reputation as one of America's great composers, and the Hutchinson Family Singers of Milford, John W. Hutchinson, *pater familia*.

About the Hutchinson family much has been written. The family put the town of Milford on the map during the middle of the nineteenth century when they were most active. The Hutchinson's were a singing group of international fame who espoused social and religious causes. They referred to themselves as of the "Tribe of Jesse." Their father, Jesse, was the son of Elisha Hutchinson who had come to Milford from Middleton, Massachusetts, in 1779. The principal singers were Judson, John, Asa, and Abby Hutchinson, all talented singers and performers. "The harmony of [their] voices has been described as exquisite in its tonal quality." (Wright, page 15)

Judson died in 1859 but the rest continued for many years, sometimes joined by others of their large family Jesse fathered sixteen children, thirteen of whom were raised in Milford. They sang at concerts and rallies for abolition, temperance, and women's rights. Their presence on the bill would insure large crowds whose emotions the singers would rouse before the speechmaking, pledge-signing, fundraising, and volunteer solicitation that accompanied all such events. The Hutchinson Family repertory consisted of sentimental and topical songs of the day and original material, some of which, like "The Snow Storm," went into popular tradition. Abby's song, "Kind Words Can Never Die," contained the memorable stanza, "Old Soldiers Never Die," that General Douglas MacArthur referred to in his farewell speech to the U.S. Congress in 1951.

The Hutchinsons frequently entertained the famous Colonel and Mrs. Tom Thumb at their North River Road home in Milford. (Wright, page 191)

Ellen Beal Morey, a descendent of Orford's first settler, Israel Morey, completed her musical education in Leipzig and Berlin. She returned to a professional life in Boston as the first female conductor and the founder of both a chorus and orchestra.

Metcalf's list of accomplished artists, native to the region, includes names that are little recognized by the general public a century later. He recognizes Larkin D. Mead, sculptor, of Chesterfield; Roswell H. Shurtleff, painter of Rindge; Alfred C. Howland, Walpole, painter;

Adna Tenney and Ulysses D. Tenney, portraitists, Hanover; Daniel C. Strain of Littleton, portraitist; and Alice Palmer of Orford, painter.

In the area of national politics, perhaps the most highly valued arena of public life to the natives of the region, Metcalf proudly offers the accomplishments of many men from the region. Levi Woodbury of Francestown served under Pres. Andrew Jackson as secretary of the navy and under Presidents Jackson and Martin Van Buren as secretary of the treasury. Metcalf reminds us that Daniel Webster served as secretary of state under Presidents Harrison, Tyler, and Fillmore.

Nathan Clifford of Rumney was attorney general under President Polk. Salmon P. Chase of Cornish was secretary of the treasury under Abraham Lincoln. Marshall Jewell of Winchester was postmaster general in the cabinet of Pres. Ulysses S. Grant and Amos T. Akerman of Keene was his attorney general. Three of these men also served on the Supreme Court; Chief Justice Chase, and Associate Justices Woodbury and Clifford. John W. Weeks of Lancaster was secretary of war to President Harding.

Franklin Pierce, the only New Hampshire president, was known for his civility. President from 1853-1857, Pierce was the first president to deliver his inaugural address without a manuscript. Franklin Pierce was held in high regard by those who knew him personally. A much talked about event locally was a

mammoth convention and barbeque at Hillsboro, August 19, 1852, for which event the ladies of Antrim and Stoddard prepared a giant fruit cake weighing 500 pound, inscribed "Pierce and King Union." (Stoddard Historical Society, pages 38-39)

Pierce was among the first scholars to attend Francestown Academy from which he graduated in 1819 before entering Bowdoin College in Maine. His father, John Pierce, had been an exemplary soldier in the Revolutionary War and much honored in New Hampshire where he settled after the war. He served in many local and state offices, including governor, Franklin Pierce first served in the New Hampshire legislature as the representative from Hillsborough in 1829 at the age of twenty-five. Later he served in the United States Senate. When he was running for the presidency, he was owner of the *Concord Monitor-Patriot*. A little known fact about Pierce is his defence of the New Hampshire Shaker communities against a suit of slander which he won on an appeal. No less a figure than Nathaniel Hawthorne wrote Franklin Pierce's biography.

The regions' nineteenth-century contributions to theater include Denman Thompson of Swanzey, who created and produced "The Old Homestead," a town tradition that continues to this day. Its production dates

always include the evening of the July full moon. Will M. Cressy, of Bradford, playwright, actor, and popular comedian and Charles H. Hoyt of Charlestown, playwright and manager, both had national reputations.

Many authors were born in the region. Among the most well known in the last century was Sarah J. Hale, (nee Buell) in Guild, (Newport), who was the editor of *Godey's Lady's Book,* the first woman's magazine in America. Her lasting claim to fame, however, is that she pioneered the official national celebration of Thanksgiving Day.

Edna Dean Proctor, often called New Hampshire's female poet laureate, was born in Henniker. Kate Sanborn was a native of Hanover. Renowned novelist, Frances Parkinson Keyes, was raised on the northern Vermont/New Hamsphire border. She married Henry W. Keyser, a young lawyer from a prominent local family. They lived for several years in the Keyser farmstead in Haverhill where Keyser began his political career. He served as New Hampshire's governor and later, as a senator from New Hampshire. A few of her novels are set in the border region and *Also the Hills,* is set on Briar Hill, North Haverhill.

Two virtually forgotten writers of nineteenth century popularity are Constance Fennimore Woolson, of Claremont and Eleanor Hodgman Porter of Littleton, creator of Pollyanna, one of the most memorable of all fictional children.

Metcalf occasionally animates important symbols of New Hampshire claiming for them the same importance that he invests in the state's important citizens. A case in point is the *Kearsarge,* a famous Civil War naval vessel built in the Portsmouth shipyards which, he tells us, was so-named because its oaken timbers were cut from the foot hills of Kearsarge Mountain in Warner by Joseph Barnard of Hopkinton. Barnard is the only "plain folks"

member of Metcalf's entire roll call of honor.

He cites Marshall P. Wilder of Rindge, founder of both the New England Horticultural Society and the American Pomological Society and Walter A. Wood of Mason, inventor of the mowing machine that helped in the mechanization of agriculture. One is puzzled, however, as to how such a thorough gleaner of New Hampshire's success stories could have neglected to mention the inventor of the first automobile, a Sunapee native.

Up to the present date [1941], from 1869, no one that we have been able to learn about or hear of, has challenged the claim of Enos Merrill Clough of Sunapee that he invented a horseless carriage or automobile, and that it was the first ever to run on any highway in the United States. This is true, although his claim has been publicized extensively. (Bartlett, page 86)

Clough's invention made its maiden trip from Sunapee to Newport, on or before July 4, 1869, when a sketch of the inventor and his machine appeared in the *Newport Argus.*

Potter's Place, Andover, is named after Richard Potter, and famed slight-of-hand artist (magician) who also misses Metcalf's list.

In addition to those on Metcalf's list, are the many other citizens, not New Hampshire natives, in whom regional pride rested. John Hay stands out as one who lived in the affection of his New Hampshire neighbors. Late in the 1890s, John Hay, former secretary to President Abraham Lincoln and secretary of state to Presidents McKinley and Theodore Roosevelt, built an estate on Lake Sunapee in Newbury which became, for awhile, the summer home of American foreign policy. "This was true

In 1923, fire destroyed Harlakenden, this beautiful residence in Cornish, site of Woodrow Wilson's first Summer White House. New Hampshire, although not a Democratic state, took great pride in the fact of Wilson's residency. The house belonged to Winston Churchill, noted American writer, who became part of the Cornish art colony in 1898. Churchill's 1906 novel, Coniston, "an acute and effective novel dealing with boss-rule in old-time New Hampshire politics led to Churchill's own active involvement in New Hampshire politics. He had been a supporter and friend of Theodore Roosevelt, who visited the area in 1902 and hunted in Corbin's Park."

(Wade, pages 61-62)
The president and his family summered here from 1913 to 1915, after which the town that had lured upper-class summer residents for decades, proved an inadequate

substitute for the New Jersey seashore haunts that Mrs. Wilson preferred. The photograph was published by Charles Skinner, Apothecaries Hall, Windsor, Vermont. Courtesy of New Hampshire Historical Society

Ira B. Allen of Allen's Lane, Hanover, 1887, Hanover Stage Coach Driver. Courtesy of Dartmouth College Library; gift of Mary A. Fletcher

during the 'Boxer' difficulties in China in 1900, and during the Panama negotiations in 1903." President Roosevelt visited Hay at Lake Sunapee August, 1902. Secretary Hay died there on July 1, 1905. (Squires, pages 432-433)

Few know of the role of Austin Corbin, born in Newport, 1827, in saving the buffalo from extinction. A talented lawyer, businessman, and empire builder, he maintained the family homestead as a summer home, greatly increasing its land holdings and eventually conceiving the idea of establishing a vast game preserve in the area for buffalo and other threatened species. When, in 1886, he learned of the National Museum's difficulty in locating buffalo in the west, he began a conservation effort. By 1888, his twenty-five thousand-acre Blue Mountain Forest Park, located on portions of Cornish, Croydon, Plainfield, Grantham, and Newport, was incorporated and stocked with 30 buffalo, 140 deer of four different species, 35 moose, 135 elk, 14 wild boar from Germany's Black Forest, 6 antelope, caribou, and bighorn mountain goats. All flourished but the caribou, goats, and moose. In time, it became a hunting ground for wealthy visitors. Locals were most excited by the buffalo and the preserve, also known locally as "Corbin's Park," was successful in providing zoos with buffalo. He didn't live "to see the full flowering of his project, for in June 1896 Austin Corbin was killed when thrown from his carriage by a runaway team. The animal kingdom had its

revenge on the jailor." (Wade, pages 95-100) In fact, this glib commentary is only partially apt for Corbin's efforts led to the eventual stabilization of the American buffalo population.

Southwestern New Hampshire is boastful of the facts that Dublin began the nation's first free library in 1822 and Peterborough, the nation's first public library in 1833.

Dublin, long a favorite resort, boasts a history of distinguished summer folk. Among the famous who lived for extended periods in the town at the foot of Mount Monadnock are Admiral Byrd, Amy Lowell, Mark Twain, and Lord Percy and family when he was British ambassador to the United States.

Among the Grand Monadnock's greatest admirers and frequent visitors were Ralph Waldo Emerson, Henry David Thoreau, and William Ellery Channing.

Area towns pay tribute to the long memories of their citizens, as does Sutton. Of its "Honorable Women," wives of the first settlers, two are remembered for their formidable intellectual powers:

Mrs. Abraham Peasley was social, kind, and cheerful, and might be called a living encyclopedia. She had a wonderful remembrance of all events connected with the first settlements and everything else.

Mrs. Cornelius Bean, who lived to be nearly 100 years of age, was always ready to assist the sick.

Historical marker, Guild (Newport).
Photo by Armand Szainer

She was cheerful and happy to the last; possessed a very strong memory. (Worthen, page 239)

The town of Sharon is justly proud of a resident trailblazer in local women's history.

Mrs. Perry, daughter of Thomas and Ellen W. Wilson, was the first woman in New Hampshire to serve in the selectman's office—in 1928. Mrs. Perry was also the first woman Representative to go from Sharon. She . . . was brought up in politics, but when she took her first office, it was almost necessity, there were at that time so few people living in the town. Her brother and young Putney wanted a town treasurer. Mrs. Perry scorned just one office, but if she could be clerk besides, she would serve. She was elected to both offices. In 1927-29, too, she was a member of the State Legislature and in 1930 and '38 a delegate to the Constitutional Convention. The Town Records of these years, in fact, and as early as 1919 show most of the local offices filled by Wilsons. Harold A. Wilson, a brother of Mrs. Perry, had been tax collector since 1926. (King, page 114)

These and countless other indiviuals have contributed to the region's sense of importance. Many untold stories lie within its boundaries, all potential sources of inspiration to those who follow in their wake.

American aviator, Amelia Earhart (1897-1937), arrived at the Twin State Airport in Lebanon early in the morning of October 4, 1933, on a speaking and promotional trip to the area. The enthusiasm of the crowds acknowledges the esteem in which she was held by local citizens of all ages. Here she is being mobbed on the College Green in Hanover before her scheduled address to the student body at Dartmouth College. After her talk, Earhart consulted with area officials and business people concerning a proposed commercial airline between the upper Connecticut River Valley and Boston which she was promoting.
Earhart had been the first woman to fly the Atlantic (1928) and the first pilot to fly between Hawaii and California in 1935. Her mysterious disappearance over the Pacific Ocean a few years after this celebrated visit to western New Hampshire turned the accomplished Earhart into an enduring national legend. Courtesy of Dartmouth College Library

The photograph of Mr. Fileau and his dog brings to mind the portraiture convention of depicting subjects surrounded by those things that best characterize them. Mr. Fileau and his wife were among twenty-eight locals who met on November 16, 1886, at the instigation of the Agricultural College's Professor Charles H. Pettee, to revive the Grange which had languished for seven years. The regenerated organization went on to flourish in Hanover for the next thirty years before beginning its decline. Courtesy of Dartmouth College Library

9
PHOTOGRAPHERS AND THE ART OF PHOTOGRAPHY

In a sense, this entire book celebrates the art of the photographer in documenting the culture of western New Hampshires's heritage. These few photographs give us a chance to make particular mention of the history of the occupation itself and some of the aspects of the art of the photographer that existing examples illustrate. Considering that photography was only invented in 1839, it is remarkable that the region supported dozens of professional photographers who, by mid-century, with camera, tripod and film of cumbersome size and weight, actively pursued business in town and countryside, at tourist attractions, private parties, businesses, civic events, and among private citizens. It is also not an exaggeration to consider the nineteenth-century photographers as pioneer promoters of tourism.

At least thirty-five professional photographers were at work in the upper New Hampshire Connecticut River Valley before 1870 and many more within the whole of the state's western regions. The earliest documented commercial photographer in Hanover was a black man by the name of Augustus Washington who, as a freshman at Dartmouth College, earned enough to settle his debts before moving south to Hartford, Connecticut, to teach school. Keene's earliest photographer opened shop in 1840! Within a decade a half-dozen or more had gone into business there.

This portrait of photographer C. E. Lewis (1844-1921), comes from an 1889 album. Greg Drake, a meticulous researcher of photographic history in the region, places him as one of the Lewis brothers, probably first working out of Northfield, Vermont. He moved to Lebanon where he worked as a photographer from 1882 to 1898. His nephew, George R. Lewis, succeeded him, being active from 1898-1902.

Drake speculates that both were at one time or another in Lebanon, part of a Lewis Brothers business. The inability of Drake to pin down the precise professional doings of this public citizen (he also served as Lebanon's Water Commissioner from about 1890) points up the elusiveness of documentary data concerning the careers of professional photographers historically. Courtesy of Dartmouth College Library

Through creative marketing, early photographers left us with a wealth of documentary photographs of our nineteenth-century ancestors. Through their cameras we see their neighbors and their times. We can only assume that they, themselves, are representatives of the tastes and values of their communities.

The approach of the first generation of photographers seems to be that of the painter. Images are well composed and inherently interesting. It is always possible to see the photographer's point of view and usually possible to discern subtleties of narrative exposition in the finished pieces. There exists a parallel between the subjects documented by writers or local historians and those documented by visual artists.

Since photography entered the realm of business so quickly, photographers directed their output toward the consumer from the beginning. In addition to personal commissions, they took pictures of what they thought the public would buy. An analysis of the body of their work, therefore, gives us clues as to what were the key interests of the mid-to late-century consumer in the region. Our ancestors valued their churches, homes, public buildings, workplaces, social groups, schools, patriotic institutions, heroes, festivals, occupations, animals, triumphs, and leisure time. A typical collection of early photographs, therefore, falls roughly into the same categories as those of a period town history.

The photographer assumed the role of the portrait painter in nineteenth-century America and brought that upper-class genre within the financial grasp of the whole population. As artists, photographers freely altered scenes to provide interesting images. This is particularly true of photographs that included people. The tenets of the portrait studio held sway. Props, costumes, and inventive poses all assumed a place in studio-made photographs. The photographer on location improvised creative attributes appropriate to the setting and subject. Photo-

graphs of picnickers, for example, would be artfully arranged against an interesting natural background. If the location was someone's home or summer camp, suitable props would find their way into the pictures.

Amateur photographers supplement to some degree our record of the past but it is to the professional photographer that our attention turns at this point. No doubt, most of the first generation of professional photographers began as rank amateurs themselves, a chapter of their history of which we know practically nothing.

Regional views were the bread and butter of the photographer's trade. It is unclear, at times, what photographs are from a particular studio and which ones are purchased from other photographers for inclusion in a studio's sales catalog. There is ample evidence that local printers and publishers cooperated with local photographers in producing and marketing their visual wares.

Jotham A. French, Keene

Keene's 1968 town history, *Upper Ashuelot*, places Jotham A. French among the first commercial photographers in Keene. He and Chester Allen opened a business in the 1840s, just a few years after jeweler and watchmaker Edward Poole's 1840 photographic experiments, the earliest known to have been done there by a local photographer. In 1861, Jotham A. French started a photography business in the old Richards Block with Daniel W. Sawyer. In 1866, the year after fire destroyed their gallery, they moved to the recently built Bridgeman Block. Five years later, French bought out his partner and by 1874 he was advertising two thousand stereoscopic views in his catalog. In 1890 he published a souvenir booklet on Keene containing sixty scenes. His business was last listed in the 1897-1898 Keene city directory which

This is one of a pair of portraits of Howard Henry Harrison Langill (1849-1914) and his wife included in an 1889 album. Both prints, mounted on heavy, gilt embossed card stock, have an elaborate business advertisement for the Langill Studio on the back.

Langill had been an itinerant photographer before he set up his Hanover studio in 1882. His body of work includes large-scale coverage of Dartmouth College events and extensive documentation of the town and its environs. His nephew and namesake, Henry Howard Barrett, worked with him after the turn of the century, eventually succeeding him. Drake places the elder Langill in a second studio at White River Junction for the year 1889. Well respected as a portrait photographer, Langill executed a fine pair of portraits of his fellow-photographer and wife, Mr. and Mrs. H. O. Bly. Courtesy of Dartmouth College Library

Henry Osgood Bly is pictured at right in this fascinating caricature-like assemblage by an unknown photographer. The identity of the two other figures is uncertain. It bears the hallmark of a private joke. The work of H. O. Bly, whose studio was active in Hanover from 1860 to 1878, is among the most striking Upper Valley photography of the period. Both a portrait and landscape artist, many of Bly's stereographic images comprise a collection at Dartmouth College Photo Archives. Courtesy of Dartmouth College Library

H. O. Bly's Photographic Trade Advertisement, Hanover. The imprint reads: FROM H. O. BLY'S Photograph Gallery HANOVER, N.H. Photographs in any style, TINTYPES, AMBROTYPES AND FERREOTYPES OF ANY SIZE. Stereoscopic Views, Stereoscopes, Chromos, Albums, Frames, &tc., for sale.

Most photographers of the period advertised their stock on the backs of their photographs. Courtesy of Dartmouth College Library

The anonymous artist who penned this simple sketch of Henry Osgood Bly's Photograpy Gallery evidences some training in scale and perspective. Situated above a hardware store on Hanover's Main Street, Bly's studio was comfortable and appropriately equipped for studio portraiture. The sketch reveals that Bly was aware of effective techniques for lighting his subjects. Few props were necessary to create the straightforward portraits in which he specialized. However, when Bly used painted backdrops, he skillfully integrated them into the studio's environment with carefully chosen, well placed props. Courtesy of Dartmouth College Library

adds up to a half century as an active documenter of the region.

Disasters

Where once had floated the harvest of the northern forests in turbulent and festive log drives, by the 1920s, it was unusual for anything of significance to disturb the tranquil passage of the seasons on the Connecticut River. For this reason alone, natural disasters like fire or flood filled the air with excitement—impending dangers or financial penalty notwithstanding. The tragic muse works hard in the lives of photographers and inspire some truly arresting visual documents of western New Hampshire's most heightened moments. As they play themselves out, the stressful events dissolve into local memory, to be kept alive by stories of the human dramas, sad, joyful, or funny, that enlivened the course of events.

Before the photographer, writers and oral tradition provided much of the documentation of local drama and tragedy. Typical examples include accounts of criminal justice, odd turns of nature, and devastating accidents.

Thos. McCoy once fancied that his corn in the field was disappearing too fast, and found a beaten track thro' the woods direct to the field. He went to Temple and borrowed a bear trap with teeth from Major Hale, and set it in the track. Mr. Treadwell made a rolling bee (black logs,) which was common in those days. The neighbors were all collected at the rolling and all at [o]nce they heard a dreadful screaming in the woods. Not knowing what could be the matter they all ran to the spot, where they found Sewall Parker, (then a boy,) in the trap. They took him out and carried him home, (poor Sewall carried the scar made by the teeth of the trap to his grave). Old Abel (his father) being absent at the time came to where they were at work and said to Tom McCoy "Where's Sewall?" The answer was,

"Gath, I vow I don't know, I'm not Sewall's keeper,"— — "you, Tom McCoy! you set a trap to catch my boy." One of Sewall's sisters was living at James Templeton's one winter and Sewall went there on an errand, and it was said she slipped a lump of butter into Sewall's bosom. Wm. Templeton, suspecting what was there invited S. to go to the barn and when there nothing would do but he must wrestle with him, and hugged him up until the butter melted and ran down through his "unmentionables." In Sewall's later days...nothing would put him in a rage so quick as to mention the name of bear trap or butter. (Peterborough Historical Society, pages 162-163)

Hanging

Josiah Burnham was executed in Haverhill on August 12, 1806, for the murders of Russell Freeman, Esquire and Capt. Joseph Starkweather. The account of the event reveals much about the criminal justice system of the time.

Burnham and his victims were in prison for debt, and occupied the same room. The cause of Burnham's murderous assault is not known, as the prisoners had conducted themselves with general mildness and submission whilst confined together. Burnham in his speech from the gallows [said], "I was carried away with my passions...."

The hanging of Burnham was a great occasion. It is estimated that fully 10,000 people gathered on the west side of Powder House hill....They came from near and far, in carts and in wagons, on horse-back and on foot, old men and young men, beaux and lassies, mothers with babes in their arms, and even invalids. The event took place with much ceremony. A military guard escorted the prisoner from the jail to the scaffold, and a long sermon,

Titled "The Miller at Home," this effectively staged portrait of a miller, not at home, but seated next to the millstone, places him right at the heart of his workplace. This is perhaps a wry comment on the lifestyle of some miller know to the artist. The typical miller would have lived in the millhouse nearby. The photograph typifies the theatricality imposed on many documentary photographs of old-time New Hampshire life. The photographer as artist and set designer is splendidly evident in this Kilburn Brothers photograph.

Familiarity with the miller's operations is implied by the arrangement of the props and saves the picture from romantic overstatement. The nineteenth-century miller ground such grains as wheat, rye, barley, and oats but by far the greatest portion of his business was the grinding of corn, both kernels and cobs. the latter made an inferior quality product that farmers used primarily for animal feed. One noted Lancaster miller was David Greenlief of whom it was said, he "was a man full of reminiscences that pleased his customers to hear while

waiting for their grists to be ground, for in those days people took their grists to the mill in a bag thrown across the back of a horse, on top of which they rode, and waited for the grain to be ground and took it home in the same way. The interval of waiting was often filled by an entertaining bit of story-telling by the miller." (Somers, page 382.)

The miller's payment was a measure of each bag of grist milled. All baskets and firkins served also as measures. What looks like a weights scale sits on the counter behind the bushel of cornhusks. Photographed and published by the Kilburn brothers of Littleton, the stereograph is No. 539 of the studio's stereographic offerings. Courtesy of New Hampshire Historical Society

Such historical reenactments were part of the social life of our nineteenth-century forebears. Here, a group of Hanover old-timers demonstrate the domestic skills of an earlier day, skills in the living memories of very few Hanover residents of the late nineteenth century. The mirror on the mantle reflects a camera shy member of the living diorama. The actors dress in old-fashioned garb, a convention in theatrical depictions of early American life. The photograph is identified as "a Burrell photo." Courtesy of Dartmouth College Library

A number of nineteenth-century professional photographers in the western regions of the state were accomplished portrait artists and Bly was among them. The annotation on the back of this Bly portrait of one of Hanover's mid-nineteenth-century residents reads: "Aunt Sophie Jones colored woman lived probably on 'Nigger Hill' W. Lebanon road out of town." Since the early nineteenth century the region had an ongoing population of Negroes, as they were

listed in early census records. Some came as servants or slaves to local settlers. Dartmouth's first president, Eleazar Wheelock, had Negros in his household. This photograph, when compared to the drawing of Bly's studio, p. 155, informs the viewer that the floor was crosshatched in a design set diagonally to the back wall, a good aesthetic choice for the space. Bly uses the table appearing in the sketch as a prop in this warm portrait of Mrs. Jones. Courtesy of Dartmouth College Library

An owner of this stereograph identified the scene, in glorious script and verbal understatement, "General view of Jaffrey Centre, N. H." It reminds one that the stereograph had multiple purposes in its heyday, one important one being public relations that communities used to lure tourists to the area. This masterful advertisement for Jaffrey downplays the Grand Monadnock and dwells, instead, on the romantic view of farmlife. The mower appears oblivious to the overseer in top hat and frock coat standing knee deep in the mown hay. The cemetery in the middle distance is an effective visual lead in to the village roofs in the valley. Identification on the back of the card stock mount identifies the photographer and publisher as George H. Scripture, No. 2, French's Block, Peterborough, New Hampshire. Courtesy of New Hampshire Historical Society

Crowd Assembled at the Warden farm, after Murder Suspect Apprehended. Courtesy of Dartmouth College Library

Although the photo is not imprinted by a photographer, it is very like the work of the H. H. H. Langill Studio, the assiduous visual chronicler of Hanover people, scenery, sights, and happenings. The starkness of the scene captures the dark mood surrounding a truly horrific event in the life of the small village.

preceded by singing and prayer, was preached by the Rev. David Southerland of Bath to the immense concourse of people who listened with deep emotion to the preacher. After these were ended Burnham was given an opportunity to address the multitude, which he did in a faltering and broken speech, the substance, however, of which was a confession of his crime and the justice of his punishment. One suggestive thing he mentions in his speech, which illustrates the peculiar theological bias of the times, vis., that he had been a believer in the doctrine of universal salvation, and but for this he would not have committed the crime for which he was about to suffer, and he admonished his hearers to beware of this doctrine. He was entirely unmoved during all the ordeal at the gallows, evincing not the slightest feeling at the eloquence and impressive words of the preacher, which melted the vast audience into tears and sobbing. (Bittinger, pages 395-396)

Lebanon—Fire of May 10, 1887

A very large area of Lebanon, indeed, was burned in this fire, including the entire O. W. Baldwin Block on Hanover Street. Commenting on the tradition of helping one's neighbors that prevailed in the region, one local historian recalls:

We are glad, too, that we have been good neighbors to the folks in next-door towns. Way back in 1816 our doctors went to Warren to help in their spotted fever epidemic. (We call it meningitis today.) Then there was the May morning in 1887 when a hill farmer shouted, "Hurry, Thomas, Leb is all afire," and we joined firefighters from all over the state.

Charles Downs writes a gripping account of the fire in his history of Lebanon (1908). It reads like a baseball announcer's running account of the last inning of the seventh game of the World's Series. A veritable melodrama, he titles it: "At Last, LEBANAN'S GREAT CALAMITY HAS COME—80 BUILDINGS BURNED—600 MEN THROWN OUT OF EMPLOYMENT—40 FAMILIES HOMELESS." The first paragraph encapsulates the tragedy, setting the before-and-after scenes:

When Monday's sun set peacefully in the west the busy hum of industry in twenty or more manufacturing establishments, large and small, on five dams, on both sides of the Mascoma River in the center village of this town, had just ceased for the day, and the 600 employees therein wended their way to their homes for the night's rest preparatory to another day's toil. When Tuesday's sun rose every one of those shops and mills was a heap of

Women are conspicuous by their absence in this photograph. The body language of the expectant crowd projects a sinister quality that emanates from the photograph to the viewer. The artist, working under poor conditions, nevertheless captures the attitude of the crowd, many of whom were personally acquainted with the victim and the murderer.

Christie Warden was murdered on July 17, 1891, in Hanover's Vale of Tempe off the road (now Reservoir Road) that led to the Warden Farm.

She was dragged away at gunpoint from her mother, sister, and a neighbor woman as the four were returning home from a Hanover Grange meeting by a former Warden Farm hired hand, Frank Almy.

Before help could arrive, Warden was dead. She had been shot and mutilated. Almy, whose criminal background was revealed only after the murder, led local townspeople and authorities on a thirty-one-day manhunt before he was discovered hiding out in the hayloft of the Warden barn. The men crowded in the Warden barnyard are waiting for a glimpse of the murderer who is about to be removed from the premises by the Sheriff. What transpired then seems shocking a century later. After surrendering his pistols, Almy was taken to the Wheelock House, now the Hanover Inn. After his wounds were

BEFORE THE FIRE MAY 10. 1887.

Hidey-hole of Christie Warden's Murderer, Warden Barn, Hanover. Courtesy of New Hampshire Historical Society

These photographs were taken on Tuesday, August 18, 1891 the date of Almy's capture.

dressed, a crowd that filled the street in front of the hotel demanded a closeup view of the murderer. Because of the crowd's ugly temper, its demands were granted and 1500 people filed past Almy, who lay in his hotel room on a narrow cot. The crowd was persuaded to disperse when Almy fainted.

He was tried and convicted of first degree murder in Plymouth courthouse, and was sentenced to hang. After a long delay, due to legal technicalities, sentence was carried out in Concord State Prison on May 16, 1893. Invitations, printed on black cards, were issued for his hanging, and a special train was run from Hanover to Concord. (Robert P. Richmond in Childs' pages 161-172)

"Before the Fire of May 10, 1887" and "Mascoma St., Looking West . . . West Park St." reads the caption of this anonymous photo. A couple of the signs are readable: TRANSIENT LIVERY STABLE on the right; STORE WARE ROOMS above PAINTS SILKS, on the building to the left of the stables implies a large general store; STOVES is on the building along the side street. In the foreground one can decipher: POND SEXTRACT. Much more of the village than that shown here was destroyed by the catastrophe. Courtesy of Dartmouth College Library

The "Burned District," as this photo was quaintly captioned at the time, depicts Lebanon, New Hampshire, after the apalling fire of May 10, 1887. The view looks east "where Everett Mill now stands," as is noted on the original photo. The scene looks as if considerable cleanup had already been accomplished with the stone foundations and various granite forms scattered through the scene looking like markers in an unintentional graveyard. Such scenes are morbidly attractive to the populace, several small groups of whom linger here and there. A few look like workers in overalls, but others are probably curiosity seekers, perhaps, mourning a neighborhood once teeming with townspeople and industry. Courtesy of New Hampshire Historical Society

The dramatic scope of this scene of devastation details the community response to the human tragedy that resulted from the derailing of the Montreal Express a few miles outside of Norwich station. A flawed section of rail caused the original calamity but it was the fire, fed by fuel from the freshly stoked stoves and lamps, that led to the horrific loss of life. The train fell on the solidly frozen surface of the White River beneath the Hartford, Vermont, rail-road bridge near the Paine farmhouse which opened its doors to the wounded. Visible are the lines of waiting horse-drawn vehicles stretching in both directions, the array of volunteers, the two assisting trains, one from each side of the river, the rail cart and the hastily constructed log path over which the victims were carried to the top of the riverbank en route to the shelter of the farmhouse. The groups of onlookers at either end of the bridge abutments, men and women, seem to wear an aspect of

mourning in keeping with the abjectness of the row of granite bridge piers that no longer carry their accustomed burden.
Courtesy of Dartmouth College Library

smouldering ruins, after a desperate fight of five hours to save them, and the devastation was being stayed for want of anything on which to feed down the river, and the interposition of brick walls and piles of green logs, as well as by the arrival of timely help, in other directions. (Downs, pages 384-385)

The fire was first noticed at 12:45 a.m. The combination of highly combustible materials, architectural structures that allowed gusts of wind to feed the fire, and the intensity of the heat prevented timely firefighting. Water power failed and the telephone to Concord was out of order. It was over an hour before help could be summoned by phone. Hanover had to be roused by messenger. (Ironically, a waterworks, as yet unbuilt, was under contract to the town.) "Our fire department, 120 men, with the appliances they had, were never intended to cope with such a fire, and were powerless before it," Downs moans. The waterwheel burnt up and "[t]here was nothing now but hand engines to fight the largest fire New Hampshire ever saw—two or

three hand engines and a little extinguisher."

The fire raced through the mills, and up the street. The firefighters had few strokes of luck to bolster their efforts. Both sides of the river became involved and the destruction was complete. Help did eventually arrive from Concord (at 5:45 a.m.) and from both sides of the border. Insurance maps of the village record that eighty buildings, not counting sheds or out buildings, were destroyed. Downs concludes his remarks with complete insurance information, the entire account a masterful verbal document that these photos nicely enhance. One unintentional comic note enters the scenario when, near its conclusion, Downs breaks the flow of his narrative to comment on the phenomenal speed of the Concord company's trip. Such a feat was remarkable in its own right and Downs gives it due respect.

Just as this last fight had been successfully made, and it became reasonably sure that the last house was burning, the steam engine Governor Hill and Kearsarge hose carriage arrived from Concord,

There were twenty views of the railroad disaster that the H. H. H. Langill Studios of Hanover offered as souvenirs. They cost from thirty to sixty cents apiece, depending on size. The view from the south abutment of the bridge looks down on the section of the ice where the cars struck. Courtesy of Dartmouth College Library

The trestle bridge that replaced the Hartford Vermont bridge following the "Great Rail Road Accident" of February 6, 1887, rests on the original stone piers and abutments which had not been destroyed in the accident. That the trestle bridge safely supports the train adds to the effectiveness of this photo when viewed in relationship to the earlier images of the burnt and mangled cars, the morgue and the defective pieces of railing that caused the wreck. Courtesy of Dartmouth College Library

Railroad Collision near Andover Centre, New Hampshire 1885. The photographer's method of advertising his documentary views of the collision that took place on a Sunday morning, October 18, 1885, implies that the victims of this accident were known to the local public. In addition to his studio advertisement, photographer W. G. C. Kimball lists by name and job, those killed. Photo by W. G. C. Kimball; Courtesy of New Hampshire Historical Society

After about 1890, the track between Contoocook and Claremont was not well-maintained. This was true for many of the lesser lines. The result was frequent delay, even derailment of trains as they traveled the deteriorating rails. Bad weather lent further hazards to the speeding trains. Inaccurate signals, mistakes in setting rail switches and other human error also took their toll. In June 1890, two Boston and Maine Passenger Division freights collided head-on at the stone culvert above Olcott Falls producing this twisted wreck. The customary crowd of people, helping out or simply curious, mills about he scene. Courtesy of Dartmouth College Library

The double-arched stone Cheshire Railroad Bridge and the Tucker Toll Bridge safely withstand the highwater of April 15, 1907 [?]. Taken from Walpole, the Bellows Falls end of the bridge is to the right. The photo was taken by the Lewis A. Brown Studio of Brattleboro, Vermont, and sold as a postcard earlier in the century. It is interesting to compare this photo with an earlier one (p. 76) showing the two bridges standing high above the falls on a normal day. Courtesy of Richard E. Roy

about 5:45 o'clock, having made the trip of 65 miles in 85 minutes with two stops, one of which was four minutes. This is the quickest time ever made on the road except possibly that in competition for the Canadian mails about thirty years ago, when an engine made the trip from White River Junction to Concord, 70 miles, in 90 minutes. (page 391)

Great Rail Road Accident! at Hartford, Vt. Feb. 5, 1887 And Other Rail Accidents

When the Montreal Express derailed on February 5, 1887, just north of Norwich Station destroying the Hartford, Vermont, railroad bridge and sending the train, its passengers, and freight down to the ice below, the tragedy touched the lives of many who lived in the Connecticut River Valley near Hanover. Among the victims were some local residents, including a couple of Dartmouth College students who had boarded the train only minutes before the derailment. An international outcry against the practice of using oil and wood fuel in the passenger compartments stemmed from the generally held belief that few lives would have been lost had the fuel not fed the fire. The furor led to the introduction of national safety code regulations for the railroads, the first in the world.

Newspaper accounts and an obituary verse ballad drawn from them focus on individual tragedies giving poignant evidence of the personal pain that citzens of the region suffered. "The Central Vermont Railroad Tragedy" was sung by local singers in the years following the event. The following version of the ballad is from the singing of the MacArthur Family who learned it from the *New Green Mountain Songster*. They called it "Central Vermont." (Morley and MacArthur, page 14)

'Twas the Montreal Express, it was speeding at its best
When at Hartford bridge it struck a broken rail.
Then with a fearful crash, to the river it was dashed
And a hundred souls went down to meet their fate.

Horror met the victims' gaze as the wreck was soon ablaze
And fainting cries of help were sad to hear.
None responded to the call, so they perished one and all
In the Central Vermont Railroad Tragedy.

.   .   .   .

There was one I'll not forget, that was little Joe Lagret.
He was with his father on that fatal night.
He wasn't injured in the fall but when he heard his father call
From the wreck he tried to save him but in vain.

"Alas, my boy," said he, "there is no hope for me."
As the flames around his head began to curl.
Little Joe began to cry when his father said, "Goodbye,
We'll meet again up in another world."

The episode of the father and son is true. Their real names were Dieu Donne Maigret, father, and Joseph Maigret, son, from Quebec. (Ballard et al, page 158)

H. H. H. Langill of Hanover was an enterprising photographer who knew what kinds of souvenir photographs would sell. An indefatigable promoter of his stock, Langill took numerous photographs of the railway accident. Perhaps to modern sensibilities some of his subjects crowd the edge of morbidity; nonetheless, the public's interest in the miniscule detail of public or

private disaster has fed the errant journalist through the centuries. Langill knew his public well. The geography of the event helped Langill's sales tremendously but there were several aspects of the disaster that made it of interest to a wider than local audience. Among them was the technical interest of engineers, manufacturers, and others. Langill accommodated such interest by photographing the pieces of flawed railing and machinery implicated as causing the fatal crash. Langill identified one photo as "Pieces of broken rail," and another as "Broken end of journal," a journal being "that part of a shaft or axle in actual contact with a bearing." *(American College Dictionary)* The archives of the Thayer School of Civil Engineering at Dartmouth has prints of the broken rails, which were studied by the engineering students.

That Langill advertised these technical views as part of a complete set indicated that he expected a wide audience for them, not merely schools of engineering. Indeed, many in the nineteenth century were vitally interested in the technical aspects of railroading, which was, after all, the most imposing of the Industrial Revolution's inventions at that time and the symbol of the opening of America. What today is of importance mainly to the railroad buff or to the civil engineer was of far more general interest a century ago. Although the majority of views of the accident, being of the scene itself, satisfied the more prurient instincts of the photographer's clientele, Langill did not forget the potential customers for his more mundane subjects.

Train wrecks were becoming increasingly common by the turn of the century. By 1900, in Temple, personal injuries escalated. "A number of people in recent years had been killed or injured when their horse-drawn vehicles were struck by trains, so the Boston & Maine finally placed flagmen at the four crossings." (Historical Society of Temple, page 20)

Perhaps the most bizarre train accident in the Peterborough area was the runaway boxcar that got

This photo probably dates from the 1927 or an earlier flood. While the date of the photo is uncertain, the enterprising "bread people," as the photo's annotator calls them, make a satisfying subject. The silhouetted human figures and the ripples emanating from the dipped oars add theatricality to the scene, empha-sized by the clouded portions of the landscape and the distorted reflection of the little boat and its burden. The mundane activity of delivering bread to Hanover suddenly becomes a lifeline to stranded customers, lending an aesthetic tension to this thoroughly captivating image.

Bread, milk, and fuel were the three commodities that took priority during periods of prolonged deprivation. In the 1936 flood, for example, Charlestown was completely closed to traffic for four days. On the fifth, "the road was opened to Bellows Falls, only to milk, bread and gas trucks. It was impossible to move milk out of Charlestown for three days, and following that period it was trucked direct to Boston." (Frizzell et al., pages 122-123) Courtesy of Dartmouth College Library

away in Jaffery and made its unattended way down to Peterborough where it shot across Main Street and into the parking lot at Centertown, hit an automobile in the Cumberland Farms parking lot and stopped. This occurrence, on October 29, 1969, caused quite a stir. Current resident Blake Tewksbury remembers being at Tom Nichols' house when Nichols, an insurance agent, got a call from a customer who said,

"My car's been run over by a railroad car."

"Where was it parked?," Tom [Nichols] asked him.

"In front of Cumberland Farms' Store." the guy said.

Then Tom says, "Go back to bed and sleep it off. You can call me tomorrow," and he hung up.

Blake laughed at the recollection, and added, "no-body would have believed a story like that right around 'Hallowe'en."

The caller may have been assistant superintendent of schools, Frank Finley who is pictured at the time, in the local paper, looking mournfully at his brand new Oldsmobile, "crushed in the freak accident." The *Petersborough Transcript* took a similarly comic tone in their comments on the event when they looked back on the highlights of the year's news. "Peterborough's last experience with 'downtown' freight 'service' was on Oct. 29, 1969, when two box cars rolled in from Jaffrey, and ended up on Main St. " The paper called it "1969's event of the year." (*Peterborough Transcript,* January 1, 1970, pages 1, 7).

Robert Richardson, longtime resident of Mill Street, remembers "railroad boxcars loading coal into Hafeli's sheds, lined up along the river, back of where Yankee is, now."

Long time residents of Eastview, Harrisville, remember that people "could set their clocks" by the morning milk trains. The children of Eastview and other towns, would take the daily train to Keene to attend high school.

Water Rising at Ledyard Bridge, 1936, Aerial View. Courtesy of Dartmouth College Library

Residents Watching Waters Rise From Ledyard Bridge 1936. Photograph Looks Toward Hanover. Courtesy of Dartmouth College Library

Few bankruptcy sales are set so effectively as is this one at the old W. S. Farnsworth Sons Company in the old Brennan Block, teetering on the corner of Summer and Main streets in Peterborough. The sign reads: "Bankrupt Stock Groceries, Hardware, Dry Goods, Shoes, Paint. Everything Must be Sold." The shadow of the wrought iron arch decorating the old water trough lies in the foreground. The swell of the floodwaters upended the porch roof support posts that have landed like Pick-up Sticks across the porch railing. Courtesy of Peterborough Historical Society

Floods and Hurricanes

Due to its rivers, lakes, and ponds, the region has an eventful history of highwater and flooding. For almost two hundred years, private and public records have kept track of the vicissitudes of the local weather. Damaging floods have been recorded in the western regions for the years 1771, 1801, 1813, 1818, 1828, 1839, 1850, 1866, 1882, 1884, 1886, 1889, 1895, 1896, 1900, 1907, 1908, 1913, 1914, 1927, 1933, 1936, 1938, and 1973. This list is incomplete and does not include highwater where flooding was not widespread.

Hurricane and Flood in 1775

Diary entry of Abner Sanger, May 28, 1775: Toward night comes up a terrible hurricane thundershower. Trees are whirled down in great plenty. After the shower is over I go up to Carpenter's to find Mother's cow. (page 45)

Diary entry of Abner Sanger, November 22, 1775: "This remarkable great rain causes a great flood." (page 68)

The Great Whirlwind of 1821

The New London account of the Great Whirlwind of 1821 represents it as a tornado, every bit as terrifying as the 1938 hurricane.

All the trees in an orchard of one hundred, without a single exception, were prostrated, and one half were carried entirely away. . . . [Debris left unclaimed until a fire], retracing the course of the tornado, burned up the greater part of the debris. . . . While the woods were on fire the odor of burning honey stored by wild bees was wafted to a great distance, and at night on Colby Hill an ordinary newspaper could be read with ease. (Myra Lord, page 128)

Charlestown Bridge

An eyewitness, Mrs. A. F. Nims, describes how the Charlestown bridge went out in a flood in 1839 when she was seven years of age.

I remember the incident well. My father (James Milliken) was watering his horse in the barnyard (#321 [i.e. town lot]) when he saw it coming. He called his family to see it and mounting his horse without saddle or bridle rode to see the fate of the Tucker Bridge (Toll bridge at Bellows Falls). The

South Charlestown Bridge rode grandly upon the current until it pitched over the first rapid when one corner struck a rock and went to pieces all at once and nothing first. (Frizell et al., page 128)

1839 was a year of remarkable weather in which four unusual storms hit the region, the first a great rainstorm in January that caused tremendous highwater all over New England from the melting of snow.

According to local sources, "[t]he ice on the Connecticut and Ashuelot Rivers broke up and many bridges were carried away." This storm overlapped with another that caused destruction throughout the entire northeast and middle Atlantic states. Two violent snowstorms closed out the year. "It took nine hours for a sleigh to get to Keene from Walpole," December 18th, after three days of snow and Sunday's mail arrived Wednesday. Less than two weeks later, another nor'easter caused an even longer delay of the mail, with "[t]he mail carrier from Concord [having] to bring the mail a portion of the way on his back." (Keene History Committee, page 558)

The 1839 account fails to note that the Tucker Toll Bridge, an uncovered bridge and only the second to have spanned the river at that spot, had survived the floodwaters. It was, however, badly damaged and replaced within the decade by the covered bridge shown on page 162.

Floods

In the autumn of '67 there was a flood. His brother Benjamin was afraid of the water and Charles [Wilson] took him on his back. The children saw a pig carried into the meadow—a terrifying sight to them. (King, page 114)

The two floods mentioned by local historians again and again are the floods of 1927 and of 1936. Although the hurricane of 1938 caused flooding and spectacular wind damage, its floods did not compare with 1936 when the state's western regions were virtually afloat. The town of Peterborough suffered a double tragedy when raging fire destroyed its handsome, historic downtown business block the afternoon of the flood.

Of the 1927 flood, one Hanover chronicler wryly comments,

[d]uring the November flood of 1927 a possibly prejudiced faculty [of Dartmouth College] felt that the students were spending more time in watching the Connecticut and White Rivers than they were on their studies. But one also remembers the long train of flat cars leaving Norwich, loaded with most of the undergraduate body, bound for Hartford, to spend a long, tedious, dirty day cleaning up the silt and muck which the receding waters had left. (Childs, page 180)

The Nubanusit River washed out the western end of the Grove Street Bridge in 1936. The floodwaters swept toward Hancock, the Contoocook River reaching fifteen feet in places. In Hancock, rescuers had to use boats and ropes to help cows swim from a rapidly submerging barn, one by one, to where each could be pulled up to dry land. Courtesy of Peterborough Historical Society

Diary entry of Abner Sanger, May 12, 1781: "The Blake's cart sand on the mill dam road between the mill and the dam." (page 359)

From the looks of this 1936 photo, no amount of sand between the mill and the dam would have helped these washed out railroad tracks at Peterboro's Noone Mills. The situation is ironic because Noone Mills "which had suffered substantially in 1927, prepared on Tuesday night for protection against the impending flood which broke with full force early Wednesday morning and continued for two days. Much of the damage was done by water but the ice was still in the rivers. The flooding of the rivers broke up the ice, which formed gorges at several points, then broke away, coming down the river in great masses and causing terrific damage. Noone's Mill was the worst sufferer. Water was up three or four feet on the first floor. (Morison, page 627) Courtesy of Peterborough Historical Society

The Main Street Bridge, Peterborough, captured here sometime prior to September 21, 1938, was a favorite photographic subject in its time. Another photo of the bridge, under construction (bottom of page 85), reveals the damage it suffered during the hurricane.

The U.S. Weather Bureau testified in 1955 that hurricanes like that of September 21, 1938, "[expend] more energy than the United States uses in electricity in fifty years!" (Squires, page 710) Historically, the western regions of New Hampshire have suffered very few damaging hurricanes, the only great ones prior to 1938 on record being a similar one in 1788 and another, not as devastating to the region, in October of 1804. Courtesy of Peterborough Historical Society

A young Charlestown girl's letter to her grandmother reveals something of the total disruption of ordinary life that floods and similar disasters cause.

> There was a cloudburst yesterday (at Cavendish) and the rain came down in torrents. This morning there was no school because the lights went out and the dam broke at Gould's Mills, and it is like a Mississippi flood. Cows and hens and pigs went down the river. This morning Mary and I went down to the river and it was just like an ocean. Barrels and hayloaders and about everything you could think of came down. And this noon Dad took us to the Cheshire Bridge and we saw a henhouse coming down the river and it bumped the bridge. (Frizzell et al., page 120)

There was concern for the Cheshire Bridge, which had just had its piers reconstructed. Although it was closed to traffic for the first day of the flood and open only to emergency vehicles the second day, by the third day, it was back in normal operation, the waters having receded as rapidly as they had risen.

Flood of 1936

In Western New Hampshire communities the annual high water watch is one calendar ritual in all but those years when spring follows an "open winter" of sparse precipitation. Where better to monitor the incremental floodwaters than at a bridge? In these photos, the usually placid waters of the Connecticut churn threateningly, carrying the potential treasures of unexpected flotsam to eager eyes stimulated by the proximity of disaster. In one photo, the people crowd the Ledyard Bridge facing the oncoming current. The aerial view, taken from the Hanover side of the river, reveals the low-lying fields on the edge of Norwich where a line of partially submerged trees mark the river's bank. (page 165)

Writing in the early 1960's, Bancroft H. Brown asserts that Hanover's general population had suffered less from floods in its history than the people of many neighboring communities. Nevertheless, if photographs and local oral history are to be trusted, the sight of rising floodwaters is irresistible to the populace. Brown acknowledges this enticement of high water:

> . . . before the river was as much restrained as it is now, the ice going out in the spring was a spine tingling spectacle. And even today any vague rumor that a barn has washed away in Lyme and is due to hit the Ledyard Bridge in an hour or two will inspire many, from College and village, to hasten down the the hill to the river in what might be called a hopeful frame of mind. (Childs, page 180)

Perhaps the curious throng middle photo, page 165, is waiting for the Lyme barn.

It is a matter of some pride to the area that the bridge survived this violent flood that came just a few months after its completion. "For a time, at the height of the flood, it was the only bridge open to traffic for a distance of four hundred miles along the river." (Childs, page 26)

The town of Peterborough also suffered severe water shortage after ice broke the Grove Street water main.

Railroad tracks all over state suffered, although railroad beds were somewhat helpful in restraining floodwaters in some places. Cakes of ice, some still visible amid the rubble in the photo of Noone Mills, page 167, increased damage to railroad tracks. Many of western New Hampshire's railroad tracks were never rebuilt.

Noone Mills stayed active in Peterborough until past mid-twentieth century, long after most other mills had disappeared. They made woolen cloth for blankets and for the military and a special sheeting for conveyor belts that were used in the making of currency at a factory in Dalton, Massachusetts, which printed money for the U.S. Mint.

The Hurricane and Fire of 1938

The severity of the "Great Hurricane of 1938" resulted from the incredibly rare occurrence of a tropical hurricane veering inland at Connecticut, moving north through western Massachusetts and entering Vermont, with New Hampshire's Connecticut River Valley in the hurricane's most violent eastern quadrant. Four days of heavy, incessant rains found many of the rivers in western New Hampshire already at flood stage when it hit at the end of the afternoon of Wednesday, September 21. Warnings had missed the mark. Weather forecasters, never anticipating its future path, had cleared ocean shipping lanes.

Accounts of the hurricane, from whatever community they come, have a similar tone and carry amazingly comparable information. An upper Connecticut River Valley account is particulary evocative of the mood preceding the storm:

> New Englanders never understood about hurricanes until September 21, 1938. . . .
> No one living in Hanover will forget that day. It had rained steadily for four days, and the ground was soaked. By noon there was something in the atmosphere that no one liked. Seasoned travelers said, "Now if we were in the Caribbean, I'd say there was a hurricane coming." And we laughed. New Hampshire isn't the Caribbean. But we were jumpy; we couldn't settle down to anything. The barometer

dropped every time you tapped it. You opened the attic door and got a rush of air in the face. The wind blew stronger. The radio stuttered something about winds of gale force, and then the electricity went off.

Out doors the elms swayed more and more. They did not break, or crash down; they simply eased down to the ground uplifting a mass of roots and earth. Pine trees, offering more resistance, broke off. (Childs, page 174)

Some chroniclers acknowledge that while people of the area "hoped that it might turn eastward and do little damage to this neighborhood, [t]he possibility of its coming and doing serious damage was, however, not unexpected." (Morison, page 628) Apparently, the fact that households all over western New Hampshire lost electricity prevented radio broadcasts and their brief warning from reaching many area residents.

The story of Peterborough's loss of trees to the hurricane is well-known. Besides the loss of the MacDowell Colony forests, single trees and groves of trees went down all over Peterborough.

Practically every road leading out of Peterborough, except the Wilton road, was blocked for several days by fallen trees. Some of the country roads were solidly blocked by trees for distances of half a mile or more. In some places as many as eight to ten trees were piled over each other. (Morison, page 630)

The fire that leveled the buildings in the center of Peterborough began next door to the Transcript. Yet, the conflagration usually is called by the name of the beautiful old landmark it destroyed. Originally a granary, the handsome and historic building had been the home of the Transcript for years. Stored grain in the farmer's supply company situated behind the Transcript building created spontaneous combustion and reduced to ashes the entire business block it shared. From Depot Street south, all of Main Street was destroyed. Fifty years later, one lifelong resident remarked that "the whole block between the Baptist Church and the bridge went."

The flood, fire, and hurricane badly battered portions of Petersborough and strained the resources of the small community. Nevertheless, townspeople "hove to" for the distressing compound calamity. The old granary building had been a revered historic landmark, the loss of which made a psychological difference to the community's sense of itself that took a full generation to overcome. The hurricane and the fire altered irrevocably the physical character of the town. The ice that had exaggerated the damage of the 1936 flood was not a factor in 1938, but "water, wind and fire all...wrought changes on the face of Peterborough that will endure for as much as seventy-

five years." (Morison, page 628)

The fire broke out in the building behind the Transcript at 3:30 in the afternoon.

...the building was under several feet of water and there was no way by which the firemen could get close enough to fight it. The rain, although torrential, was not enough to stop the fire, which was fanned by a high wind. Help came from neighboring towns, from Wilton, Milford and later from Nashua, and as the water lines were intact and there was high ground at the lower end of Pine Street, these fire companies were of some help fighting the fire from the bridge. However, through the afternoon the fire gradually spread and finally every building along Main Street from the river to Depot Street were completely destroyed. Washouts along the road prevented help arriving that had been summoned from Keene and some of the western towns. But even then the worst was yet to come. (Morison, page 629)

The hurricane's force as it "funneled between Barrett and Temple Mountains," tore into town blowing wildly for three hours.

Pine forests had been subject to torrential rains for four days; the ground was soft, the wind striking the pine trees matted them together so that it could not get through, building up terrific pressure against them on the southeast side. After swaying back and forth for a few minutes, acres of pine forest were leveled at once. (Morison, page 629)

The fire continued even after the winds died down and was still burning the next morning. An eyewitness who lived on the Old Jaffrey Road wrote about the storm.

The full force of the storm...came in with appalling swiftness. It tore down trees first on one side of the house and then the other. They cracked and fell as if they were twigs. This went steadily on into the night. Some time before we went to bed, we saw the glow of a fire. It was a chicken house. Then another glow came, and this was the Transcript office and adjoining buildings in Peterborough, which, of course, we did not know until the next morning. The storm seemed to grow a little less about midnight. I think we went to bed then.

The following morning the sky was clear and

beautiful, but devastation was all around us. . . .We were completely blocked in. A great tree fell across the entrance to the garage, and many across the road, especially near the entrance. . . . [He walked into town.] The fire was not yet out, the river was still flowing through a part of the town. As I stood looking up the street to the left of the Unitarian Church, I saw a pretty white house, curtains at the windows, but no smoke coming out of the chimneys, with the river sweeping around it. I said to the man standing beside me, "I wonder if anyone is in that house." He said "No." I said, "Are you sure?" He said, "Yes. That's my house. I'm watching it go." But it never did. Everybody was in Peterborough.

Friday morning, I awoke at 6:45, and heard men in the road chopping. It took me just five minutes to dress. I rushed out into the main road. The foreman came down the road to speak to me. When I told him our plight and asked how we could get chopped out, he said he had eight men working, and he would give us four. He immediately called them, and as we went in I asked if they didn't want some coffee. They were enthusiastic! I led them to the kitchen, and soon we had all eight working for us. (quoted in Morison, pages 630-631)

Hardly a town or village was spared. Scenes like the ones pictured here repeated themselves in community after community. The town of Hancock lost three stained glass windows in the church.

but although the beautiful Christopher Wren steeple swayed badly, it managed to withstand the gale. Both chimneys were torn from the grammar school building and timbers on the south side were loosened and moved several inches. (Hancock History Committee, page 81)

In Charlestown, many residents lost roofs, windows, barns, and hen houses. Unharvested fields were ruined. The diary entry written by Clarence Bailey of North Charlestown gives a glimpse of the event in that area.

We rode down to S. C. [South Charlestown] to look at the high water this P. M. It is almost in the road in several places. About five o'clock a hurricane struck us, taking off part of the n. side of the barn roof and damaging the south side where I had just shingled new. It blew out 6 big house windows and most of the barn windows, tore the lightning rods off the buildings, took the corn barn off its base and set it flat on the ground. Fortunately Mr. F. had put the corn into the silo the 12th or it would have been almost impossible to cut it. For about a mile each

way from our house it was impossible to travel except on foot the next morning because of the tangle of trees, brush and wires. We had the road cleared before night. It was the same everywhere in New England where such a storm was never seen before. (reprinted in Frizzel et al., page 123)

Frizzell describes the uprooting of trees with the "worm's eye view of the root system exposed to the southeast from whence the storm had come." She notes that the town did not suffer from flood as so many others in the area had and concludes her account on an uplifting note.

From the mass of debris on Main Street it seemed that Charleston would have lost its beautiful tree-shaded thoroughfare. When all was cleared away the trees were less abundant, but still beautiful. (Frizzel et al., page 123)

After the Hurricane

Many hands were hired to clean up and repair the damage from the hurricane, including WPA workers whose wages had risen to forty cents an hour and foreman's wages to fifty cents an hour. In addition, by presidential order, the Timber Salvage branch of the Forest Service, was organized under the auspices of the United States Department of Agriculture.

The Civilian Conservation Corps was a very successful program in New Hampshire from 1933, a few months after Congress passed the legislation establishing it and Pres. Franklin D. Roosevelt signed it into law, and 1942, when the final camp closed. Camp Wildwood, not far from Woodsville, was the first of approximately forty CCC camps established in New Hampshire and one of about a dozen in the western part of the state. Crews from the CCC were active in many local forestry and land projects and were pressed into active service for such local emergencies as the 1936 and 1938 hurricane clean-ups. Lena Bourne Fish of Jaffrey, noted ballad singer and local writer, printed her poem, "The Flood at Squantum," about the 1936 flood, in her local newspaper, excerpted here:.

I thought of the time when Noah built the Ark.
Of that terror that shall be no more.
When I saw turbid waters rush down through
 our street.
And heard that mad torrent's wild roar.

· · · ·

But good Messrs. Ferry and Tilton as well.

Flood and Fire: Peterborough, New Hampshire, Sept. 28, 1938. Courtesy of Peterborough Historical Society

Still-smoking Transcript Ruins, Looking West. The photo carries the inscription: "Transcript Fire Disaster, Main Street Bridge, Peterborough, September 28, 1938." Courtesy of Peterborough Historical Society

This photo of local men "Examining the Ruins After the Transcript Fire," shows the community coming to life in the first stage of community renewal. "Ah, yes, there they are. the inquisitive old men," one Peterborough native aptly remarked when he saw this picture. Courtesy of Peterborough Historical Society

With their jolly brave CCC crew,
Sure proved to be helpe[r]s in our time of need,
For they fixed that old dam good as new.

. . . .

(*Jaffrey Record and Monadnock Breeze,* 27 March 1936, cited in Draves, page 109)

Although Peterborough's damage much exceeded that of Andover, several miles to the north, Andover's summary of repairs, carried out by the end of 1939, reflects the situation in towns throughout the state:

8.4	Miles of town roads rebuilt
13.2	miles of town roads resurfaced
10,600	cubic yards of gravel spread
8,000	cubic yards of fill used in washouts
694	lineal feet of metal culverts installed
516	lineal feet of cement culverts laid
4	new bridges constructed
1	covered bridge abutment rebuilt
6.3	miles of road given a blacktop treatment
1.6	miles of road treated with calcium chloride
670	lineal feet of stone and metal culverts relaid

Andover also salvaged "an estimated three million board feet of white pine and hardwood timber blown down all over town." (Chaffee, page 194) In 1939, Milford formed a Timber Salvage Association to take care of their sixty million feet of timber that was felled. Milford reported winds of one hundred miles an hour force and "an eerie bronze-colored sky frightened many people."

(Wright, page 36)

Peterborough's MacDowell Dam, one of four dams built in the state before 1950, and an Army Corps of Engineers Flood Control effort that takes in portions of the western region of the state represent substantive action taken as preventive measures against future flooding. Both projects continue in their respective locations.

Diary entry of Abner Sanger, May 10, 1781:
Warm good weather. waters are very high. People to see it and etc. (page 358)

There is probably not a town in New Hampshire that does not remember the hurricane of 1938 in its records. Many local historians and oral accounts mention the fact that the hurricane came without warning. One gets the impression from accounts of the devastation it wrought and from the many photographs of its effects that survive, that advance notice would have done little or no good.

A legendary elm that had stood outside the Taggart homestead in Sharon, is said to have

[sprung] from a sapling whip Joe Barnes idly stuck into the ground after a Fourth-of-July ride to Jaffrey for rum. William Taggart's wife was Hannah Barnes, and Joe Barnes stopping to visit his sister on his return inadvertently planted a tree—or so the tale goes. At any rate there was the tree, a landmark, and beautiful to look upon. Mr Keeler, who counted the number of its rings at the time the Hurricane blew it down, found it to be one hundred-seventy years old. (King, pages 202-203)

shops, including the Winged Pig. Another eatery stood where Nonie's is now. The town rebuilt its stone bridge and the rebuilt downtown is proportionate in scale to the surrounding area. The fact remains, however, that the face of Peterborough was forever altered by the events of September 1938.

The humorous focus of this photo transcends time and place. Then, as now, it takes several onlookers and a couple of workers to tow a friend out of a ditch. This driver-in-trouble is at the corner of Grove and School streets. Notice that the knitted toque remains the hat of choice among New Hampshire men in 1938.

Such tragi-comedy, amusing in retrospect, occurred throughout western New Hampshire. For example, in 1913, when Woodrow Wilson summered at "Harlakenden," in Cornish," [h]is secret service guards strung a telephone line through the dense pine woods around the house to guard against interlopers. This line was hung on six-inch nails spiked into the trees, and were never removed. These spikes, covered by later growth, raised havoc with the saws of a portable mill set up close by after the 1938 hurricane, which did great damage in these magnificent woods." (Wade, page 76) Courtesy of Peterborough Historical Society

For all the devastation of natural disasters, such catastrophes often create the opportunity for a town to rearrange itself the better to accommodate changes that the passage of time imposes upon even the most thoughtfully planned community. Among several changes to the business area of the town, the Diner, pictured here, was moved over to Depot Square, next to the present (1988) Yankee building. What was Lloyd's Grocery Store now houses several small

The hurricane affected Peterborough more dramatically than it did most towns. The winds left the MacDowell Colony with an astronomical eighty-nine thousand stumps, barely believable. Clearing them took a few years at the approximate cost of $50,000. The Colony was forced to cancel its residencies for 1939. This buckled barn in the town itself gives testimony to the hurricane's wanton destruction. Courtesy of Peterborough Historical Society

In his autobiography, Orozco remarked on the fact "sports [were] very important at Dartmouth, especially skiing in winter and football in summer." He was especially enamoured of the winter carnival and its attendant ice sculpture competition. (page 72)

Apparently, many share his enthusiasm for the Carnival Show. This 1923 crowd predates Orozco's residency at Dartmouth by more than a decade. *Courtesy of Dartmouth College Library*

10
NATURAL WONDERS AND THE SEASONS

Rivers

The Contoocook River flows north from Peterborough to the Merrimack River above Concord which unusual fact is often cited as a natural wonder, claimed by few rivers in the northern hemisphere. Some kayakers claim it to have the best "white water" of any New Hampshire river.

Winter

The blizzard of 1888 left a powerful impression on the people of western New Hampshire which they expressed in numerous accounts and stories that have come down to us. George Olcott's diary account, describes the nature and effects of the storm in vivid detail.

In Charlestown, [t]wo-and-one-half feet of snow has fallen, and is piled promiscuously in drifts anywhere from four to fourteen feet in depth. . . . The Acworth stage is snowed in here. . . . Main St. was broken out Tuesday P.M., by an advance squad of heavy men with snow shovels, who pushed their bodies through the snow in advance of D. G. Stoughton's pair of heavy team horses. . . . Several parties were bewildered on Main St. Monday night, one gentleman being guided to the Eagle Hotel only by the glimmer of the street light in front. G. W. Foggett

This companionable duo from Lyme provide the quintessential example of "a picture worth a thousand words." The citizens of the region have a healthy respect for the animals of the wild who *share their habitat. When one of their own exercises unusual mastery over a wild creature, it becomes an instance of curiosity and pride for everyone. The unidentified man in this snapshot* *expresses his satisfaction by the mere hint of a smile. Courtesy of New Hampshire Historical Society*

in returning to his office from the residence of his sister, Mrs. Chadborn, on East St., struggled long in the snow, often lying prostrate in the drifts to regain his breath, and wandering wide from the familiar sidewalk, finally reached Corbin's store in an utterly exhausted condition, and feeling if he had been exposed much longer to the storm that death must have resulted; some hours later on closing his office, he noticed a lantern gleam in the street below, and zigzagging around in a strange manner; finally the light disappeared, and realizing that someone was dazed in the storm, he called "Who is lost in the drifts?" and pushing toward the faint reply, he found Mr. Partridge, an old soldier in feeble health and partially blind, who had started from his place of business in J. C. Carmody's saloon to reach his home on upper Main St.; he was taken by Mr. Foggett to the Eagle where he passed the night. Many similar experiences have been reported and "Lost on Main St." will be a fruitful theme to recall for the benefit of a future generation. (Frizzell et al., page 118)

Hancock memories include two items concerning the 1888 blizzard.

Poultry farmer C. E. L. Hayward had a flourishing business with so many hens that he hired six men working full-time, year-round to care for them. At the Hayward farm, "[d]uring the blizzard of 1888 the snow drifts were so deep that it was impossible to reach the hen houses for three whole days. The hens kept alive during

this time by eating snow." (Hancock History Committee, page 189)

Elsewhere in Hancock, Ella Robinson recalled the event as experienced at Elmwood Farm which was situated "in the northeastern corner of Hancock on Moose Brook as it flows into the Contoocook River. . . .

A trainload of people were stranded at the house during the great blizzard of 1888. The last trains to reach Elmwood on the twelfth of March were stalled there for four days. The passengers and train crews were marooned. They prepared supper for thirty-five people that night. Those who could not be lodged in the house slept in the barn. In these days of easy access to markets, no house would have been so well stocked with provisions. The Robinsons were then milking seventeen cows and making seventy-five pounds of butter a week. The cellar was filled with potatoes, vegetables, apples and cider. Besides poultry and eggs, they had on hand a side of beef and a dressed pig. The men brought in wood and kept the fires going and helped the women with the housework and cooking. There was only one woman among the guests. They made biscuits by the peck and cooked other things in proportion. They beguiled the hours while the storm raged and the snow drifted to the tops of the windows, with much singing, card playing and impromptu entertainment. Each person contributed his

Shoveling Out the Freight Cars of the Boston and Maine Line, near Hanover. Courtesy of Dartmouth College Library

One of the hazards of travel in the age of the railroad was the capriciousness of nature. In the early decades of railroad service, dealing with the snow on the tracks was sort of like on-the-job-training. Railway workers figured it out as they went along. Of course, long experience of regional winters had given locals plenty of experience to glean for creative solutions to snow clearing. A combination of snow plows, or flanges, and hand shovels got the train crews through most, but certainly not all, storms. A legendary storm on Friday, February 21, 1873, forced weekend passengers en route to points west from Concord to debark in Bradford and find lodgings while a few hardy souls who continued the trek westward were stranded for three days between there and Newport.

These undated photos mark a particularly heavy snowfall requiring a vast volunteer army of snow shovelers to clear the Boston and Maine line near Hanover/Norwich station. Such instances are looked upon as great social times by townspeople who chew on the memories through storytelling for years afterward. Some truly dramatic accounts of wintertime are to be found in local lore throughout the years. Courtesy of Dartmouth College Library

specialty. There was a minister and a lawyer in the company besides the popular lecturer, George Makepeace Fowle, who delivered the lecture that he was scheduled to give in Concord at that time. (Hancock History Committee, pages 204-206)

Nature's splendor and oddities hold enough fascination for the public to motivate tourists the world over. Photographs of these attractions tend to speak for themselves and those included here are good examples. Seasons each bring unique beauty to the region but it is nature in extremity that lures the photographer's gaze most often—the sight of an altered landscape or one that confounds the expectations.

New Englanders are notoriously compulsive weather-watchers. For some, it supplies the whole of their conversational gamut and for others the ideal conversational gambit. The subject breaks the ice between strangers and seems always a safe topic for social exchange. The western regions of New Hampshire pay appropriate obeisance to the weather in its local histories. A few examples are broadly representative. Keene's most recent town history devotes twenty-two pages to the vagaries and wonders of the weather. Many histories excerpt weather-related entries from local diaries. New London's is a case in point. An appendix includes notes kept by Mrs. Fred W. Knowlton of which excerpts appear from between 1917 and 1949. These are followed by F. Eldred Hodge's observations from the local U.S. Weather Bureau sub-station from 1946 to 1950. These, in turn, are

followed by a list of "The Dates for the Break-up of the Ice on Lake Sunapee, 1900-1950." It is particularly interesting to compare the data among the three sets of statistics. For instance, of 1917, Mrs. Knowlton records: "A late spring—cattle were in the barn until May 18." In the same year, the ice broke up on Lake Sunapee on May 7. In 1940, the late spring (ice out on Lake Sunapee, May 7) was not as noteworthy to the editors of Mrs. Knowlton's weather diary as were other occurrences:

> June 22 had a white frost—August 25 had a white frost—October 21 had snow—Nov. 28 snow plows were out—December 1 12 inches of snow—Dec. 20 and 24 had two earthquakes early in the morning—December 30 a thunder shower.

Or, as excerpted from her records of 1948:

> Very cold and lots of snow in January and February—late spring—no planting done until June—warm fall—hard rain on December 30—frost coming out of ground on December 31. (Squires, 1952, pages 332-333)

Similar records have been kept by local residents since the first days of settlement. Abner Sanger rarely fails to mention the weather in his journal written over a period of years, the dates between October 1, 1774 and December 11, 1794 being extant. Noting the date of the barn animals to pasture is a tradition in the region:

Winter View: North Factory, Peterborough, 1890s. Courtesy of Peterborough Historical Society

Late Spring, Early Summer View: North Factory, Peterborough, 1890s.
  The North Factory of Peterborough is the location of Wilder's Thermometer Factory. The family business was founded by Charles Wilder, an inventor. It manufactured thermometers and barometers of such superior quality that even the United States Weather bureau relied on them. Wilder instruments were shipped from Peterborough to all corners of the globe. The factory is gone but the farmhouse remains at this time. The picturesque has given way to safety, the road having been "straightened" with a modern bridge angled across the river to ease the flow of traffic. *Courtesy of Peterborough Historical Society*

"Abandoned Pro Tem: Mud Season in the Upper Valley." To one resident of Weare, the first hint of spring is the appearance of "Frost Heaves" signs that road crews plant along country roads in late January and early February as the deep frost beneath the road beds begins to thaw. For a good many of the locals, however, it is mud season that ushers in springtime. In a year of heavy snowfall, mud season can last for a few weeks. Rural residents have many ingenious ways of coping with mud season. Dartmouth College's "Duckboards," wooden platforms that were built over the paths on the Green in front of Baker Library, became something of a town conversation piece, historically. *Courtesy of Dartmouth College Library*

Larry McDonald took this expressive photo, "Made it This Time," in 1978. It could be anywhere in the western regions of the state but is located in the upper Connecticut River Valley area. The two Hancock men who adapted Model T Fords as early snowmobiles, Ron Perry and Bill Hanson, are credited with applying their creativity to the annual problem of early spring roads. "During the mud season, when many roads were impassable, the ingenious pair of mechanics devised mud drums which they bolted to a vehicle's rear wheels to prevent it from becoming mired." (Hancock History Committee, page 62)

This brings to mind the local farmer hitching up the horse to move it along. An old joke of rural New England tells of the farmer who wore himself out pulling mired motor vehicles out of the mud hole at the bottom of his hill all day long. Then, he was faced with wearing himself out by carrying pails of water to the dip in the road all night long to keep it muddy. Courtesy of Dartmouth College Library

Spots of natural beauty have always been prized by sightseers and nature lovers. The turn of the century photographers of scenery such as this of a glen near Lowellville were genuine artists. The design and narrative tension in this picture is strong. It is made even more compelling by the double image in this stereograph. By the contrast of the still figure casually seated against the rushing water and of the placid stream gliding calmly behind the falls, the artist creates a narrative statement. The resulting aesthetic tension pleases the viewer.

One of a series of Marlborough Harbor, New Hampshire, views, it was produced by the Keene photographic studio of French and Sawyer and sold by them and by the Sawyer and Davis studio of Marlborough. The photo was taken before 1871, the year French bought out his partner's share in their Keene studio. Courtesy of the New Hampshire Historical Society.

June 13, 1832, diary entry of Denison Gould, Hillsborough:

> We have had 2 hot days. Turned our oxen out to pasture today for the first time this summer. They have been in the yoke or in the barn every day since the 14th of April and nights too.

Gould's account predates Mrs. Knowlton's by almost a century.

Late snows are recorded several times in the first half of the nineteenth century and 1816 was variously called the "year without a summer," "poverty year" or, as one local wag put it, "eighteen hundred and froze to death." According to Keene oral history, the seeds froze in the ground that year.

This preoccupation with the weather is true of most diaries and led to the immediate and continuing success of the *Old Farmer's Almanac,* A Dublin, New Hampshire, enterprise, in continuous publication since 1792.

The Upended Lake, 1989

Described in the news as "one of the more bizarre environmental events of the season," the inversion of Stoddard's Highland Lake in the spring of 1989 is, indeed, one of the more astounding weather phenomena in recent history. "[A] round Easter Sunday. . . : Like the return of Atlantis, the lake bottom dislodged and rose to the surface." The lake had been drained for dam repairs and left unfilled through an open winter that had provided too little snow to insulate the lake bed which froze to a depth of four feet. A " 'flashy' lake, one that fills quickly," Highland Lake rises about thirty inches for every inch of rainfall. A three-inch spring rain "filled the lake faster than it could be drained." Residents, who had taken advantage of the dry lake to clean and refurbish their beaches, lost their investments and gained an uncharted lake as the vast ice block thawed, depositing its detrius wherever it fell (*Braile*)

These two samples of George H. Scripture's "Monadnock Mountain Views" are interesting portrayals of the attractions that the Monadnock area held for the tourists. The inclusion of human figures adds interest to the natural rock formations, Jupiter's Pyramids and Fairy's Archway, as Scripture identifies them, and provides a measure of scale to the viewer. Scripture was a Peterborough photographer with a studio at No. 2 French's Block. Courtesy of New Hampshire Historical Society

This view of Mount Kearsarge, also a Monadnock geological formation, is taken from Route 89 at Warner, looking northwest toward Sutton. It is this kind of scenery that garnered national highway design awards for the interstate when it opened. Residents of the towns surrounding Kearsarge Mountain are very affected by its powerful presence. The summit of Kearsarge was bare rock at the turn of the nineteenth century, a fire having burnt off the stunted forest growth and soil in the early 1800s. Today, forest growth crowds the still barren summits. Elsewhere in this book hang-gliders take off from an outcrop of rock high on the mountainside. Photo by the author

The people posing add amusement to this photograph that features one of the natural curiosities of the area. What is probably the original of this image appears in the 1892 town history of Swanzey with the citation, "Boulder by Charles H. Holbrook's House near West Swanzey." Small lettering at the bottom identifies its engraver: Autoglyph Print, W. P. Allen, Gardner, Massachusetts. Courtesy of the New Hampshire Historical Society

Peterborough's Central School Graduation Class of 1907 presents a typical array of young adolescents ready for bigger and better things. Central School, built in 1888, consolidated some of the town school districts, gradually absorbing more students as overall town population increased and certain of the rural school districts closed. Located on Vine Street, the school was in use until 1955 and was taken down in 1960. The students pictured here are: Front row: John Perry, Rice "Sunny" Caldwell, Martin "Pat" Keenan, Billy McNeal, Danny Mahoney, and Charlie "Daw" Dailey. Second row: Francis Burpee, Clara Driscoll, George Widener, Teacher, Miss Effie Pritchard (Mrs. Herbert Moore), Alfred Thomas, Mary Jewell, Forest "Jack" Frost, and Annie Teto. Third row: Dow Hannon, Marguerite Hawkins, Madolin Mitchell, Eleanor O'Donohue, Theo Ames, Leona Weeks, and Sadie Harvey. Courtesy of Peterborough Historical Society

11
RELIGION
AND
EDUCATION

Religion

Community social life was entwined with church life in the western regions of the state. The original charters provided a glebe, the parcel of land set aside for the meeting house. New Hampshire's settlers made the building of the meeting house the first of their community concerns. The early records of all the towns along the western regions of the state are filled with the matters of building the meeting house and hiring the minister.

In western New Hampshire, the principal established church was the Congregational Church. However, within a few decades of settlement, other established churches made their appearance. The very first of New Hampshire's Methodist congregations, for example, was formed in Chesterfield in 1795. During the religious revivals starting in the middle of the eighteenth century and continuing well into the nineteenth, diverse religious sects found membership throughout the area.

The age of political freedom that followed the War of Independence found its counterpart in religious thought, as well: By the end of the eighteenth century, more and more citizens were claiming exemptions from religious taxes in their communities, professing affiliation with religions other than the town's official denomination. An example of the difficulties this created is found in Keene. Although the town's minister

was personally liked and respected, a tax for the support of the established Congregational Society of Keene which had been required since colonial days

For several years, Mr. Morrison's Sunday School met in Peterborough. An annual picnic in the area was well attended by the participants, those photographed here are enjoying the occasion in 1910.

Mortier Morrison, Civil War veteran, was treasurer of the Peterborough Savings Bank and an active Peterborough politician. He served in the New Hampshire House of Representatives in 1879, 1881, and 1915. He was on the Governor's Council for 1885 and 1886. He served as town moderator for twenty-five years and served a three year term as selectman.

Morrison himself is not pictured here. Perhaps, he took the photo which includes, front row, left to right: Jesse Martin, William H. Caldwell, Forest Field, Jeremiah Driscoll, James Brennan, George H. Scripture, Lewis

Wilson, and Fred Robbe. Second Row: Andrew Walbridge, Robert Bass, Thomas D. Winch, Charles Jellison, and Arthur Spaulding. Third row: Timothy Driscoll, George A. Hamilton, Herbert F. Nichols, and Algernon Holt. Fourth Row:

Charles Baldwin, Arthur Miller, Walter Bailey, and Hiram Cram. Some of these men appear elsewhere in this volume. Some of Scripture's photos are also represented herein. Photo courtesy of Peterborough Historical Society

was not universally appreciated. It was challenged in 1797 by Dr. Ziba Hall, who claimed to be Universalist. The selectmen supported the established church and fought Dr. Hall's suit to recover his church tax. A sharp controversy followed, but on the grounds that the Universalists were not a recognized denomination, the court ruled against Dr. Hall, and he was forced to pay the required sum, as were several pioneer Baptists a few years later. The legislature soon recognized Universalists [1805] and other religious denominations, and compulsory support of the Congregational Church ended. (Keene History Committee, pages 41-42)

Revivalist Preaching

The relatively late settlement of the western regions of the state accounts, in part, for the early and enthusiastic appearance of religious practices influenced by revivalist preachers. Dartmouth College was founded by a minister whose training at Yale coincided with the emergence, there, of the New Lights. A 1733 graduate of Yale College, Eleazar Wheelock was one of the New Lights, revivalist preachers who espoused extemporaneous preaching done with vigor and passion. Long before he brought his missions to the Indians in New Hampshire, he was vocal in defending the ordained minister's practice of such sermonizing. A leader, with Jonathan Edwards, of the New Lights, he was the cousin of James Davenport, one of the fanatical practitioners who was seen as insane and demented by some of the old guard (Old Lights).

The flamboyance of the extempore style was a threat to the supremacy of the more sedate, traditional preachers who read from prepared texts carefully crafted and adhering to the proscriptions of established church authority. The religious revival of 1740 suffered a backlash of angry

criticism by academics at Harvard and Yale and eloquent church legislative assemblies.

Significantly, formal religious support of the patriots' cause in revolt against British authority in the second half of the eighteenth century had its first expression in the views of the New Light revivalist preachers. Within a generation of their early assertions, their radical thought had worked its way, through the sermons of many influential preachers, to being the standard orthodoxy of the New England preacher. Jonathan Edwards' fast sermons were important in fostering these free ideas. The effect of these ideas spread far beyond the academic centers where their primary exponents found their radical voices.

New Light preachers proseletized along the Connecticut River Valley (Yale College graduates) and eastern Massachusetts (Harvard College graduates). Ironically, the eschewing of lengthy notetaking and note making by the revivalists led to the development of a carefully constructed literature of sermonizing—somewhat in response to the brief notes used by the extemporaneous speakers. New methods of preaching were favored by graduates of Yale like Eleazar Wheelock and there is no doubt that he found the increasing religious toleration to his liking and set the tone for more liberal thinking in the region. Many Dartmouth College graduates took up teaching and preaching posts throughout the area and beyond.

Of note during this same era, are the following bits of history. When Rev. Ezra Carpenter brought his family to Keene, October 4, 1753, he also brought as part of his household "Probably the first Negro slave in the region." (*Upper Ashuelot*, page 16.) Rev. Jonathan Leavitt was the first pastor of the Church of Walpole serving from 1761 to 1764. He was fired apparently because a church member saw him on horseback with one end of a rope tied to the

Harvest decorations are a direct carry over from England, brought with the settlers to their American church communities. Historically the work of women's church groups, assisted, of course, by church sextons, harvest ornaments incorporate traditional motifs that are still familiar. An autumn "Harvest Home" or other harvest celebration is often the occasion for these decorations, made from natural grains, flowers and other items found in nature. The women of Claremont depend on bouquets of flowers, hanging garlands, and an arched centerpiece dominating the altar to achieve their festive appearance. G. E. Stevens, Bailey Block, Claremont, took this undated autumnal photo of the interior of Claremont's Universalist Church. Courtesy of New Hampshire Historical Society

Christmas decorations are a later phenomenon in American churches. Among protestant congregations, they represent the response of organized religion to the secularization of Christmas. Perhaps the more flam-boyant celebrations of the immigrant Catholic Churches also had their impact on the more sedate practices of American churches. Church decorations borrow motifs and designs from the European cultures of the population's ancestors. In addition, the elaborate ornamentation of homes and public buildings practiced in Dickensian England, profoundly influenced the look of Christmas in America. Claremont's Universalist Church presents a muted display utilizing greens found locally. The motifs are similar to those used in the autumn display, although the Christmas star is decidedly seasonal. The Coffrin Photo Studio of Claremont published this undated photograph. Courtesy of New Hampshire Historical Society

The simplicity of this 1823 Quaker Meeting House at "Quaker City" in Unity reflects the plainness of the Quaker lifestyle and belief system. A great many towns in western New Hampshire have locales known by similar place names: Quaker Hill, Quaker Road, and Quaker Meeting Hill are examples. Shaker place names are found in the area, as well, although not in as great numbers. Courtesy of New Hampshire Historical Society

Brother John Cummings and his work mate, probably another brother of the Enfield Society, pause for this informal photograph in the midst of moving a piece of granite. The simple tools they employ, a small roller and two wooden staffs, remind us of how our ancestors were able to attack the prodigious tasks of building settlements in the wilderness. This photograph, taken between 1875 and 1890, comes originally from the collections of the Shaker Library in Sabbathday Lake, Maine. Brother John Cummings is on the left. Courtesy of New Hampshire Historical Society

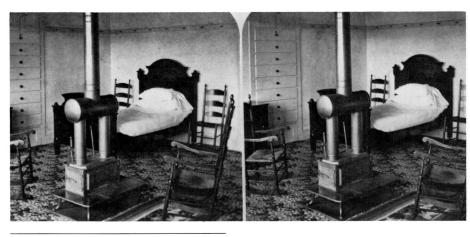

This bedroom contains two of the items most associated in the mind of the public with Shaker living quarters, the built-in sets of drawers and the wood stoves that occupied every room in frequent use for work or relaxation. According to former Enfield Society elder, Henry Cumings, there were approximately one thousand drawers built into the dwelling house. (cited by Emlen, page 77) The furniture is simple and elegant, a hallmark of Shaker artisanship that attracted contemporary buyers and have made such pieces collector's items of high value at the present time. Along the upper walls is a peg rail on which the room's occupants could hang their clothing while they slept and hang their chairs while they cleaned. Note that the design of the chairs allows this efficient system. The Shaker found no contradiction between spirituality and creature comforts. They objected to excess but considered basic comfort to assist productive work. The inclusion of several chairs indicates that some socializing may have been done in this room. Courtesy of New Hampshire Historical Society

pommel of his horse and the other around the neck of a female slave who had run away. (Roberts, page 432).

Religious Milestones in the Western Regions

Religious milestones associated with the area include the founding of several important sects. The Enfield Shakers trace their spiritual genealogy back to the Great Awakening, both through their foundress, Ann Lee, and the preacher George Whitefield who visited New Hampshire in the 1770's, inspiring "hearers." His influence on the Free Will Baptists in Canterbury led to the founding of the Shaker Community there and in Enfield. The General Convention of the Universalists met in Winchester to adopt its confession of Faith, in 1803.

Mormonism had early adherents in southwestern New Hampshire due to the fact that Lucy Mack Smith, the mother of Joseph Smith, its founder, was from Gilsum. Lucy's husband and son, John, preached in the Keene area in 1836. The Seventh Day Adventist faith began in Washington in the 1840's, its first church organized there in 1862.

Some towns in the Keene area were founded by religious settlers. Richmond was founded by Quakers and Baptists, for example. At the end of the eighteenth century,

> Keene was surrounded by dissident religious groups. Methodists in Chesterfield established a church in 1789 [correct date is 1795]. Baptists and Quakers founded the town of Richmond. Universalism developed from the preaching of Caleb Rich in Richmond and the organization of Hosea Ballou, a native of Richmond. Baptist settlers from Middleboro, Mass, met in Westmoreland by 1771. Most of these separatists shunned any formal organization or established ministry at first. (Stabler, in *ASJ* page 130, note 3)

No theological seminary of importance was situated in the western regions, but Dartmouth historian William Cogswell assumed the leadership of the state's influential Gilmanton Seminary in 1844, attracting a number of Dartmouth graduates as students.

Toleration Act of 1819

The single most important act for religious liberty in New Hampshire was the passage of the Toleration Act of 1819 repealing the requirement that towns support ministers and meeting houses. The debate had been going on for nearly thirty years.

Reference to God, long a unique feature of New Hampshire's state Constitution, was deleted by a 1968 amendment, by a 142,112 to 67,697 vote. It had long been claimed that no other state Constitution in the nation, nor the federal Constitution, contained any mention of the Deity

Article 6 of the First Part of the state Constitution, which extolled the public worship of God, had become a center of controversy in several Constitutional Conventions of the previous century. But this 1968 deletion, as sponsored by the Constitutional Convention of 1964, was approved without editorial or other public argument as to its merit.

In sum, the importance of the Act was the total separation of church and state in actual practice. Towns were, by law, secularized in their governance. In

This anonymous photo gives evidence of the beauty of the Shaker Village at Enfield. The compact village with its several styles of architecture make a handsome sight. The village was known for its agricultural and animal husbandry. Enfield's Lake Mascoma, formerly Pleasant Pond, is five miles by one-half mile in area. At the time of the photo, it is probable that the Northern Railroad ran along its eastern shore. The village of North Enfield is situated on about one-half mile of the southwestern shore and Shaker Village owns the rest of the southwestern bank, the entire length of the pond. The land they owned in Enfield and vicinity was approximately 2,500 acres, most of it in productive use. Courtesy of New Hampshire Historical Society

Judging from the number of photographs taken there, the steps in front of the Office of the Great Stone House was a favorite spot for photographs of Enfield Village families. The elders and eldresses of Enfield Village pose in this undated photo. The picture shows clearly the conventional garb of the community. It makes evident, as well, that there was some slight variation in dress. In general, the Society kept a fairly strict conformity of attire. Courtesy of New Hampshire Historical Society

The girls are here joined by the boys of the village in this photograph of Enfield Shaker Village children taken at the same photo session as most of the images included here. An additional prop, the banjo, reminds us that music, singing and dancing were all part of both the religious and social life of the community. The boys' dress shows just a little more uniformity than the girls' dress. The hats on the little ones draw the eye directly to them. Courtesy of New Hampshire Historical Society

This separate photo of the boys shows the clapboard construction typical of the Village buildings, only three of which are stone and a few of brick. Two of the boys carry items that are probably dear to their hearts. The banjo shows up here, again, carried by the same child as before. The boy on the right is holding what looks like a mouth harp or harmonica. The older boy's beard, brimmed hat and frock coat identify him as on the verge of manhood. In all these portraits, the anonymous photographer has taken pains to arrange to good effect both the placement of the figures and the placement of their hands. Courtesy of New Hampshire Historical Society

practice, of course, the separation of religious from civil affairs was less clear. Such traditional practices as prayer at civic gatherings (to open Memorial Day or Old Home Day exercises, for example), or sacred hymns sung at various other informal town events, continued unabated throughout the state. Indeed, some such practices continue to the present day.

The establishment of non-English faiths began in the 1820s with the Roman Catholicism of the French Canadian and Irish immigrant. A Roman Catholic congregation began in Claremont in 1823; Old St. Mary's Church in that city was the first Catholic church in New Hampshire. Later waves of immigration from southern and eastern Europe led to the establishment of a Russian Orthodox Church in Claremont at the end of the century and a Greek Orthodox Church in Keene before 1910. A Jewish Temple was opened on Court Street in Keene in 1947. The Congregation Ahavas Achim remains the only formal Jewish congregation in the western regions. Dartmouth College has an active Hillel Society, a branch of the international Jewish collegiate organization.

"The Cathedral of the Pines, at Rindge, is, perhaps, the most remarkable religious project in New Hampshire not associated with any one church." (Squires, page 805) A memorial to summer resident Sanderson Sloan, who was killed in the war in 1944, the Cathedral in the Pines consists of a stone altar set high in the hills amid beautiful pine groves. Completely non-denominational, services of any faith are held there, including marriages. The first service was held in the summer of 1945 and the first sunrise service on Easter Sunday, 1946. In its first ten years, one-and-one-half million people from all over the world visited the site.

Sects of Interest in the Western Regions

While numerous sects found audiences and congregations in the western regions of New Hampshire, the ones most referred to by historians include the Millerites, probably because they were novel for the period, and the Moravians, most likely because they were uncommon in New England. The Osgoodites found most of their adherents in the western New Hampshire town of Warner and the Shaker Society enjoys the most notoriety of any religious sect in the area.

Millerites

William Millers' followers were scattered throughout New England. In Keene, their meetings became frequent

as 1843, the year they believed would bring the

end of the world, approached. In December 1842 they held a 10-day series of Keene meetings under Mr. Preble of Nashua, a traveling preacher. Reports that numbers of them, wearing white ascension robes, actually waited on the hills about Keene valley to be gathered up into heaven are probably true. (Keene History Committee, page 94)

They gathered, ready for the end of the world, on December 25, 1842, on Beech Hill in Keene, among other places across the state. When Miller's early predictions proved inaccurate, he explained it as a difference between earthly time and spiritual time, and moved his prediction ahead, the final time to October 11, 1844. (Squires, page 338) Considering their faith compatible with the beliefs of the Shaker Society, many Millerites joined that sect when their own disbanded.

Moravians

A "short-lived Moravian Community in Hanover was characteristic of similar experiments throughout the country. It was located on the first left hand road off Ruddsboro Road." (Childs, page 75)

Osgoodites

A number of unique, short-lived sects made their appearance in western new Hampshire. One interesting local sect, the Osgoodites, practiced in Warner.

Jacob Osgood (1777-1844), a man of great girth, had grown up in South Hampton where the Free Will Baptists had been most active.

He was a man of considerable ability and of the warmest sympathies. . . . In their best days, and perhaps always, these people claim miraculous gifts, such as the healing of the sick. Their meetings were peculiar, consisting of one service, all taking part. Songs, prayers, and exhortations were intermixed without much regularity. When there came a lull, unlike the Quakers, they did not sit in silence. Bro. Osgood, without rising, would close the exercises in these words: "If there's no more to be said, meeting's done." (Harriman, pages 511-512)

Like so many of the sects that arose out of the Great Awakening, they were pacifists. A few Osgoodites were incarcerated briefly in Hopkinton when they "pleaded 'conscientious scruples,' but refused to pay an 'equivalent'. . . . But the military authorities, seeing that these men rather gloried in their 'martyrdom,' went and released them." (Harriman, page 512)

Under normal circumstances, the building that houses the Enfield Village Trustees Office would be considered an imposing structure. Only its proximity to the Great Stone House shrinks it somewhat in the viewer's eyes. The angle effectively enhances its size while the horse-drawn carriage lends additional appeal. The wheel marks of village vehicles lay an interesting pattern on the foreground.

The bell in the belfry weighs 800 lbs., the second bell hung by the Shakers in the Dwelling Houses's belfry. The bell rang for meals and prayers.

The six story building was the largest stone structure in New England and an early example of the new Greek Revival style that was to dominate the architectural style of the next several decades. Courtesy New Hampshire Historical Society

The Shaker Society dining room on the first floor of Enfield Village's Great Stone Dwelling House is here decorated for Christmas with modest flower bouquets at the tables and hand-made paper chains hung in garlands from the ceiling and lamp flues. The Shaker Village tables are set for family style eating. Pitchers and bowls hold food and beverages for passing around the table. Condiments in their cruets are also shared among several diners.

The low backs of the chairs are designed for storage under the tables when not in use. The posts are of hand-turned maple and the shutters of solid boards. The built-in cupboards and drawers so characteristic of Shaker

interiors are also evident.

In this photograph, a hand bell sits under the clock on the far wall. The shuttered windows are capable of letting in a quantity of light, enhanced, when needed, by gas or oil lamps hanging from the pillars throughout the room. The lamps are hung under flues that connect with the stove pipe that carries the smoke out of the room through the chimney in the far wall, another example of the celebrated Shaker ingenuity. The LaSalette fathers once produced a print of this photo with a short bi-lingual English/French description of the room. A copy hangs in the room today. Courtesy of New Hampshire Historical Society

Shaker Village, including the Old Stone House, Enfield, 1988. Photo by Armand Szainer

FOUNDING OF DARTMOUTH COLLEGE
779 ly Wheelock removed his family and school from Lebanon, Conn. a the erection of a college in a forest. In the open air with his numerous l offered morning and evening prayer, and the surrounding forest resound e solemn sound of supplication and praise.

S. E. Brown's 1839 lithograph depicting the founding of Dartmouth College incorporates the principal motifs associated with the story of Eleazar Wheelock's wilderness college. Frequently reproduced, the sketch features the tools for carving civilization out of the wilderness and those who hefted the tools. The raw materials, the few hewn boards and the two small but sound buildings surround Wheelock and his students. Brown's assertive design summarizes the familiar narrative outline of the school's beginnings. The College motto's biblical allusions are apt corollaries to the legend of the school's beginning. The New Testament quotation in context is "The voice of one crying in the wilderness/Prepare ye the Way of the Lord/Make His paths straight." (Matthew. 3:3) The phrase echoes the prophet Isaiah, "The voice of him that cryeth in the wilderness." (Isaiah 40:3) Courtesy of Dartmouth College Library

The group was already virtually defunct in 1890, when the following account was published.

> They claimed to be "the saints;" and it was a part of their religion to denounce all denominations in general, and the Free-Will Baptists in particular. In connection with much that seemed spiritual in their worship, they indulge in low and personal remarks, objectionable songs, and, finally, in kissing and dancing.
>
> After a career of more than forty years, Osgood died, and the surviving adherents were scattered; but as late as 1849 the present writer remembers to have attended, for the first and only time, one of their evening meetings, held in a private house in Warner village. On this occasion a few persons, among them the school-master, who had ventured in out of curiosity, though perfectly quiet and respectful, got soundly reproved by one of the "saints"—a female "saint"—on account of the smartness of their dress.
>
> One of their number had recently died, almost instantaneously, and, as was not unnatural, most of their prayers and exhortations bore reference to the sad event. One of the prayers uttered contained the following sentence, so peculiar that it has not been forgotten by the listener to this late day: "Thou knowest, O lord, Thou didst call for her while she stood at the table washing up her dishes."
>
> The wife of Jacob Osgood, founder of the Osgoodites, was a daughter of Jonathan Stevens and wife, who were among the early settlers of Sutton, in which town Mrs. Osgood was born, September 12, 1779. Her name is found among the centenarians of Sutton. (Worthen, Pages 433-434)

Shakers

By far the most important Shaker communities in New Hampshire were at Canterbury, in the Merrimack Valley, and at Enfield, near Hanover. There were, however, Shaker properties of varying sizes in many towns in southwestern New Hampshire in the first half of the nineteenth century. Some communities refused to allow Shakers to settle among them but others seem to have accepted their presence with little notice. The Enfield Community began in October, 1782, a mere eight years after Ann Lee had landed in New York with her followers to pursue missionary work in America, and was formalized in 1795.

The Shaker movement arrived in New Hampshire during a flash of Baptist revivalism sparked by radical New Light Free Will Baptist preacher, Benjamin Randall, a follower of George Whitefield who had preached in the region when he visited America several years earlier. Ann Lee had been one of Whitefield's "hearers" in England where he was a leader of the Great Awakening.

Westmoreland is the site of an early example of religious intolerance in western New Hampshire. Churchgoers there were disturbed in 1784 to find that a Quaker settler had moved to their community. His presence so threatened the spirituality of the residents that the Town appointed a committee of fifteen to expel the "Shaking Quaker" from their midst. It seems that the use of the term "Shaker" was not yet in general usage just two years after the Society moved to Enfield.

The Shakers were generally liked within the state, but this tolerance was by no means universal and it took a number of years of observation for others to realize that the Shaker Society posed no threat to other religions and made, indeed, compatible neighbors.

In 1782, Job Bishop and Hannah Goodrich went to the New Hampshire communities as ministers and the New Hampshire communities were formally organized the next year. In Enfield, the community developed on "Shaker Hill," the prosperous farmstead of James Jewitt where they met for ten years "... until they decided to consolidate their holdings and purchased land on Mascoma Lake in 1792." (HABS No. NH-75, Report, pages 6, 7)

Maximum membership at Enfield was about 330 and total membership between its founding and dissolution was 511. The last seven Shakers moved to Canterbury in 1923.

In her anti-Shaker, *A Portraiture of Shakerism*, published in 1822, Mary Dyer, who had lived in the Enfield community for a short period, describes the Enfield Shaker meetings. "[T]here were pipes to smoke, cider to drink, and melons, apples, and nuts to eat; and where the participants sang such "merry love songs" as

> I love the brethren the brethren love me
> Oh! how happy, how happy I be.
> I love the sisters, the sisters love me,
> Oh! how happy, how happy I be.
> How pretty they look, how clever they feel,
> And this we will sing when we love a good deal.
> (quoted in Andrews, page 180)

To the late twentieth-century reader, Dyer seems to describe behavior that is innocent enough. We find people partaking of ample, yet simple, celebratory food and a mere children's rhyme, retaining nothing of the suggestiveness Dyer meant her description to elicit and which, apparently, it did elicit for some readers at the time.

Another area resident presents local memory of the Enfield Shakers quite differently. Lillian Kenison Bailey of Hanover writes her praiseful assessment in 1969. We know that the memory refers to a time much earlier in the century, since the surviving Shakers at Enfield left in 1923 to go live in Canterbury. Bailey recalls that

> . . . [t]heir model farms, excellent seeds and prizewinning stock helped make better farming all around. The Shaker peddler wagons were always welcome and a favorite outing for many a farm boy was to hitch up and take his girl over to the Enfield Shaker Colony for dinner and shopping. One girl recalls buying at various times pressed ginger, herbs, sweet flag, broadcloth and sweaters. (Childs, pages 76-77)

Shaker Beliefs

Like the Universalists, the Shakers believed in universal salvation. Like many sects spawned by the Great Awakening, Shakers were pacifists. They believed in the separation of the sexes, the confession of sins and the imminence of the millenium.

The Shakers, or, as they were officially known, the United Society of Believers in Christ's Second Appearing, believed "that all good actions of men are done under the influence of God. . . . They adopted no creeds, believing that His spirit" was omnipresent. (Chandler, page 3)

Believing the Bible to be historical, not inspired, and that Christ was mortal, although of God's spirit, they believed that the mortal spirit was eternal but eshewed the notion of bodily resurrection. "Departed spirits may give help to earthly spirits," however.

Joseph Meacham, one of Ann Lee's successors, brought the cardinal virtues of the Shaker Society to the congregations in New Hampshire. They included

1. virgin life;
2. honesty and integrity of purpose;
3. humanity and kindess to all;
4. diligence in business, labor for all; industrious but not lavish;
5. prudence, economy, temperance and frugality without parsimony;
6. absolute freedom from debt;
7. education of children in scriptural, secular and scientific knowledge;
8. a universal interest in all things;
9. ample provision for all in health, sickness, old age. (Chandler, page 8)

As one chronicler puts it, "[t]heir teachings were too kindly and forgiving for the traditional theology of sin and eternal punishment, and they made relatively few converts." (Squires, page 339)

The Millenial Laws, Part III (Concerning Temporal Economy), Section III (Orders Concerning Clothing) articulates the Society's policy. The rules laid down address issues of worldliness.

> If brethren desire any garments or fixtures to garments, as pockets, etc. etc. or new articles of manufacture, that come in the sisters line of business, which are not common to the brethren in general, they must apply to the Elders.
> 2. Silk hat bands may not be worn, save on fur hats, for nice use.
> 3. Dark colored hat bands may not be worn, on summer hats.
> 4. All should remember that these are not the true heirs of the Kingdom of Heaven, who multiply to themselves, needless treasures of this world's goods. (Andrews, pages 281-282)

Shakers observed numerous regulations concerning meals, including groups assembling for prayers in designated areas before meals while awaiting the bell to call all to the dining rooms. Additional prayers were said in place at the tables. Monitors helped children with the cutting of their food and men and women ate at separate tables. They ate in silence, observing a code of good manners that Emily Post would consider exemplary. The Millenial Laws, Part II (More Particular Orders for Justification and Protection), Section VII (Orders concerning Attending to Meals, Eating, Etc. Etc.) list sixteen orders. Included among them are dietary laws that reflect the folk wisdom of the time and general practice a generation later. Meals were early breakfast, noon dinner and six o'clock supper.

Enfield Shakers

There has not been a difinitive study of the Enfield Shakers but a number of interesting items have been published. A great deal of manuscript material is also available, the Shakers being inveterate and careful chroniclers of their lives. Enfield's Shaker Village was "more pretentious and extensive, perhaps, than any other Shaker settlement." (Chandler, page 27) Its 1828 population, in four families, came to 262 members. They occupied

> 23 dwelling and store houses [with a] spacious and valuable Grist mill, 3 saw mills, 3 cider mills, one carding machine, a machine for the manufacture of pails, a trip hammer shop, and a lead aqueduct manufactory. 70 cows, 12 horses and 12 yoke of oxen. [They had an] elegant Church in their

principal village for public worship. 70 X 50, two stories high. (Carleton, page 200)

The Historic American Buildings Survey, which documented the Shaker Great Stone Dwelling House at Enfield in 1959, proves these dimensions to be inaccurate. The building's dimensions are 58'1" by 100'2½". The trustees decided on a dwelling of such hugh proportions because of the tremendous growth in the Society's population at the time. By regulation, no building could exceed the meeting house in size. To solve this problem, the elders decided to incorporate the meeting house into the dwelling house. Technical solutions to the problem of an open room of this size are described in the HABS survey.

A truss system concealed within the floor, ceiling and central walls of the third and fourth stories supports the upper stories of the structure. This system allows a second-story meeting room to run the full width of the building (54' - 4") without the need for interior supporting columns (columns were added in the 20th century.) Heavy timber members are joined with pegged mortise and tennon joints....

Several bits of Enfield Shaker history are available in miscellaneous sources. One interesting item concerns the outcome of an 1810 lawsuit brought against Enfield Shakers. The judgment confirmed the nature of the Shaker convenant as a binding contract and some of the court's remarks on this case reveal a strong value system in the outside world at the time that supported the Shaker lifestyle:

No one can see the improvements made in hus-bandry and manufactures by this sect and at the same time believe the existence of the sect to be against the policy of the law. Whatever we may think of their faith, their works are good, and charity bids us think well of the tree when the fruits are salutary. (quoted in Andrews, page 206)

It was a later lawsuit, filed in 1848, that Franklin Pierce successfully defended. The choice of Pierce as defense lawyer was a logical one for the Society of Shakers to make. Pierce had been a leader in the effort

to remove the Protestant qualification for office holding from the State Constitution....His advocacy of this change, beginning in 1844, had marked him as one devoted to the cause of religious liberty. (Upton, page 3)

Pierce's eloquent argument before the court ran from 3:00 in the afternoon until 5:30 and, after a supper recess, from 6:10 to 7:50, on December 29, 1848. The case

was won on appeal several weeks later.

Elder Briggs of Enfield, New Hampshire, described a social aspect to the Shaker's work. He recalls

that wood-chopping and maple-sugaring were gala times, like picnics, and mention[s] the diversion of fishing, swimming, and playing ball, the half-holidays once a week during warm weather, the refreshments during haying, which consisted of sweet buttermilk; lemon, peppermint, chickerberry, raspberry, and current shrub; cake, cheese, and smoked herring. (quoted in Andrews, pages 189-90)

One disadvantage of a life of simplicity was expressed by Enfield, New Hampshire's Elder Briggs, for forty years a Shaker. He often found it trying to be subject to the judgment of others whose knowledge of the world was inadequate. He laid the cause to Shaker life, saying those leaders "educated to be like children, usually remain children and the product of their teaching is again children." (quoted in Andrews, page 237)

One facet of Shaker life that is stressed in Shaker literature is the fact that no child raised by the Shakers is encouraged or coerced into membership. Children wishing to go out into the world are given clothing and a kind of dowry to tide them over until they can put to use the skills they'd acquired by living among the Shakers. Shaker schools were renowned for their thoroughness.

A tragic murder mars the serene history of the Enfield Society. A man named Thomas Weir had placed his children with the Shakers while he fought in the Civil War. Upon his return, he visited his children and wanted them back. Apparently, the children were unwilling to leave. One evening, the community's administrator, Caleb Dyer, refused to allow Weir to visit his children at a later than usual hour. When Weir returned, he shot Mr. Dyer who died a short time later. Weir, fifty-two years old at the time, was sentenced to thirty years and a day in the state prison for the crime.

"Division of each community into family units" made a useful structure for the Shaker lifestyle, bringing

...distinct advantages. It led to a certain flexibility of production. Each family carried on its industrial activities independently, buying from and selling to the world or other families and societies....Prefer-ential discounts and exchange policies prevailed. Experience proved that the ideal size was about fifty members...(Andrews, pages 106-107)

The Trustees, also called office deacons, had responsibility for the fixed property of the Society, serving as its representatives in the legal sense. They conducted business with the outside world on behalf of the Society. Other deacons, with such titles as farm deacon, garden deaconness, etc., had responsibility for goods and property within the Society. The Trustees Office served "as a supply depot and clearing house for outgoing or incoming goods." (Andrews, pages 105-107)

One historian describes Enfield architecture as consisting of "modest buildings...built for convenience and durability over beauty although some of them have an expensive appearance." (Carleton, page 200) One can hardly doubt that the reference to "expensive appearance," belongs to the Great Stone Building in front of which the Elders and Eldresses pose for an anonymous photographer, probably another Shaker. (page 187)

The privately owned Great Stone House, on the site of Enfield's Shaker Village, is known today as The Shaker Inn and Conference Center. There is a curious appropriateness to this use since the original building, the center of the Church Family, served as the main dwelling house of Enfield's Shaker Society. The massive building dwarfs everything that surrounds it. Today, the first floor of the granite structure houses a museum, bar and restaurant; the second floor contains conference and lounge rooms; the third floor consists of guest rooms. There were two other stone buildings erected by the Shaker community. One is the Laundry, first stone building in Enfield (1849) across from the Inn, in which is located the store for the LaSalette Father's Shrine. There is also a brick building on the east side of Rt. 4-A.

In 1985, the Lower Shaker Village Partnership purchased all but thirty acres of the original twelve hundred plus acres on both sides of Route 4 in Enfield that the Shaker Society sold to the LaSalette fathers in 1928. The property once called by its Shaker residents "God's Chosen Vale," is being developed by the Lower Shaker Village Partnership who run the Shaker Inn in the Great Stone House.

The imposing porticoed building next to the Shaker building is a Roman Catholic Church, built by the priests who purchased the Village. The LaSalette fathers is a Roman Catholic religious order with antecedents in French Canada. They have ministered throughout New England for several generations. The cupola of the belfry on the Great Stone House carries what at first might seem to be a weathervane but is, instead, a cross, placed there when the LaSalette fathers used the building. The LaSalette order of priests had, over the years, put the property to a variety of uses, including a seminary, boy's boarding school, summer camp, retreat house and conference center. Today, the LaSalette fathers have retained the land on which their shrine to Our Lady of LaSalette stands and a couple of administration buildings associated with the shrine. It attracts thousands of visitors annually, with Christmas and May celebrations being the highlights of the year. The front of the Greek Revival Church carries a plaque on the side of the main entrance that reads: "Gift of our Illustrious Benefactress Mary A.

Keane God Bless Her." The words above the pediment are: EUNTES ERGO DOCETE OMNES GENTES (Go, therefore and teach all nations), a Latin phrase taken from the New Testament.

The church today is owned by the Shaker Village Partnership and leased back to the order for occasional church services. Special events, concerts, lectures and the like, are held there throughout the year and the Church, still consecrated, has become a popular site for non-denominational weddings.

Oral legend has it that the Shakers had an offer that was four times higher at the same time that the LaSalette Fathers made their bid for the property. The other bid allegedly came from a group of New Yorkers who wanted to start a game preserve. One version of the story goes that when the Shakers considered the potential uses to which the property would be put, that they felt the order of priests who intended to open a seminary and school there were planning a use for the facilities more in keeping with the spirit and intent of their own beliefs. Therefore, they accepted the lower bid.

In his 1875 *Gazetteer* of New Hampshire, Alonzo Fogg makes the remark that the Shakers "were not in the early days, distinguished from others in their dress, and would not to-day, if the world did not yield to the calls of fashion. They now dress as every one did a hundred years ago." (page 146)

Talented and industrious farmers, the Shakers became known in New Hampshire for their seeds, herbs, boxes, brooms, measures, pails, and baskets. At Enfield, they kept a herd of fifteen hundred sheep as well as oxen and cows whose milk and milk products were processed for private consumption and public sale. The Enfield Shakers raised and sold seed on twenty-five hundred acres of land, some argue that they were the first of the Shaker communities to do so.

Shakers were entirely approving of technological advances; in 1854, the Enfield community bought one of the first two circular knitting machines made by a Franklin inventor. By the 1870s, the Society was doing almost a half-million dollars of annual business through farming and manufacturing.

Presidential Visit

President Monroe visited the Enfield community in June 1817 when he toured the region. A Lebanon chronicler recalls the event.

In the summer of this year (1817) the people of this vicinity had their first sight of a president of the United States....At Enfield, coming by the Fourth

New Hampshire Turnpike, he stopped at the habitation of the Shaker community. The elder came forth from the principal house in the settlement and thus addressed the president: "I, Joseph Goodrich, welcome James Monroe to our habitation." The president then offered his hand to the eldress, when she said: "I respect thee, but I cannot take thy hand." The president examined the institution and their manufactures for about an hour and was highly pleased with the beauty of their fields, their exemplary habits, their improvements in agriculture and the neatness of their substantial but plain buildings. (Downs, pages 232-233)

Two years later, Monroe visited a Shaker community in Kentucky.

A smaller Shaker community developed after Lot 20, Range 1 of the Grand Monadnock, Dublin, was settled by Benjamin Spaulding at the close of the eighteenth century. Upon his death, two of his three sons deeded the land in 1814 to a representative of the Shaker Community at Shirley, Massachusetts. The Shakers used the property as pasturage. In 1883, they sold it along with all of their other local property (about six hundred acres in all). (Chamberlain, page 139)

Lot 1, Range 1 of the Grand Monadnock, Jaffrey, was settled by Shakers from the Shirley Community about 1810. Nathaniel Turner bought it of Matthew Thornton of Merrimack in 1787 who turned around and deeded it to Elijah Wild, Jr., of Shirley, for sixty pounds. Elijah deeded some of the land to Ivory Wild, of Shirley, in October 1800 and on October 23, 1810, the remainder to the Shakers. The next day, Ivory did the same with his portion. Ivory had converted to Shakerism in Shirley upon hearing Mother Ann Lee preach; he was one of four prosperous farmers to break with Shirley's Congregational Church, the first such breach in that church's history. This deed was made in the year of the great Shaker Revival. In addition to the Dublin property mentioned above, the Shakers also bought a farm in Marlborough in 1839 and, in 1860 and 1872 additional Dublin and Jaffrey land.

Education in the Western Regions

Formal education at all levels goes back to the early days of the settlement in western New Hampshire. Among the first considerations of town meetings was the building and upkeep of village schools. It was really the first basic concern addressed by our ancestors once the meeting house was built and issues surrounding it had been settled. In some communities "dame schools" held in the homes of local women preceded town public schools. Nevertheless, within a few years of stabilization, settlements built town schools and arranged school terms

around the agricultural calendar. Basic Colonial law requiring the establishment of grammar and elementary schools strengthened in the new republic. Few communities dragged their feet, even the most reluctant voters capitulating within a few years of discussion on the issue. Probably, the later settlement of the frontier by former residents of Massachusetts and Connecticut prevented delay in establishing schools, for the western regions did not repeat the history of poor cooperation on the founding of schools that marked the east coast settlements years earlier. The communities of the Connecticut River Valley responded quickly to state laws concerning education. By mid-nineteenth century, the average number of weeks in the school year along the Connecticut River was fifteen, fewer in the rural towns, more in the commercial centers. Quality may have been minimal at first, but the appearance of private seminaries, religious and secular, and enhanced state educational laws, eventually raised the standards of universal public education.

Charlie Wilson [born c. 1857, Sharon] told us he never went to school for the summer terms after he was seven years old. He said that in '68 he attended seventeen weeks and that was the longest he ever went to school. (King, page 114)

A number of citizens, schooled in the area, made important contributions to education at home and far beyond. Dartmouth College students filled education posts throughout New England, sometime only briefly, as a means of working their way through school. Ada C. Howard of Temple was the first president of Wellesley College. Gen. John Eaton, also raised and educated in the area, served as the first commissioner of the United States Bureau of Education established under President Grant and forerunner of the federal Department of Education. Another significant contribution to education was the founding of the nation's first Normal School by R. Samuel Reed Hall, LL. D., born in Croydon, October 17, 1795. He was also the originator of America's System of Teacher training and the author of the first textbook on teaching in the United States.

Dartmouth

Another factor shoring up the timely establishment of schools in the region was the extraordinary fact of its frontier college at Hanover, chartered in 1769. The town of Hanover and Dartmouth College are indistinguishable from each other in the first years of their establishment. The town *was* the college. Town records indicate that the citizens of the area have generally taken pride in their proximity to Dartmouth. The cultural events that Dartmouth's presence makes possible in the region

By the looks of the children in this May 9, 1885, photo of School No. 8, Fitzwilliam Depot, Rhoda J. Colburn, the teacher, ran a tight ship. Richard Bradley sent this annotated document from Santa Ana, California. The children are all identified, a welcome addition to what would have been another virtually anonymous photo. Back row: Winifred Ward, Erwin Wilson, George Baldwin, Arthur Handy, George Couloom, Herbert Hohman, Oscar Flagg, John Bruno Todd, Arno Ward, and Herbert Pease. Second row: Mary Tatro, Ada Baldwin Whitcomb, Walter Grout, Sarah Hayden, Netie Whitney, Lillian Baldwin, Hattie Baldwin, Florence Whitney, Alice Burbank, Annie Bigelow, Nellie Handy, and Lottie Pease. Third Row: Simon Bruno, Hormidas [?] Plante, Charles Williams, Robert Stone, Harry Hohman, Eva Grant, and Herman Todd. Again, we see the range of ages of the young scholars and the neat dress donned for the occasion. Courtesy of New Hampshire Historical Society

Tilden's Ladies Academy in West Lebanon, a well-respected private boarding school for young women, was named after its principal benefactor, William Tilden, Esquire. Built in 1854, it was operated under its original Board of Trustees until Hiram Orcutt, then its principal, leased the school in 1865 and ran it concurrently with another school in Brattleboro, Vermont, for three years.

A few years later William Tilden added two imposing wings to the original structure. He sought and obtained a new charter from the New Hampshire legislature and a new board of trustees was named. Facilities included "a spacious gymnasium, dining-hall, rooms for the family of the principal, studio, a reading, historical, and library room, and some fifty pleasant rooms for boarders." (Fogg, page 528) It thrived under the new circumstances for many years. This photo, from the Langill Photo Studio, in Hanover, was taken in the 1880s. Its students, as is evident from this photograph, were drawn from upper middle-class families living within a radius of about a hundred miles. Courtesy of Dartmouth College Library

Situated on the town Common, this Washington schoolhouse is flanked by the Washington Town House (1789) and the Congregational Meeting House (foreground), completed in 1841. The schoolhouse was built in 1883 and, as this recent photograph shows, is still in active use. The three buildings comprise one of the loveliest town commons in the region, a source of much pride to town residents.

This picture calls to mind the fact that there are school plagrounds in western New Hampshire that cover portions of public streets. For the well-being of children and teachers, the towns involved continue to make appropriate arrangements to bar the areas from motorized traffic at specified times. One of Newport's schools enjoys such a privilege even today. A document in the WPA files at the University of New Hampshire reports that Ackworth's "Main Street goes through the school-yard," and is "closed at lunchtime for children's play." This would have been in the late 1930s or early 1940s. Photo by Bob LaPree; courtesy of New Hampshire Historical Society

Keene Teacher's College was founded by the New Hampshire General Court of 1909. Situated in the heart of the great mill city, the college celebrated its half-centenary in 1959 with an enrollment of 770 students. Since that date, the college has grown tremendously. In 1963, it became a division of the University of New Hampshire. It has become an important cultural center in the area helping to spark a revival of urban renewal that continues to the present. Pictured is the Young Student Union Building on Main Street, Keene. Photo by Armand Szainer

greatly enhance the quality of life and contribute to Hanover's summer tourism.

Dartmouth's early founding by Eleazar Wheelock, a New Lights minister who graduated from Yale in 1733, has an extremely interesting history. Its charter was granted in 1769 by John Wentworth II, nephew of Benning Wentworth and last of the royal governors of New Hampshire. He generously endowed it with forty thousand acres of land and supported the college in other meaningful ways. (see lithograph, page 189)

In Connecticut, Yale graduate Rev. Eleazar Wheelock had tutored Samsom Occum, a Mohegan Indian of exceptional intelligence, and became fired with the idea of establishing a school for Indians. Such a school was endorsed by the Convention of Congregational Ministers in 1762. On behalf of Wheelock's dream, Occum traveled to England to raise funds. He preached to enthusiastic audiences and raised large contributions for the College, including a large sum from the earl of Dartmouth. The earl also prevailed upon the king of England who gave 200 pounds.

Meanwhile, Wheelock decided that he wanted to enlarge his endeavor to include higher education as well and applied to Gov. John Wentworth, himself a learned man with degrees from Harvard, Oxford, and Aberdeen, to establish a college for "education and instruction of Youth of the Indian Tribes...and also of English Youth and any others." Wentworth gave him the charter and his continuing support. Among other things, he granted forty thousand acres, encouraged its petition to the first state legislature for a lottery to raise 3,000 pounds, in 1773, and served on its first Board of Trustees.

A footnote to the founding of Dartmouth College is the fact that the first meeting of its Trustees took place in the northeast parlor of Wyman's Tavern in Keene, October 22, 1770. The Tavern, located midway between Lebanon, Connecticut, where Wheelock started out, and Hanover, to which he was relocating, was easier to reach at the time. For many years, the road north through Northampton, Massachusetts, Hinsdale, Keene, and Charlestown to Hanover, was known as Dartmouth College Highway. At the historic Wyman Tavern, 339 Main Street, Keene's patriots gathered at dawn for their enlistment march, under the command of William Wyman, innkeeper, to Cambridge, Massachusetts, April 20, 1775. Today the building is a museum of the Historical Society of Cheshire County.

Hanover was little more than a frontier when Wheelock moved there with his household and a handful of students in 1770 at the generous invitation of the settlers who gave Wheelock three thousand acres of land along the river, labor, funds, building materials, and additional property at the eastern edge of the township. Ironically, Occum never followed Wheelock to Hanover, having had a falling out with him. Ironically, also, the college educated practically no Indians until late in the twentieth century, in part, perhaps because few Indians lived in the upper Connecticut River area after the French and Indian War was over, a situation Wheelock, doubtless, did not expect. Dartmouth's motto, the biblical text, *Vox clamantis in Deserto* ("A Voice Crying in the Wilderness"), like Brown's sketch (p. 189), appropriately symbolizes the college's original goal. In the early 1970s, the neglected pledge of the school's charter to educate and instruct "Youth of the Indian Tribes" was taken out and dusted off. After consideration by a College-wide planning group, a successful Indian Studies program was introduced at Dartmouth College.

A succinct history of the college appears in the autobiography of the famous Mexican Muralist, Jose Clemente Orozco, written after he had been artist-in-residence there in the 1930s. He writes vividly of Dartmouth College, his remarks a lively combination of romanticism, wit, perception, and honesty. He says,

Dartmouth College in Hanover, New Hampshire, is one of the oldest of educational institutions in the American Union. Several years before the War of Independence it was founded by a missionary who wished to educate the Indians of the neighborhood. Eleazar Wheelock came among them with a grammar, a Bible, a drum, and more than five thousand quarts of whiskey. To the sound of his drum, the Indians assembled, drank his whiskey, and learned the idiom of the New Testament. Today there are no more Indians left to be educated after this admirable plan. The College preserves Wheelock's grammer, his Bible, and his drum. It now has great halls, stadiums, and laboratories, which are worth millions of dollars. In the midst of it all stands Baker Library, the pride of the College, with a collection of books in Spanish which by itself is greater than many very important libraries in Spanish America.

On the ground floor of the library I painted a series of murals....My stay in Dartmouth, from 1932 to 1934, was altogether agreeable and satisfactory. Dartmouth is one of the best examples of Liberalism in the North and of New England hospitality. New Englanders are completely different from other groups of Americans. Country folk, hostile and formal in their dealings with outlanders and new arrivals, but most cordial on closer acquaintance, and anxious to be neighborly, to understand one, and to help out with the greatest good will, disinterest, and courtesy....When I had finished my work, faculty and students bade me a most cordial farewell."(pages 158-160.)

Much is made in the history books and local lore of

Long admired for its architecture, Hanover can count the buildings along the east side of the Green among its most enduring and handsome assets. The famous engraver, N. Currier, once published an engraving of College Row, entitled "Dartmouth College" This photo of "Dartmouth Row," taken in the 1800s, includes, left to right, Thornton, Dartmouth, Wentworth and Reed Halls, essentially, the entire College at mid-nineteenth century. Reed Hall is the oldest, being on the site of Wheelock's homestead which was moved in 1839 to make way for it. The Wheelock mansion, now on West Wheelock Street, became Howe Library. The first buildings were planned by Eleazar Wheelock in consultation with architect Comfort Sever who had come to Hanover in 1773 under Wheelock's patronage. Phinehas Annis completed the cupola on Dartmouth Hall in 1791. Courtesy of Dartmouth College Library

One-room schoolhouses dotted the American landscape in the nineteenth century. Those photographed here are typical. This traditional school photo illustrates the extreme range of ages of the children who attended the local school. The toddlers seated on the bottom granite step at Lebanon in 1891, appear to be unusually young for matriculation, although, typically, enrollment began at four years of age.

The boys wear caps but only one girl and the teacher do likewise. In general, those assembled appear to be willing subjects for the camera lens. The clothing seems rather formal for "everyday." Young men, often students earning their way through college, or unmarried women, were hired for the instruction of children. As secondary schools increased, the teaching of the elementary grades was usually left in the hands of women.

Lebanon was quick to establish a Teacher's Institute after the N.H. legislature, in its June 1846 session, authorized towns to raise money to support teacher training institutions. Within three years the town voted a " 'Teacher's Institute' in the Western Judicial District of the County of Grafton." In 1855, the town was divided into twelve school districts. Courtesy of New Hampshire Historical Society

"School House, District No. 1, 1844," reads the sign below the flagpole. The original photograph is identified as having been taken before 1919 in Fitzwilliam. The older couple, dressed in historic costume, sit in the rather elegant surrey with the fringe on top. Perhaps, the occasion is an Old Home Day or other heritage event in the town which were often held at local schools like this one. Courtesy of New Hampshire Historical Society

the legendary grave robbing on the part of Dartmouth medical students. Apocryphal though the stories may have been, many residents in the surrounding communities took them at face value. Two anecdotes from Andover illustrate the point.

One grave in the old North Church Cemetery at East Andover has no tenant, for the body of Mary Wadleigh Hilton was stolen by grave robbers on the night of the burial and presumably taken to the medical college at Hanover. This happened a long time ago in 1824. A small marble monument in the Hilton family row bears the inscription "BODY STOLEN AFTER BURIAL." The occurrence greatly disturbed the community.

The second anecdote concerns "the first wife of Jonathan Emery [who] died twenty years later." Recalling the Hilton incident, her husband buried her "in the front yard of his home and...protected [her grave] against robbery by a wire and bell in the house." (Chaffee, page 212)

Lyman Flint kept careful accounts of his expenses while a student at Dartmouth College. Expenses remained surprisingly consistent in the period of over a half-century, to judge by Flint's records, a sample of which includes, for his sophomore year 1838-1839, Fall term tuition of $9.00, miscellaneous books, $6.66 and thirteen weeks board, $15.56 plus 1½ bushels of wheat at $3.00.

High school expenses of mid-nineteenth century were also modest, by our standards. For the 1844-1845 school year of Francestown's District No. 4, the following account survives:

August 1844	Paid Lucretia Batcheldor for teaching Summer School	18.00
	Paid Richard Fuller for wood	4.68
May 16	Paid for Washing House	1.00
Dec 5	To Peins of Glass & seting the same	30
	Paid for Brome & tin diper	28
March/45	Paid James Pitee for teaching Winter School	52.50
	Paid Joseph Willard for Black Board	75
		————
		$77.51

(Schott, page 94)

Similar discrepancy between men's and women's teaching salaries continued in New Hampshire for well over a hundred years.

Such proverbial expressions in currency at the time as "a penny saved is a penny earned" and "every penny counts" take on enhanced meaning when reflected against these accounts. The wonder is that the expressions are still in active usage a century and more later.

One-Room Schoolhouses

One-room schoolhouses were modest buildings, with a door at one end and the teacher's desk at the other. Typically, they contained but one room with plank benches down the sides. The desks would have been locally made. Boys sat on one side of the room and girls on the other, smaller children in the front where they enjoyed the heat of the great stove that was in the center of the room. On cold days, the bigger boys and girls seated against the back wall were near freezing. Aside from the desks and benches, the only other furnishings would have been a blackboard and occasionally, in some schools, a few outline maps. Textbooks were the saving grace of education.

The success of the schools in towns like Coventry-Benton was due in no small degree to the excellence of the text books. There were not many of these, but among them were some of the best. It is doubtful if there was ever compressed into small text book compass so many of the essentials of a first-class English education as were found in Webster's spelling book, supplemented by Adams' and Colburns' arithmetic, Morse's geography and the American Preceptor. (Whitcher, page 208)

One assumes that Whitcher's own formality of style harkens back to these very tomes.

Early schools in western New Hampshire followed the agricultural calendar with one eight-to-ten week term in the winter; later, another term of the same length was instituted in the summer. School was never in session during hoeing or haying seasons. Even today, the school calendar reminds us of the agricultural work year of our ancestors. Northern New England's winter vacations are a survival of the era when classes were dismissed for the sugaring season in late February or early March. In many regions of the country winter school vacations are unheard of.

Enrollment ranged from a few pupils to seventy-five or so, aged four to twenty-one and, if unmarried, even older, with all grades in the one room. Formal graduation ceremonies are a twentieth-century innovation in most local schools, although there were end-of-the-year exercises that townspeople were invited to attend. Curriculum was unregulated. Memorable examples of effective teaching methods sometimes found their way into the oral and written history of the community.

Emma F. Orcutt found many of her [Benton] pupils unable except by dint of great effort to master the multiplication table. She finally induced the whole school to sing it to the tune of "Yankee Doodle," and the thing was done before the boys and girls realized that they had been learning the detested table. (Whitcher, page 207)

The vividness of the recollection leads one to suspect that Miss Orcutt was the town historian's own teacher which would date her services to the 1850s or early 60s. Children would recite, read compositions, and put dramatic programs, public performances being considered good practice for adult participation in town affairs. Supplementary to the formal schooling were such enriching activities as spelling schools, singing schools, and dance programs arranged by families on a private basis.

The curriculum included the basic disciplines of reading, writing, history, literature, geography, arithmetic, music, elocution, and declamation. Depending on the individual skills of the teacher, further enrichment in art or music would be possible. As is true today, many children took private lessons to supplement their schooling.

At least once a year, the public would be invited to a school program during which children would recite, sing, dance, or otherwise show off the fruits of their learning.

The stereotype of the stern, even violent, school master, is documented in anecdotes passed on orally and in the media. Town histories reinforce this idea, as well. Whitcher perpetuates the stereotype, recalling that " 'keeping order'. . . was one of the great essentials in the early days. Birch withes and heavy rock maple rulers, with physical courage and strength to wield them, were regarded among the things of first importance." He elaborates,

As has been previously noted, to "keep school" successfully, first of all it was necessary to "keep order," and the various tortures were invented by various teachers to accomplish this end. "Lickings" were nothing, but to bend over and hold down a nail in the floor, or to hold out a book at arm's length, or to be sent over to sit with the homliest girl in school, or, worst of all, to be sent to Squire William Whitcher's house to have that rigid old puritan just talk to you, some of these were genuine punishments. (page 208)

Clearly, these were primarily boys' punishments although some would apply equally to either sex. And some, perhaps, are apocryphal.

The highpoint of Francestown Academy's long, uneven history is said to have been during the principalship of Hervey S. Cowell who arrived at the school in 1876 at the age of twenty-one. Academy trustees said of him that the successful enlargement of enrollment during his tenure was due to: "the gentlemanly bearing, the mode of governing and the thorough and systematic teaching of our present teacher H. S. Cowell and his assistant." [the latter being Miss Flora C. Cobb, who soon became Mrs. Cowell.]

Coincident with Cowell's years at the Academy, the town's cultural life also took a turn for the better with "musicales, several lecture series, public recitations and concerts enliven[ing] the town." Under his direction, the high school started a student newspaper that included contributions from alumni. He reinstituted graduation exercises in 1882, "[t]o the delight of both townspeople and pupils. . . a full five days were given over 'to feasting and merriment' with the actual graduation exercises being witnessed by some 600 people" When he and his wife left Francestown in 1883, it was to the dismay of everyone. (Schott, page 99)

School reunions are a mid-nineteenth century phenomenon in western New Hampshire. In Sharon, they date from 1891, the event conducted very much on the order of Old Home Days. This fact led some in town to believe that the idea for Old Home Week germinated there.

It is an indication of the insularity of the small towns and villages in the area that such a notion could survive in Sharon. Reunions are a much older custom. Francestown Academy's reunions predate Sharon's, for example, by at least five years. Nevertheless, in smaller communities, town reunions and school reunions are virtually indistinguishable from each other. Traditionally held in Willard Bass Park (formerly Hadley's Grove), the Sharon reunion of 1939 was held inside the Brick Schoolhouse because of hurricane damage to the accustomed site. The group present in 1939 took on the task of clearing the Park "of its blowdown trees" and do so with dispatch. They again met at Willard Bass Park in 1940. (King, page 205)

Schoolhouse Museum

In Enfield, the historical society runs the Schoolhouse Museum, given to them by two former local scholars who bought and restored it. Harry Nichols and Wilson Roberts opened the Lockehaven Schoolhouse as a Museum in 1947 and turned it over to the Enfield Historical Society thirty-one years later.

In this late nineteenth-century panorama, Beech Hill offers a tempting
vantage point from which to survey the
town of Keene spread below. Although
the photographer is not identified,
"Village of Keene f'm Beech Hill," is
listed among French & Sawyer's
Stereoscopic Views of Keene and
Vicinity. Beech Hill, located east of the
village, figures prominently in the history
of the town. It became a mill settlement
in the late 1860s. Its high elevation made
it a favorite recreation area by the
1880s. In 1886, an octagonal auxiliary
reservoir was built which was given to
the town in 1929 for a swimming pool.
In 1890, a fish hatchery was added and
a tract of land was given to the town for
park land that became known as
"Children's Wood." Its twelve acres

adjoined City Park and was the gift of
George A. Wheelock, Keene's first parks
commissioner. In the first part of the
twentieth century, a ski jump was active
on its heights and motorcycle hill-
climbing competitions took place at
Cole's Pasture. In the late nineteenth
century, the road to Beech Hill was via
Roxbury Street.

Otter Brook Dam, completed April,
1958, was one of five dams built after
1950 as part of a second phase of the
Flood Control Project that was spawned
after the great Hurricane of 1938.
(Another regional dam, on the Cold
River in Walpole, was built about the
same time. The others were in the White
Mountains area.) Otter Brook, a
tributary of the Ashuelot River, like most
other rivers in the region, was already at

flood stage when the hurricane swept up
the Connecticut River Valley that
September.

One peculiar occasion also distin-
guishes the history of Beech Hill. A ten-
day meeting of Millerites ended
December 25, 1842: "These people,
some of them substantial citizens, were
the followers of William Miller who
interpreted the scriptures as forecasting
a certain day when the world would
come to an end . . . . [A] few of his
followers disposed of some of their
worldly goods, clothed themselves in
white robes, and gathered at 'Sun Set
Rock' on Beech Hill and waited patiently
for this great event to occur. The
following morning at daybreak, it is
said, 'they humbly and quietly walked
back to their respective homes much

12
TOWN AND VALLEY VIEWS

T he notion of village and town is central to the world-view of the citizens of New Hampshire's western regions. Expressions of local self-consciousness are found in various historical documents and artifacts. The paintings of Harrisville's village of Eastview that Willard Richardson executed on old molding planes are one example of this value expressed by a village native. The carvings of his sister, Louisa Richardson Fairfield, made of the schoolchildren of Hancock, when she lived there, is another. Their brother, Robert's, portrait-dolls of their great-grandparents, Moses and Rebecca Eaton, nineteenth-century residents of Eastview, are still another. Some of these artifacts are pictured elsewhere in the book, among the color photos.

Town histories, in more concentrated form than any other, perhaps, pay tribute to the idea and ideals of town and village life. Each locale seems to have found one or more points, events or persons to enshrine as representative of local values. These photos have been selected as apt visual expressions of pride in town or village. Interspersed among them are vignettes from local sources evincing special meaning for individual communities as defined by their towns or villages.

The village of Orford, disdained as insignificant in the eighteenth century, today enjoys distinction as the location of seven elegant homes situated atop "The Ridge," commanding fine views of the Connecticut River. Samuel Morey's house, discussed earlier, is one of their number (third from the right). The one

north of his was a dower house he built for his daughter.

This southeasterly view, taken from Fairlee Cliff around 1900, shows the sparsely settled village spread out between the Connecticut River and Lime Hill in the background. Orford's unusual Common runs north-south

along the west side of the highway that divides the village. The West Congregational Church is noted for the two long horse sheds that line its north and west sides. Orford Covered Bridge leads the eye into the scene from right. Courtesy of New Hampshire Historical Society

Contemporary Views

The emphasis on vintage photographs in this historical survey of western New Hampshire removes attention from its recent development. The last century has wrought enormous physical and social changes on the area. Yet, there is much that harkens back to an earlier age. Highways and real estate development have altered the face of the state, more dramatically in some locations than in others. The Connecticut River Valley has grown gracefully, on the whole.

Perhaps the most visible change results from the decline of farmland, the increase of forestation, and the proliferation of housing developments with architectural designs that reflect, to some degree, urban and suburban lifestyles encroaching into a rural environment. The results receive mixed reviews from long-time residents of the area, although there are those who profit substantially from these changes.

At the same time, there are many citizens of the area whose interest in heritage and conservation leads to their active support of measures that limit the nature and pace of growth in their respective communities and across the state. Effective activists wage and win environmental battles that contribute to the strengthening or reinstatement of values that societal change has eroded in the twentieth century. The physical changes wrought by development are often the very stimuli that motivates residents of the state's western regions to attempt local conservation. The nineteen eighties have aroused the consciousness of many, old-timers and recent residents alike.

Some sections of western New Hampshire remain relatively isolated from large population centers. Time moves slowly there. Towns have long memories and continuity is as evident as change in many places. These regions of the state enjoy their rural identity and strive to maintain some vestiges of it. They recognize, as well, that to lose their heritage would be detrimental to many concerns, including commercial interest. Nevertheless, it cannot be denied that without conscious and conscientious effort, maintaining the mark of history may prove to be elusive for western New Hampshire.

The abbreviated, handwritten identification jotted on back of this French & Sawyer View of Keene, says simply, "Looking s e 1st Cong. Ch. on l." At the time of this photo, before 1880 when it suffered a disastrous fire, the stores to the right of the church were known collectively as Clarke's Block, after Elbridge Clarke who owned the commercial buildings. Among the businesses housed in Clarke's Block, billiards, sewing machine sales room, ice cream parlor, bootery, harness shop, and stove shop are all identifiable on both parts of this clean image. Courtesy of New Hampshire Historical Society

This stereoscope is French & Sawyer's "View No. 306: Bridgeman's Block and Town Hall." The major visual focus of this view, however, and what makes it interesting, is that it presents a rare rear view of businesses in the center of the town's commercial district. The right hand section of a print of this stereograph in Keene's 1968 town history is identified as having been taken from the steeple of the Baptist Church. Attention is drawn to the "old Unitarian Church, corner of Main and Church Streets and the old Catholic Church on Marlboro Street." Here, we see the rear of businesses beside the First Congregational Church not visible in the preceding view. At the time of the photo, they are contained in Ball's Block, a commercial building that included at least one large meeting hall. Groups as disparate as the Odd Fellows and the first congregation of St. George's Greek Orthodox Church met at various times in Ball's Block. Keene's first High School was founded on that location in 1828, the year that the building was built by the Wilder brothers. French & Sawyer's photographic gallery was in the Bridgeman Block. Courtesy of New Hampshire Historical Society

E. C. Clark's photo of Troy Village depicts a mill village whose buildings are huddled around the oldest family-owned mill in the state, the third oldest in the country. (Ripley, The Fabric of Troy, page i) Incorporated in 1815, Troy was comprised of portions of Fitzwilliam and Marlborough from Monadnock Grants Nos. 4 and 5. According to local history, repeated petitions to separate beginning in 1791 were denied Troy settlers even after the village built a meeting house in 1813. Locals persuaded an investigative committee appointed by the New Hampshire legislature to "take the buggy ride to the town center (Marlboro[ugh]). This rough and tortuous ride convinced the committee...." (Fuller, page 5) The Troy Mill chimney dominates the town while the beautiful mill pond in the foreground and Mount Monadnock in the background emphasize its natural beauty. Courtesy of New Hampshire Historical Society

The gentleman lounging against the portico pillar of Charlestown's Eagle Hotel reminds us that the towns along the Connecticut had adequate amenities by the middle of the nineteenth century to satisfy their out-of-town guests, whether on business or pleasure. The large wood-frame building was one of several that burned in 1904, in a fire set by a prisoner in the town jail. The hotel had been built by Stephen Hassam for his son Stephen D.

The Eagle Hotel also ran the town's busiest livery stable. In 1830, the proprietor advertised in the Sullivan Mercury of January 1: " '30 cents in cash will be paid for any quantity of good oats less than 1000 Bushels on delivery at my stables. . . . S. D. Hassam.' " (quoted in Frizell et al., page 280) Courtesy of New Hampshire Historical Society

It is an all too rare pleasure to come across a well-documented photograph in a public archive. This view, "East Haverhill Village, 1886 or 1887, [a gift of] John F. Page, 10/1/79," is one of the happy exceptions. The stamp of Fred L. Hunkins, Out-door Photographer, Laconia, N. H., is nicely supplemented by detailed identification of the village, penned in a neat hand:

Left foreground: Potato starch mill. Center foreground: B. C. & M. R. R. Station (years later moved to Pike for a Library); Left Center, rear, the first East Haverhill Church, built 1836, burned 1902-03. House and Barns, center right—The Wm. Gannett, then ALONZO

SMITH farm. The splendid house later owned by daughter Bertha (Smith) Douglas. Road in center rear to Number Six District of East Haverhill—The large barn & white house site first settled by Issac Pike. Later home of Royal Noyes, Hiram Cross, in 1960-1970s by Maurice Naylor. Barn gone, house half torn down; now 1970s a small house, no sheds. In addition, Black Mountain and Sugar Loaf are noted.

Together, the image and its annotation are a model photographic legacy for present and future generations. Courtesy of New Hampshire Historical Society

The Claremont commercial district bears a striking resemblance to parts of Keene, their principal buildings obviously of the same vintage. The apothecary shop on the far left and the tailor shop far right are the only clearly discernible businesses. The long tree-lined avenues leading into the business blocks were the pride of regional communities. When avenues of old chestnuts and elms succumbed to disease or fell to hurricane winds in mid-twentieth century, the change wrought on the townscape saddened the populace. The awnings, common when these photos were taken, are charming accents to the period buildings they

grace. Towns along the Connecticut seem to our eyes a nice balance of rural and town life. Courtesy of New Hampshire Historical Society

Its title, "Monadnock House, Troy," but weakly describes this photo in which the artist tosses off the commercial establishment by placing visual interest on the delicate lines of the bandstand on the Common. Only the closest scrutiny rewards one a glimpse of hotel guests relaxing on the porches and the group standing companionably by the corner. The anonymous photographer has a genius for design. The fences, porchs, trees, posts, poles, and electric wires all conspire to achieve a stunning portrait that meets our most idealistic conception of a New England village. In this way, the photographic artists of the nineteenth century feed our imaginations and form our historical memories. Courtesy of New Hampshire Historical Society

Jotham A. French lists this stereoscope of Winchester as, "Over the Bridge from Depot Grounds." Such titles confirm that the clientele for many of the items in a photography studio's lists were townspeople themselves. Occasionally the name of a prominent resident will be used to identify a scene. French was one of many photographers who drew on an understanding of his neighbors' values and interests in creating a body of work

for sale. He had views of Keene and all of the surrounding towns and villages in his catalog.

Such stereotyped views as this, of a town's broad, tree-lined streets and avenues, were extremely popular. Here,

the pedestrians, posing for the camera, set up an interesting foreground and the buggy, wheeling off into the distance as it leaves the little bridge, adds to the depth of the image. Courtesy of New Hampshire Historical Society.

This view of the Observatory at Dartmouth College, is taken from almost the same vantage point as the stereoscopic view which illustrates the artist-photographer as humorist. (page 156) It looks south from Bartlett Tower. Like the view of Peterborough from East Hill, this view of Hanover is an uncommon one. What impresses is the marvelous setting in which Eliazer Wheelock placed his Indian College. The hills in the distance are dwarfed by the Hanover prospect which rises above the Connecticut River. This view was sold by the Detroit Publishing Company, in business around the turn of the century. They seem to have specialized in photographs for such commercial use as public relations business brochures, postcards, and calendars. Courtesy of Library of Congress, Photograph and Print Division

Newport's Town Common in 1988 presents a picture postcard scene to motorists passing on Route 10. The Newport Town Common hosts numerous public activities in summertime, including weekly band concerts, and weekend flea markets. Band concerts are a summer attraction in many towns in the region and this quaint gazebo provides a pleasant setting for such community events. The electric lights delineating the cross over the Methodists' Church of the Good Shepherd, entrance are uncommon decorative elements of traditional church architecture in western New Hampshire. In the heart of the Sunapee region, Newport, an active year-round community, attracts many summer residents. Photo by Armand Szainer

Enfield's Main Street in 1988 appears to be almost frozen in time. Similar scenes, reflective of an earlier period of the twentieth century, are found in many western New Hampshire towns. Even the use of the buildings in this village has undergone little change. Stanford & Sons Hardware Store carries a typical inventory. The hair salon on the second floor is appropriately named "Enfield Cutting Loft." Photo by Armand Szainer

Recent businesses often opt for locations and quarters that emphasize the rural past. While log cabins have never been widespread in western New Hampshire, they do have a long presence in the area.

"Granite-Northland Associates" spells out its services to the passersby on the prime commercial location at the corner of Routes 118 and 4 in Canaan. The family owned business is situated in a mixed residential/commercial section of the town. Photo by Armand Szainer

In 1985, the Lower Shaker Village Partnership purchased all but thirty acres of the original twelve hundred acres on both sides of Route 4 in Enfield that the Shaker Society sold to the LaSalette fathers several years ago. The property once called by its Shaker residents "Gods Chosen Vale," is being developed by the Lower Shaker Village Partnership who run the Shaker Inn in the Great Stone House.

The developers of these condominiums in Enfield incorporate the clean lines associated with Shaker architecture with a contemporary arrangement of housing units. This quasi-historical look is a popular one in western New Hampshire's newer "contained communities." Photo by Armand Szainer

Many contemporary developers in the state's western regions strive to blend their modern structures into the existing environment. A row of trees lining the riverbank discretely screens these modern buildings from the road. The roofs visible above the tree line belong to Hillside Terrace, a senior citizen community whose new brick buildings serve visually to tie together the areas on either bank of the Sugar River in Claremont. Photo by Armand Szainer

Mount Monadnock, Jaffrey, August 1988. This is the original of the sepia-toned image on the front cover of the book jacket. Photo by Armand Szainer

Hang gliding from Kearsarge Mountain, 1977. When this photograph was taken, the hang gliding craze was at its height in New Hampshire and Mount Kearsarge was a favorite launching place for experienced gliders. Photo by Armand Szainer

Bathers at Newbury Harbor, southern tip of Lake Sunapee. Photo by Armand Szainer

Picnicking at Mount Sunapee State Park, Newbury, 1972. Photo by Armand Szainer

Frye's Measure Mill, Wilton, is one of the most important historical sites in the Monadnock region and is listed on the National Register of Historic Buildings. In operation as a measure mill since 1860, the mill has had only three owners, Daniel Cragin, E. B. Frye, and the Savage Family who bought it in 1962. The colonial boxes manufactured by the mill are prized by collectors. The mill also manufactures hand carders for wool or cotton. Photo by the author

The residence on the left, occupied by members of the Savage family, is attached to the main mill by a walkway across the mill brook. Supplying power even today, the mill falls are visible in the background. Photo by the author

Shop display of colonial boxes, including a piggin into which colonial housewives put table scraps for feeding the pigs, hangs on the right. Photo by Armand Szainer

This bronze sculpture by Jacques Lipchitz, Mother and Child, sits outside the main entrance to Dartmouth College's Hopkins Center for the Performing Arts in Hanover. A gift of Evelyn A. and William B. Jaffe, it is one of many masterpieces from the extensive collection that Dartmouth College shares with the public. As a contemporary of the great innovators called Cubists, among whom Picasso is the most important, Lipchitz was greatly influenced by them. Measuring fifty-five inches, it was executed between 1949 and 1958. His works appear in the collections of many important contemporary private and museum collections. Photos by Armand Szainer

This eighteenth-century farmhouse is situated in southwestern New Hampshire. Farm architecture is one of New England's significant contributions to the nation's sense of its building-design heritage through our ancestor's artful manipulation of the rural landscape. Pictured as it stands today, several vintage photographs of the old farm are discussed in detail in the text, pages 18-21. The family who bought it in 1940 have kept it very much as it was originally. In the nineteenth century, the house was painted with a red, lead-based paint. The current owners have replaced its painted clapboards with darkly stained shingles. Photo by Armand Szainer

Early American cemeteries often sheltered symbolic meaning for their patrons. Puritan graves faced the rising sun, for example, to be ready for the Second Coming. David Watters, a scholar of Puritanism and a gravestone specialist at the University of New Hampshire, notes what he considers "to be a folk pattern" in the placement of early cemeteries in the Cornish region.

In that part of the state "communities placed cemeteries on prominent ridges to be in view of the surrounding community, as here." Dr. Watters points out, "with the fine federal house on the next hilltop. The stones date from the 1780s-1880s." (private correspondence) This cemetery is in Cornish Flats. Photo by David Walters

Miller's State Park, autumn 1978. Photo by Armand Szainer

The central Connecticut River Valley has nourished several stone carvers of considerable standing, among the most renowned the so-called Rockingham Carvers who worked on all sides of the Massachusetts/Vermont/New Hampshire borders at the turn of the nineteenth century. A New Hampshire carver of considerable repute was Paul Colburn of Hollis who worked in the late eighteenth and early nineteenth centuries. "Remember death," this beautiful example of his work reads, a continuing reminder from the grave of Elizabeth Cochran of New Boston. The stone and its carver are discussed by Theodore Chase and Laurel K. Gabel in their interesting essay on Colburn and his peers. Photo by David Watters

Village of New Boston, October 1969. Photo by Armand Szainer

Hilltop farm, February 1960. Photo by Armand Szainer

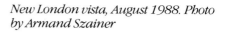

New London vista, August 1988. Photo by Armand Szainer

All three of the Richardsons, whose work appears here, are at home with carved and painted wood. Willard's four painted molding planes depict important components of the tiny village of Eastview in Harrisville where the artist grew up. They aptly illustrate the importance of the village in town organization and in the residents' sense of personal identity in early New Hampshire. The village center is still useful to the historian or local history buff because it supplies clues to the history of a town and often helps to locate the area's oldest buildings. Selected from a series of views painted on antique planes, many of which had been used at the family farm, these pictures preserve scenes he remembers or heard about in his boyhood. The painted surfaces measure approximately 3½ by 9½ inches and were executed since 1982. Photo by the author

The Eastview School No. 10 was within minutes of the Richardson farm. The gap between the stone wall and the school gave entrance to the woods where the teacher led Willard and his schoolmates on well-remembered natural history lessons. It served as a painting studio for one of the Richardson girls for a few years after the town discontinued its use as a school. The slate roof caved in under the weight of snow one winter about thirty-five years ago. Photo by the author

Eastview Train Station was on the route from Boston to Keene. Villagers heard its dependable whistle every morning and evening. The Richardson girls traveled to school in Hancock on the train, "so they could go to basketball," Willard says. The train route was discontinued after the devastating hurricane of 1938 tore up the tracks which were taken up finally in 1941. Photo by the author

Eastview Clothespin Mill employed many of the villagers of Eastview and surrounding communities. Extant only as ruins in Willard's youth, the mill operated until about the turn of the century. Village memory places Fortune Little, an Eastview resident and a former slave, as a mill hand in the clothespin mill. Photo by the author

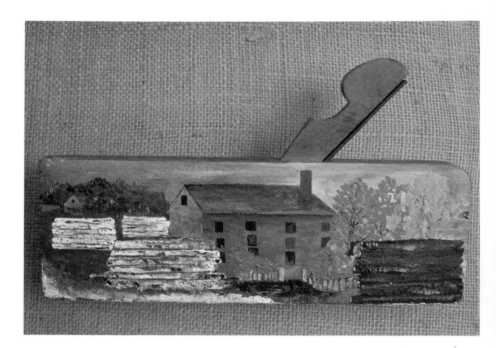

Benny Stevens was a neighbor to the Richardsons and is a favorite subject of Willard's stories and artistry. He has carved portraits of Benny in gemstones and ivory and has painted several versions of his house. It impresses Willard that Benny built this house including barn and woodshed single-handedly. Benny's pragmatism as evidenced by the untrimmed boards of the barn's siding tickles his imagination. Willard explains that Benny would just go out and cut off whatever length of board he needed, at the time he needed it. This made storage of the scrap lumber unnecessary. Benny loved his geese, hence the prominence of the gaggle of geese marching through the yard. Willard claims that Benny fed them fruit. At some point, itinerant thieves stole his geese and, Willard remembers, Benny was so devastated that he never kept geese again. There are many other stories about Benny attesting to his worthiness to be memorialized among the Eastview Village scenes. Photo by the author.

Louisa Richardson Fairfield has been recognized for her talents as a woodcarver for many years. She represented New Hampshire at the American Folklife Pavilion at the Montreal World's Fair and has received many other honors. She is also an expert needleworker and a fantastic cook. This set of figures, inspired by Browning's great "Pied Piper of Hamlin," might more accurately be called "Pied Piper of Hancock," for the children following the fabled Piper are, according to Louisa, the schoolchildren of Hancock, New Hampshire, some of

her own among them, whom she watched "troop up the hill to the Hancock School" every morning when she and her husband were raising their family there. She knows each and every child pictured here. Louisa has been carving this set of figures for over ten years and, she says, "it is almost complete. I finished one a while ago and there are only two or three more left." Like her brothers, Louisa brings her sense of homelife and her memories to her art, hallmarks of the traditonal artist. Photo by the author

Four views of the Cornish, New Hampshire-Windsor, Vermont, bridge August 1988. Photos by Armand Szainer

The Richardson family presented a Humanities Program, August 14, 1988, at the 55th Annual League of New Hampshire Craftsmen's Fair at Sunapee State Park. Left to right they are: Robert Richardson, his granddaughter, Sarah Richardson, Barbara Fairfield Barss, Willard Richardson, and Louisa Richardson Fairfield. The Humanities Program was a feature of a special annual program, Meet the Folk Artists, funded by the state Councils on the Arts and Humanities and the League of New Hampshire Craftsmen Foundation. The Richardson family has participated in that program since its inception. Louisa was, herself, a founding member of the Hancock Chapter of the League of New Hampshire Craftsmen, now part of the Sharon Arts Center where Willard is a current juried member. Sarah was visiting her grandparents at the time of the Fair and agreed to come along. She is a musician and, as her grandfather puts it, "she carves some." Photo by the author

The bridge's span against the New Hampshire hills.

View south from inside the bridge framing a nearby railroad bridge.

Entrance to the barricaded bridge from the Windsor, Vermont, side.

Allen, Richard Sanders. *Covered Bridges of the Northeast: The Complete Story in Words and Pictures.* Brattleboro, Vermont: The Stephen Greene Press, 1957.

Allison, Henry Darracott. *Dublin Days Old and New: New Hampshire Fact and Fancy.* New York: Exposition Press, 1952.

Andrews, Edwin Deming. *The People Called Shakers: A Search for the Perfect Society.* New York: Oxford University Press, 1953.

Antrim History Committee, The. *Parades and Promenades: Antrim, New Hampshire, the Second Hundred Years.* Canaan, New Hampshire: Phoenix Publishing, 1977.

Armstrong, John Bordon. *Factory Under the Elms: History of Harrisville, New Hampshire 1774-1969.* Cambridge, Massachusetts: MIT Press for The Merrimack Valley Textile Museum, [Andover, Massachusetts), 1969.

Bartlett, John Henry. *The Story of Sunapee.* Privately printed, 1941.

Bemis, Charles A. *History of the Town of Marlborough Cheshire County, New Hampshire.* Marlborough, New Hampshire: The Frost Free Library, 1974.

Bittinger, Rev. J. Q. *History of Haverhill, N. H.* Haverhill, 1888.

Blaisdell, Katharine. *Over the River and Through the Woods.* Vols. I, 6. Bradford, Vermont and Woodsville, New Hampshire: The Journal Opinion, 1979.

Braile, Robert. "Lake Goes Bottoms Up When N.H. Pulls Plug," *Boston Sunday Globe,* April 23, 1989, pages 79 and 81.

Carlton, Edwin Alonzo, compiler. *New Hampshire as It is.* Claremont, New Hampshire: Tracy and Company, 1856.

Chaffee, Ralph G. *History of Andover New Hampshire, 1900-1965.* Andover: Selectmen of Andover, 1966.

Chamberlain, Allen. *Annals of the Grand Monadnock.* Concord. New Hampshire: Society for the Preservation of New Hampshire Forests, 1975.

Chandler, Lloyd H. "The New Hampshire Shakers," *Historical New Hampshire,* Vol. 8, no. 1, March, 1952, pp. 3-32.

Chase, Theodore and Laurel K. Gabel. "The Coleman Connections: Hollis, New Hampshire, Stonecarvers, 1780-1820," *Markers III,* edited by David Watters, *The Journal of the Association for Gravestone Studies,* 1985, Lanham, Maryland: University Press of America, pp. 93-146.

Child, Hamilton, compiler and publisher. *Gazetteer of Grafton County, N. H. 1709-1816.* Syracuse, New York: The Syracuse Journal Company, Printers and Binders, June 1886.

Child, William H. *History of the Town of Cornish, New Hampshire With Genealogical record 1763-1910.* 2 vols. Concord, New Hampshire: Rumford Press. [1911?].

Childs, Francis Lane, ed. *Hanover, New Hampshire a bicentennial book: Essays in Celebration of the Town's 200th Anniversary.* [Town of] Hanover, 1961.

Clark, Charles E. *The Eastern Frontier: the Settlement of Northern New England, 1610-1732.* New York: Alfred A. Knopf, 1970.

Cohen, Charles Lloyd. *The Psychology of Puritan Religious Experience.* New York: Oxford University Press, 1986.

Cole, Luane, ed. *Lyme, New Hampshire: Patterns and Pieces. 1761/1976.* Canaan, New Hampshire: Phoenix Publishing, 1976.

Copeley, William. "A Busy Life Recalled." *New Hampshire Historical Society Newsletter.* 26:1 (Spring 1988), pp. 1-2.

Daniell, Jere R. *Colonial New Hampshire: A History.* Millwood, New York: KTO Press, 1981.

Diebold, Robert Kent. "A Critical Edition of Mrs. Mary Rowlandson's Captivity Narrative." Ph. D. dissertation, Yale University, 1972, pp. 28-38.

Downs, Rev. Charles A. *History of Lebanon, N. H. 1761-1887.* Concord: Rumford Printing Co., 1908.

Draves, David D. "The Civilian Conservation Corps in New Hampshire," *Historical New Hampshire,* Vol. 43, no. 2, Summer 1988, pp. 89-119.

Emlen, Robert P. "The Great Stone Dwelling of the Enfield, New Hampshire Shakers," *Old-Time New England* Vol. 69, nos. 3-4, Winter-Spring Issue, January-June 1979, pp. 69-85.

Fish, Lena M. [Bourne]. "The Flood at Squantum," *Jaffrey Recorder and Monadnock Breeze.* Friday, March 27, 1936, p. 8, col. 2.

[Fitzwilliam] Town History Committee, *Fitzwilliam: the Profile of a New Hampshire Town 1884-1984.* Published by the town of Fitzwilliam. Canaan, New Hampshire: Phoenix 1985.

Flanders, Helen Hartness. *Vermont Folk Songs and Ballads.* Hatboro, Pennsylvania: Folklore Associates, 1960, pp. 19-26.

———. et al., eds. *The New Green Mountain Songster.* New Haven, Connecticut: Yale University Press, 1939, pp. 156-158.

Fogg, Alonzo J. *The Statistics and Gazetteer of New-Hampshire.* Seventh edition. Concord, New Hampshire: D. L. Guernsey, Bookseller and Publisher, 1875.

Frazier, Ian. "A Reporter at Large: Great Plains-III," *The New Yorker,* March 6, 1989, pp. 41-68.

Frizzell, Martha McD., *et al. Second History of Charlestown, New Hampshire, The Old Number Four.* Charlestown, New Hampshire, 1955.

Garvin, Donna-Belle and James L. Garvin. *On the Roads North of Boston: New Hampshire Taverns and Turnpikes 1700-1900.* Concord, New Hampshire: N. H. Historical Society, 1988.

Gould, Denison. *"Rains finely Today:" The diary and account book of Denison Gould During the years 1817 to 1865.* Harrison C. Baldwin, D. M. D. ed., Privately printed, 1974.

Gould, Isaiah. *History of Stoddard, Cheshire County, N. H. 1774-1854.* Keene, New Hampshire Published by Mrs. Maria A. (Gould) Giffin, 1897. Reprint edition, Stoddard Historical Society, 1971.

Grantham, Shelby. "Bonfire! An illuminating look at the history of Dartmouth's infernos." *Dartmouth Alumni Magazine,* Vol. 79, no. 2, October 1986.

———. "Native American Studies: The Long-Deferred Promise." *Dartmouth Alumni Magazine,* Vol. 73, no. 9, pp. 24-29.

Griffin, S. G., M. A. *A History of the Town of Keene From 1732, when the Township was Granted by Massachusetts, to 1874, when it Became a City.* Keene, New Hampshire: Sentinel Printing Company, 1904.

Hancock History Committee, eds. *The Second Hundred Years of Hancock, New Hampshire.* Published by the Town of Hancock. Canaan, New Hampshire: Phoenix Publishing, 1979.

Hard, Walter. *The Connecticut.* Rivers of America Series. New York: Rinehart & Company, Inc., 1947.

Harriman, Walter. *The History of Warner, New Hampshire, for One Hundred and Forty-Four Years, from 1735 to 1879.* Concord, New Hampshire: The Republican Press Association, 1879. Warner American Revolution Bicentennial Committee edition, 1975.

Historical Society of Temple, New Hampshire. *A History of Temple New Hampshire 1768-1976.* Dublin, New Hampshire: William L. Bauhan Publisher, 1976.

"Historic Pageant at Swanzy," *Manchester, (N. H.): the Union,* June 11, 1936.

Hodgson, Alice Doan. *Thanks to the Past: The Story of Orford, N. H.* Orford, New Hampshire: Historical Fact Publications, 1965.

Hosley, William N. "The Rockingham Stonecarvers: Patterns of Stylistic Concentration and Diffusion in the Upper Connecticut River Valley, 1790-1817," *Puritan Gravestone Art II,* edited by Peter Benes, *The Dublin Seminar for New England Folklife Annual Proceedings 1978.* Boston: Boston University, pp. 66-78.

Jager, Ronald and Grace Jager. *New Hampshire: An Illustrated History of the Granite State.* "Partners in Progress" by Kathryn Grover. Woodland Hills, California: Windsor Publications, Inc., 1983.

———. *Portrait of a Hill Town: A History of Washington. New*

Hampshire 1876-1976. Washington, New Hampshire: Washington History Committee, 1977.

Jaffrey, Town of. *Annual Reports* for years 1947-1950.

Keene History Committee. *"Upper Ashuelot": a history of Keene, New Hampshire by the Keene History Committee.* Keene: City of Keene, New Hampshire, 1968.

Kenyon, Thedia Cox. *New Hampshire's Covered Bridges.* Illustrated by Stan Snow. Sanbornville, New Hampshire: Wake-Brook House, 1957.

King, H. Thorn, Jr. *Sliptown: The History of Sharon, New Hampshire 1738-1941.* Rutland, Vermont: Charles E. Tuttle Company, Inc. 1965.

Kipling, Rudyard. "How the Whale Got His Throat," in *Just-So Stories.* [original publication, 1902]. Middlesex, England: Penguin Books, 1987, p. 29; cited in Walter Hard; *The Connecticut,* p. 293.

Lehtinen, Alice E. E. *History of Jaffrey New Hampshire: Narrative and Geneology,* 3 vols. Town of Jaffrey, New Hampshire: Transcript Printing Company, Peterborough, 1971.

Lord, John King. *A History of the Town of Hanover, N. H.* Hanover: The Dartmouth Press, 1928.

Lord, Myra B. *A History of the Town of New London, Merrimack County New Hampshire.* Reprint of 1899 edition with Foreword by J. Duane Squires. Somersworth, New Hampshire: New Hampshire Publishing Company, 1972.

Lyford, James O., ed. *History of Concord, N. H. From the Original Grant in Seventeen Hundred and Twenty Five to the Opening of the Twentieth Century.* Concord History Committee Project. 2 vols. Concord, New Hampshire: The Rumford Press, 1903.

Mac Dowell Colony. *M Colony News.* Winter 1987/1988, vol. 15, no. 2.

Malmberg, Carl, ed. *Warner, New Hampshire 1880-1974.* Warner: Warner Historical Society, 1974.

Mandel, Peter. "Native Americans at Dartmouth: the People and the Program." *Darmouth Alumni Magazine.* May, 1986, vol. 78, no. 8, pp. 36-40.

[Marlborough, New Hampshire, Town of]. *Marlborough Through the Years 1776-1976.* Marlborough, 1976.

McClintock, John N[orris]. *History of New Hampshire: Colony, Province, State 1623-1888.* Boston: B.B. Russell, Cornhill, 1888.

Mead, Edgar T., Jr. *Through Covered Bridges at Concord; A Recollection of Concord and Claremont Railroad (N H).* Brattleboro, Vermont: The Stephen Greene Press, 1970.

Metcalf, Henry Harrison. *New Hampshire in History; The Contributions of the Granite State to the Development of the Nation.* Concord, New Hampshire: W. B. Ranney Company, Printers, 1922.

Morley, Linda and Margaret MacArthur. *"Margaret MacArthur & Family of Marlboro, Vermont on the Mountains High."* Cambridge, Massachusetts: Living Folk Records, 1971, [pp. 14-15].

Morison, George Abbot, *History of Peterborough New Hampshire.* Book One: Narrative. Book Two: Genealogies by Etta M. Smith. Rindge, New Hampshire: Richard R. Smith, Publishers, Inc., 1954.

Morse, Victor. *Windham County's Famous Covered Bridges.* Revised edition edited by Richard Sanders Allen. Brattleboro, Vermont: The Book Cellar, 1960.

New Hampshire Historical Society *Newsletter.* Vol. 18, no. 6, November/December 1984. "Uncovered: A Missing Link to New Hampshire's Legal History," pp. 1-2.

Nickerson, Louise. *Way Back When: Louise Nickerson recalls early Peterborough.* Peterborough, New Hampshire: Peterborough Historical Society, August, 1985.

Orozco, Jose Clemente. *Jose Clemente Orozco: An Autobiography.* Translated by Robert C. Stephenson. Texas-Pan-American Series. Austin: University of Texas Press, 1962.

Peterborough Bicentennial Committee. *Peterborough in Pictures 1876-1976.* Town of Peterborough, 1976.

Peterborough Historical Society. *Historical Sketches of Peterborough New Hampshire Portraying events and data contributing to the history of the Town.* Peterborough Historical Society, 1938. All references from Peterborough Historical Society are from the 1938 history unless otherwise noted.

[Peterborough, New Hampshire, Town of]. *Peterborough: A Good Town to Live In.* Peterborough, New Hampshire: Transcript Printing Company, 1926.

———. *1739-1939 Commemorative Booklet (Brief Historical Sketch of Peterborough from 1889-1939) Bicentennial of Peterborough New Hampshire October 21, 1939.*

Pike, Robert E. *Tall Trees, Tough Men: An anecdotal and pictorial history of logging and log-driving in New England.* New York: W. W. Norton & Company, Inc., 1984.

Poling, Evangeline Klee. *Welcome Home to Deering, New Hampshire.* Published for the Deering National Bicentennial Historical Committee. Canaan, New Hampshire: Phoenix Publishing, 1977.

Powers, Grant, *Historical Sketches of the Coos Country, 1754-1785.* Haverhill, New Hampshire: 1847, reprint 1880.

Ramsdell, George A. *The History of Milford.* Town of Milford, New Hampshire, Publishers. Concord, New Hampshire: The Rumford Press, 1901.

Read, Benjamin, *The History of Swanzey, New Hampshire from 1734-1890.* Salem, Massachusetts: The Salem Press Publishers and Printing Company, 1892.

Richardson, Robert. Hillsborough, New Hampshire. Personal communication, August 16, 1988.

Ripley, F. Fuller. *The Fabric of Troy: A History of Troy Mills.* Troy, New Hampshire: Troy Mills, Inc., 1986.

Roberts, George S. *Historic Towns of the Connecticut River Valley.* Schenectady, New York: Robson & Adee, Publishers, 1906.

Rowlandson, Mary (see Diebold, Robert Kent)

Russell, Howard S. *A Long, Deep Furrow: Three Centuries of Farming in New England.* Abridged and with a foreword by Mark Lapping. Hanover, New Hampshire: University Press of New England, 1982.

Sandburg, Carl. "Good Morning, America's Little Album: New Hampshire Again." *The Complete Poems.* New York: Harcourt Brace Jovanovich, Inc., 1969, pp. 378-79.

Sanger, Abner. *Very Poor and of a Lo Make: The Journal of Abner Sanger.* Lois K. Stabler, ed. Keene, New Hampshire: Historical Society of Cheshire County, 1987.

Schott, John R. *Frances' Town: A History of Francestown. New Hampshire.* The Town of Francestown, New Hampshire, Publishers, 1972.

Silver, Helenette. *History of New Hampshire game and furbearers.* Concord, New Hampshire: New Hampshire Fish and Game Department, 1957.

Smith, Charles James. *Annals of the Town of Hillsborough. Hillsborough County, N.H. From its first Settlement to the Year 1841.* Sandbornton, New Hampshire: Printed for the publisher, by J.C. Wilson, 1841. Reprint edition, Hillsborough Historical Society, 1979.

Smith, Etta M. see George Abbot Morison.

Smith, Marjorie Whalen. *Historic Homes of Cheshire County New Hampshire.* Brattleboro, Vermont: privately printed, 1968.

Society for the Protection of New Hampshire Forests. *The Grand Monadnock: A Literary Artistic & Social History.* Exhibition catalog, Thorne Art Gallery, Keene, 1974.

Somers, Rev. A. N. *History of Lancaster, New Hampshire.* Concord, New Hampshire: The Rumford Press, 1899.

Squires, James Duane. *Mirror to America: A History of New London, New Hampshire 1900-1950.* Concord, New Hampshire: Evans Printing Company, Inc., 1952. All references from Squires are from his 1956 history of New Hampshire unless otherwise noted.

———. *The Granite State Of The United States: A History of New Hampshire from 1623 to the Present.* New York: The American Historical Company, Inc., 1956.

State of New Hampshire, *New Hampshire Anniversaries: Development of the Constitution of New Hampshire. 1979-Biennium-1980.* Information prepared by Legislative Historian Leon W. Anderson. Published by Secretary of State William M. Gardner, unpaginated.

———. Writers of the Federal Writer's Project of the Works Progress Administration. *New Hampshire: A Guide to the Granite State.* American Guide Series. Boston: Houghton, Mifflin Company, 1938.

Stoddard (N.H.) Historical Society, History Committee of. *The History of the Town of Stoddard, New Hampshire Formerly known as Monadnock No. 7 and Limerick From its incorporation on Nov. 4, 1774 to 1974.* Stoddard, New Hampshire: Stoddard Historical Society, 1974.

Stout, Harry S. *The New England Soul: Preaching and Religious Culture in Colonial New England.* New York: Oxford University Press, 1986.

[Sunapee, Town of]. *Sunapee, New Hampshire Bicentennial 1768-1968: Historical Pictures and Stories.* Privately printed, 1968.

[Sutton, Town of]. *200th Annual Report of the Town of Sutton, 1984.*

Turner, Lynn Warren. *The Ninth State: New Hampshire's Formative Years.* Chapel Hill: University of North Carolina Press, 1983.

Wade, Hugh Mason. *A Brief History of Cornish (N.H.) 1763-1974.* Hanover, New Hampshire: The University Press of New England and The Town of Cornish, 1976

Wallace, William Allen. *The History of Canaan, New Hampshire.* James Burns Wallace, editor. Concord, New Hampshire: The Rumford Press, 1910.

Wasserman, Nancy. "Main Street." *Dartmouth Alumni Magazine.* June, 1982, vol. 74, no. 9, pp. 41-45.

Waterman, W. R. "The Story of a Bridge," *Historical New Hampshire,* vol. 22, no. 1, Spring 1965, pp. 3-26.

Wheeler, Edmund. *The History of Newport, New Hampshire, From 1766 to 1878.* Concord, New Hampshire: Printed by the Republican Press Association, 1879.

Whitcher, William F[rederick]. *Some Things About Coventry-Benton, New Hampshire.* Woodsville, New Hampshire: News Print, 1905.

White, W. Edward. *Covered Bridges of New Hampshire.* Plymouth, New Hampshire, privately printed, 1942.

Worthen, Augusta H. *The History of Sutton, New Hampshire.* A facsimile of the 1880 edition. Town of Sutton, New Hampshire [publishers], 1975.

WPA Guide, see State of New Hampshire, writers of.

Wright, Winifred A. *The Granite Town: Milford, New Hampshire 1901/1978.* Published for the Town of Milford. Canaan, New Hampshire: Phoenix Publishing, 1979.

Yesteryear Scenes of Keene. . . and Surrounding Areas. Photos from "The Old Timers" Calendars. Text by David Proper. Keene, New Hampshire: The Hampshire Press, n.d.

Collections

Cheshire County [New Hampshire] Historical Society, Photo Collections.

Dartmouth College Manuscripts and Photo Collections.

Library of Congress, Manuscripts and Photographs and Prints Divisions.

Manchester Public Library, New Hampshire Room Collections.

New Hampshire Historical Society, Manuscripts and Photo Collections.

New Hampshire State Library Collections.

Peterborough Historical Society, Manuscripts and Photo Collections.

University of New Hampshire, Dimond Library, Special Collections. WPA files.

Manuscripts

HABS NH-Mss., Library of Congress, Prints and Photograph Division; UNH Dimond Library Special Collections.

Richardson, Robert. Personal communication, n.d. [October, 1988].

Sky, Patrick. "The Search for Margery Gray," Honors Thesis, Goddard College, 1978, pp. 3, 20-21, 28-29.

Watters, David. University of New Hampshire, Durham, personal communication, August 10, 1988.

Sound Recordings

"Marjorie Gray," sung by Margaret MacArthur on *Music from Augusta "Concert Cassettes",* No. 620, SCS Sound, 1340 W. Irving Park Road, Suite 202, Chicago, Illinois, 60613.

"Hartford Wreck," sung by Margaret and Megan MacArthur on Margaret MacArthur and Family, on the Mountains High, No. F-LFR-100. Cambridge, Massachusetts: Living Folk Records, 1971. [Reissued and distributed by Alcazar Productions, Inc., Box 429, Waterbury, Vermont, 05676.]

INDEX

ABOUT THE AUTHOR

Folklorist Linda Morley has been collecting, teaching, and writing about New England folklife and culture for over twenty years. A resident of New Hampshire since 1973, Morley earned an M.A. in English at Villanova University and a Ph.D. in Folklore and Folklife at the University of Pennsylvania. She has taught at the college level for over twenty-five years and is currently a lecturer in folklore in the English Department at the University of New Hampshire in Durham and is Associate of the Committee on Degrees in Folklore and Mythology at Harvard University.

As New Hampshire's State Folklorist, Dr. Morley organized a Folk Arts program for the state's Arts Commission. She is consultant and lecturer on traditional culture for organizations and communities throughout New Hampshire and the northeast. She is the author of *New Hampshire Folk Arts and Artists: A Directory of Resources* and has written extensively on New England's culture for the scholarly and popular press, radio, television, and films. She consults for national and regional media as a cultural specialist and for such cultural institutions as the Smithsonian Institution, the Boston Children's Museum, and the DeCordova Museum of Contemporary Art.

Morley is the 1988 recipient of Southeastern Massachusetts University's Eisteddfod Award for service to the traditional arts and now serves on the University's Eisteddfod Advisory Board. Dr. Morley resides in Manchester and Hillsborough.

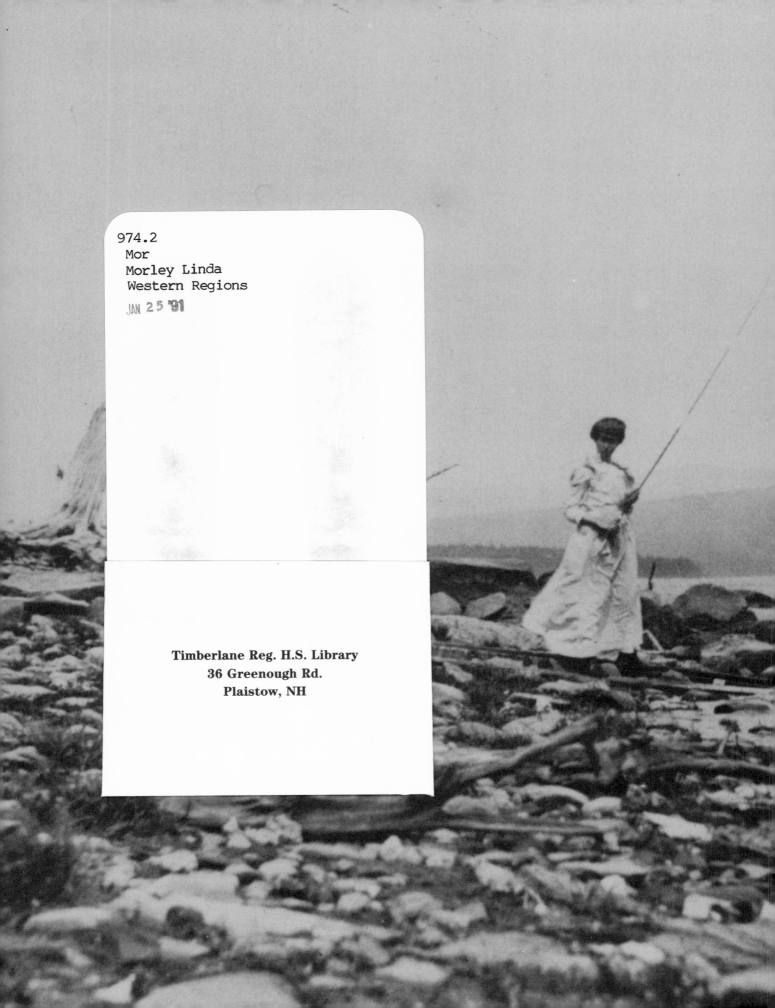